Guide to
Rocky Mountain
VEGETABLE GARDENING

Bob Gough & Cheryl Moore-Gough

COOL
SPRINGS
PRESS

Growing Successful Gardeners™
www.coolspringspress.com
BRENTWOOD, TENNESSEE

Published by Cool Springs Press
P.O. Box 2828
Brentwood, Tennessee 37024

EAN: 978-1-59186-457-8

First Printing 2009
Printed in the United States of America
10 9 8 7 6 5 4 3 2 1

Managing Editor: Billie Brownell
Art Director: Marc Pewitt

Photography and Illustration
Ferry-Morse Seed Company: 46
iStockphoto and its artists: 262, 271, 303
Bill Kersey, Kersey Graphics: 25, 27, 81, 124, 148
Kevin Mathias: 132
Ed Rode: 288
Neil Soderstrom: 57, 58, 80, 87, 98, 106, 107, 113
All other photographs used courtesy of Jupiter Images.

THE VEGETABLES

Dedication

To Rocky Mountain Vegetable Gardeners—our colleagues, students, and inspiration. You spend three months each year in a blaze of activity: planting, watering, fertilizing, nurturing, and harvesting. You battle wind, hail, insects, and weeds in order to produce the freshest, tastiest, and most nutritious vegetables possible for your families. You experiment with heirloom varieties and hybrids, and sometimes even save your seeds from year to year. You eat fresh food when you are able, then freeze, can, pickle, and dehydrate until 3:00 in the morning to preserve the rest. And then it's over. Nine months of snow and ice, gray skies and slippery roads, during which time you still enjoy the fruits of your summertime labors, read books and catalogs, and plan for your next vegetable garden.

This book is for you.

Bob & Cheryl

WELCOME TO GARDENING IN THE ROCKIES

Are you tired of boring grocery store carrots and tasteless tomatoes? Are you spending your food dollars on less than ideal greens? Would you like to pick your own, juicy, mouthwateringly delicious vegetables, harvested at their peak of flavor? Would you like to enjoy your children's eager squeals as they taste freshly picked sugar-snap peas—full of natural goodness? Do you love to be out in the beautiful Rocky Mountain air and sunshine? Then join us as we help get you started vegetable gardening!

There's nothing like growing your own vegetables *your* way! You may choose to garden organically, minimizing chemicals that you may not want your family exposed to. Or you may choose to use modern technology and chemicals. Or, you might decide to just use the least toxic methods possible, whether that means handpicking fat tomato hornworms, spraying insecticidal soap on aphids, or using that great old Christmas-sounding weed control—Hoe Hoe Hoe! There are many ways to garden successfully, even in our short seasons. But how you garden is *your* choice; you have the control when you grow your own vegetables!

Another benefit of growing your own vegetables is greater selection due to the wide variety of edibles offered in today's gardening catalogs, like yellow-fleshed watermelons, "black" tomatoes, and blue potatoes. Did you ever fall in love with an exotic plant while you were on vacation? We did! We had callaloo in Jamaica, found some seeds for sale in a catalog, put them in the ground, and watched them *not* grow. While we really didn't expect a tropical plant to thrive in Montana, it was a fun experiment. But there are so many "good eats" available to gardeners that just aren't in the produce section or, if they are, you'll pay a ridiculous price for them!

This brings to mind another important point—a packet of seeds will result in *hundreds* of plants and costs *far less* than the same number of vegetables purchased at a market. Of course, you have to figure in water, fertilizer, and your time when you consider costs, but many gardeners feel they are getting quite a bargain with their garden.

A beginning vegetable gardener often doesn't realize just how limited our Rocky Mountain growing conditions are. She just wants help "getting growing," and a good gardening book will do just that. A more experienced vegetable gardener transplanted into the Rocky Mountain region may be tempted to throw in his trowel in despair, but once he finds resources to become more familiar with this new locale and its limitations, he sticks out his jaw and defies our diverse and challenging conditions. He *can* grow abundant food for his family and to share with others.

As gardeners and authors, we relate to each of these circumstances. Dr. Bob started gardening at the age of five in Rhode Island. He moved to the Rocky Mountain region and had to modify his gardening techniques to adapt to the adverse climate, rocky and alkaline soils, and shorter growing season found here. Cheryl started her gardening experience in the Gallatin Valley of Montana, and didn't know anything other than the unexpected summer snows, strong winds, and tough weeds, and grew up gardening under these conditions.

Each of us would have welcomed a book like this one. While trial and error works, it helps to have good, solid guidance right from the start. Whether you are a beginning gardener, just starting down the path of producing your own food, or have a few plots under your belt, the information found in these pages is meant to help you, the eager reader, understand how to go about vegetable gardening in this tricky region. We've included references if you need further information and a handy glossary to define less-than-familiar terms. Don't be intimidated by gardening in the Rocky Mountains; it's fun and very rewarding!

The Lay of the Land: Climate and Soils

Knowing your growing season is essential for good gardening, but that's not an easy task. You can go online to find our USDA Hardiness Zones, or call your local county extension office, but the USDA Hardiness Zones *only* describe the *average* cold temperatures a region may experience. Since most vegetables are grown as annuals, this information is of relatively little consequence. More important to gardeners is the length of a growing season; that is, the number of days between the average date of the last killing frost of spring and the average date of the first killing frost of fall. And even that information is a little dicey as the "average" dates are usually plus or minus two full weeks. In many areas of the country the USDA Hardiness Zone designation can be roughly translated into length of the growing season, but

not in ours. Sometimes the colder the winter, the longer the growing season, as is the case for the upper Yellowstone areas of eastern Montana. Get to know your resources; ask your neighboring gardener friends when they usually plant certain vegetables and how long your local growing season is. Call the local extension office, but ask the right questions; don't ask what zone you are in, but, how long a growing season you can expect. Never plant vegetables whose maturity dates are longer than you have in your local growing season (with the possible exception of root crops like parsnips and salsify, which can take the late-season cold temperatures and even sweeten in them).

Rocky Mountain soil types are varied. While some areas have fertile, moist soils, others have soils that are dry, rocky, and compacted. Adapting your gardening techniques to your soil type is a must. We'll tell you how.

Starting at the Beginning: Seeds

It's surprising, but true: many gardeners purchase vegetable seeds based on the photograph on the packet. We'll show you how to read seed packets and interpret the essential information you need for a successful Rocky Mountain garden. Do you want to save seeds from the vegetables you grow, or do you prefer to grow vegetables that have been hybridized and bred for certain characteristics, like good freezing, canning, and other storage qualities? It's exciting to save your own seeds, but if you save them from a hybrid plant you will be disappointed. It has to do with the genetic background of the seeds. We'll tell you how to tell which seeds will "come true" and which ones won't.

Planning Your Garden

How big a garden should you plant? Most of us have planted too much one year or another, and the garden became an unenjoyable chore. We'll help you determine your garden size, how many feet of each plant to sow, and how to site your plot to maximize exposure to sunlight. Designing your general garden layout in advance of planting will help you avoid disappointment—and extra work!

What's in a Name? Soil

Getting to know your garden soil is a must! If you have compacted soil, you know it. It's hard as a rock, and your carrots will be split and funny looking, if they can even penetrate the soil. Soils that are compacted generally have more clay present than the other two mineral elements of soil, sand and silt. The relative proportions of these three soil components determine your soil texture and greatly affect what you can plant, how you should plant it, and how you take care of it by watering and fertilizing.

Soils in the Rocky Mountain region are generally higher in pH levels than those in other parts of the country, and it's important to know the pH in your garden. Why? Because some soil nutrients are less available for plants to use at certain pH levels, and you need to know how to apply fertilizer, in correct types and amounts, to remedy any imbalance.

Getting the Most From Your Garden

You'll have plenty of ideas about getting the most out of your garden after reading this chapter! By rotating vegetables, you'll be able to break insect and disease cycles in your garden, and avoid the depletion of nutrients by vegetables that have heavier feeding requirements. Interplanting can make sense if you have deeply rooted and more shallowly rooted crops planted together, or that otherwise complement one another. If you know you have an insect problem, and you know that insect's preferred vegetable treat, and you have the room, you can plant a trap crop to lure them away.

Do you have limited planting area but big ideas? We'll tell you how to use raised beds, trellising, and other smart space savers.

In addition to these basics, we'll tell you which vegetable seeds may be sown directly in the garden and which should be started as

transplants, and you will even be able to start your own transplants to get a jump on the growing season! You'll learn some options for weed and pest control, how to extend our short growing seasons, and how to water efficiently. Knowing when and how to harvest and store

your vegetables is another essential topic. You'll be all set for a great gardening experience!

The Stars

The vegetable stars of this book have an entire section of their own. Vegetables may be perennials, like asparagus and rhubarb, returning each year to welcome you back to the garden; or annuals that are grown from seed each year and produce seed for the following year; or biennials, like cabbage and parsnip, that take two years to form seed (though they are grown as annuals). We'll explain why knowing this information is important.

Each vegetable profile tells you *exactly* what you need to know to grow it successfully. We've also included important tidbits like how deeply to plant the seed, how closely to plant within a row, how far to place the rows apart, and how much produce you can expect to harvest for the number of feet in your row.

We've noted the vegetables as cool season or warm season for a very good reason: in the Rockies, we cannot plant warm-season vegetables like corn or beans too early or the seeds will rot in the ground. Cool-season vegetables like peas will stop producing when the heat of summer hits and will be a bust if they're planted too late. This type of information alone can make or break your garden. Plant cool-season vegetables early, and buy a soil thermometer to know when it's safe to plant your warm-season vegetables.

Finally, some words of encouragement. If a transplant like Dr. Bob and a previous novice like Cheryl can grow vegetables successfully in the Rocky Mountain region's challenging conditions—and we do—so can you!

Have fun. Enjoy your garden. Allow your children to pull weeds and graze on the peas and carrots. Give yourself and your family the gift of knowing where food comes from, and of eating fresh, nutritious, and *really* tasty vegetables. You will not be sorry.

We'll see *you* in the garden!

Bob & Cheryl

Chapter One

THE LAY OF THE LAND: CLIMATE AND SOILS

Of all the information that we will share with you in this book, the most important thing for you to know is the specific climate and soil type of *your* area. Our five-state area covers more than a half million square miles from the flats of the western Great Plains west beyond the alpine peaks of the Rockies. Wow! But what you'll need to know to get started can be found in our state-by-state general discussions of the soils, precipitation, temperatures, and storms that will have an influence on *your* garden. Ours is a region of extremes, and gardening here can be a challenge. The most important issue is elevation, for elevation has the most significant impact on temperature, precipitation, and local weather conditions. Sometimes there's as much as 30 to 40°F of difference between daytime and nighttime temperatures, and the intense sunlight can burn plant foliage and rapidly dry soil and leaves. Soils become thinner at higher elevations and hence are less suitable for vegetable gardens. You'll quickly learn to amend and enrich your garden soil to be successful, but it's important to know the type of soil in your garden to determine what additions may be needed.

Gardeners can expect about an 11°F reduction in temperature for every 3,300-foot increase in elevation. But even small differences in elevation can cause marked differences in growing conditions. For example, we used to live six miles south of Bozeman, Montana, where our garden was about 200 feet higher than Bozeman proper, yet our growing season was about a month shorter than that in town. Part of the reason was the heat sink effect (heat retaining effect) of towns, but another was the small difference in elevation.

We've included tables in the Appendix containing elevation, average length of the growing season, and the range in the length of the growing season of twelve cities for each state included in the Rocky Mountain region. The length of a season is based on the average number of days between the first and last frosts (that is, 32.5°F temperatures). Using these figures you can estimate the length of your garden's growing season pretty closely.

Our extreme variability in growing season length is the result of the highly variable climatic conditions that make our gardens such a challenge. There may be multiple sets of data for the same town, depending upon whether the information was collected at the airport, in the town center, or at the local agricultural experiment station. Elevations and season lengths vary widely, so we encourage you to explore the website following each table to find a locale closest to your garden if you don't live in one of the cities featured.

COLORADO

Colorado is the highest state in the United States, with an average elevation of 6,800 feet. About 40 percent of the state is the High Plains, which slope gently higher as you move westward from the eastern border at elevations of 3,350 to 4,000 feet, through the Front Range. The High Plains are usually hot on summer mornings and cool during an afternoon thunderstorm. Those thunderstorms can sometimes be severe and the hail they contain can destroy gardens in minutes. The daily maximum summer temperature is about 95°F at elevations below 5,000 feet but cools at higher elevations to the west. There are wide variations in temperatures within short distances. For example, the difference in average annual temperature between two gardens only 90 miles apart can be equivalent to differences in temperature between Florida and Iceland. About 85 percent of its annual precipitation falls in summer. Gardeners in the northeastern areas enjoy a respectable growing season of about 140 days; those in the southeastern areas, an even longer season of about 160 days; and the fortunate few in the extreme southeastern corner of Colorado relish their 180-day seasons.

About 200 miles west of the eastern border lie the Foothills, with elevations of about 7,000 to 9,000 feet. Gardening here becomes challenging, with an average July temperature of 60°F and daily highs in the 70s and 80s°F. Nights are particularly cool all summer long, which will limit your vegetable selection. Cool-season crops will do well but warm-season crops will be more of a challenge. Beyond the Foothills lie the mountains, rising from 9,000 to 14,000 feet, and beyond them is the high plateau that extends to the western border at elevations above 10,000 feet. While there may be some gardens in the low western valleys, much of the mountainous area simply does not have a growing season long enough to make it worthwhile. Nights are so cool above about

8,000 feet that many folks simply do not garden. Gardeners in the valleys of the Gunnison, Dolores, and Colorado Rivers enjoy especially long growing seasons, with the area around Grand Junction having up to 221 frost-free days in some years. Summers are wet in the eastern areas of the state but they are pretty dry in the western areas.

Productive Colorado soils, like those throughout the lower elevations of our region, have low acidity, which can cause some nutrient deficiencies. Front Range soils tend to be heavy clays that need amendments. Adding coarse sand equal to about 50 to 80 percent of the top eight inches or so of garden soil will go far to amend what you have.

The soils along river valleys are most productive, as are soils in the moister northeastern parts of the state. Drier soils on the plains of southern Colorado and on the mountain slopes and plateaus are thin and can be relatively unproductive.

IDAHO

Idaho's elevation rises from north to south, with the lowest location at the confluence of the Clearwater and Snake Rivers (738 feet) and the highest at Mt. Borah in Custer County, (12,655 feet). Large parts of the state, especially northern areas, are strongly influenced by Pacific Ocean air, though eastern Idaho is not. Temperatures are highest at the lower elevations of the Clearwater and Little Salmon River basins and along parts of the Snake River Valley from Bliss to Lewiston. Gardeners in Swan Falls enjoy the highest annual average temperature for the state (55°F) while those in Obsidian, at 6,780 feet, experience the lowest (35.4°F). Daily temperature fluctuations are most extreme in the high valleys and the semi-arid plains of the Snake River. In fact, the daily temperature from July to September can vary by more than 30°F at Boise.

Idaho precipitation patterns are complex. Average valley precipitation is greater in the southern sections, with large areas of the Clearwater, Payette, and Boise River basins getting 40 to 50 inches or more per year. On the other hand, large areas in the northeastern valleys, much of the Upper Snake River plains, the Central plains, and the lower elevations of the southwestern valleys receive fewer than ten inches per year. In the northeastern valleys and the eastern highlands less than half the rain falls between April and September, while in the Boise, Payette, and Weiser River drainage basins less than a third falls in those same months. Low relative humidities throughout the state mean dry air and rapid drying of soils and plants.

Wind throughout the state can be highly destructive, and savvy Idaho gardeners plant in protected areas.

As in other states, the growing season varies greatly depending on elevation, soil type, topography, and vegetation cover. Lewiston and its immediately surrounding areas have the longest seasons in the state. The central Snake, and lower Payette, Boise, and Weiser River basins enjoy about 150-day seasons, while upstream areas of the Snake near Pocatello and Idaho Falls have about 125-day growing seasons. Some high valleys have no growing season at all.

The most productive Idaho soils are the desert soils along the Snake River and the prairie soils in the western part of the state around Lewiston and Moscow. In general, the rest of the state has relatively poor soil.

MONTANA

Montana has great climatic variations. The western part of the state is mountainous while the eastern two-thirds is part of the Great Plains. Elevations vary from a low of 1,800 feet in the northwestern part of the state where the Kootenai River enters

Idaho to 12,850 feet at Granite Peak near Yellowstone Park. About half the state lies above 4,000 feet. Land west of the Continental Divide enjoys a modified northern Pacific Coast climate, with milder winters, more even distribution of annual precipitation, cooler summers, stronger winds, more cloudiness, higher relative humidity, and shorter growing seasons than those of eastern Montana. In western Montana hot spells are rare in summer and of relatively short duration, though temperatures can sometimes top 100°F in the low valleys. Above 4,000 feet it is almost never "very hot." Eastern Montana has a more extreme climate with average July temperatures of 74°F in southern areas. Midsummer days are warm but nights cool into the 50s and 60s°F. Miles City is one of the warmest parts of the state, having a July minimum of 60°F and an average maximum temperature of 90°F.

Precipitation is highly variable. The western mountains are the wettest area and nearly half of the annual precipitation falls from May to July. Heron is the wettest location, receiving 34.7 inches of rain on average each year. North-central Montana is the driest part of the state, although the absolute driest spot is near Belfry along the Clark Fork of the Yellowstone River in Carbon County. Belfry receives an average annual precipitation of only 6.59 inches.

Summer storms are frequent, with hailstorms in July and August causing about five million dollars of crop damage annually.

The average growing season for Montana is about 130 days. Most of the agricultural areas enjoy a growing season of more than 120 days, while the middle Yellowstone River Valley in the area around Miles City can expect a 150-day season. The higher valleys of western Montana have no growing season at all.

Soils in the eastern parts of the state are rich and can be quite productive, as can be the soils along major rivers like the Yellowstone, the Milk, and the Missouri.

UTAH

Most of Utah is mountainous, varying from an elevation of about 2,500 feet in the Virgin River Valley in southwestern Utah to 13,498 feet at Kings Peak in the Uinta Mountains. Most of the state receives only light precipitation throughout the year.

The lower elevations generally are warmer than elevated valleys and mountains. In general, the southern counties are 6 to 8°F warmer than the northern counties. There are wide daily fluctuations in temperatures, and in winter on clear nights the cold air settles in the valley bottoms while the benches and foothills remain warmer. Experienced gardeners know that the best growing areas are the higher lands at the valley edges. Although there is no orderly or extensive zone of equal length growing season, most agricultural areas of the state enjoy 130- to 150-day seasons.

Precipitation is highly variable, ranging from fewer than five inches per year over the Great Salt Lake Desert to more than forty inches in some areas of the Wasatch Mountains. The annual average for agricultural areas is about ten to fifteen inches. Areas of the state below 4,000 feet receive less than ten inches. Northwestern and eastern Utah are also quite dry.

The loam soils in the narrow belt at the base of the Wasatch Range are highly productive, as are the dry soils and the gray desert soils in much of western and some parts of eastern Utah.

WYOMING

Wyoming's elevation rises from north to south, with an average elevation of 6,700 feet. The lowest elevation is 3,125 feet near the northeastern corner of the state; the highest is the 13,785-foot Gannet Peak in the west central part of the state. Eastern Wyoming has an average elevation of 4,500 feet while the foothills to the west rise to 6,000 feet and more.

The entire state is relatively cool and areas above 6,000 feet rarely experience temperatures of 100°F. The average maximum temperature in July is 85 to 95°F, though areas above 9,000 feet have an average July maximum of only about 70°F. The lower part of the Big Horn basin, the lower elevations of central Wyoming, and the northeastern and eastern sections along the border are the warmest. Summer nights are cool.

Late spring and early fall frosts are common. The average growing season in the main agricultural areas is about 125 days.

Areas along the eastern border west to the foothills can experience growing seasons from 100 to 130 days, while Farson, near Sandy Creek off the Green River, has only a 42-day season. There is practically no growing season for tender plants in the upper Green River Valley, Star Valley, and the Jackson Hole area.

Elevations greater than 7,000 feet receive annual precipitation of up to thirty inches, with about a third of that falling during the growing season. Southwestern Wyoming at elevations of 6,500 to 8,500 feet receives 7 to 10 inches. Lower elevations at 4,000 to 5,500 feet in the northeastern parts of the state and along the eastern border can expect about 12 to 16 inches per year. The southwestern sections are very dry. The lower part of the Big Horn Basin, with 5 to 8 inches, is the driest. Seaver, at 4,105 feet, receives 5.5 inches. Worland, near the southern part of the basin, receives 7 to 8 inches; Thermopolis, 11 to12 inches; and Laramie, in the southeast corner of the state at 7,236 feet, about 10 inches. As an example of how quickly conditions change in the West, Centennial, only thirty miles west of Laramie but at an elevation of 8,074 feet, receives about 16 inches per year. The High Plains area receives about 10 to 15 inches per year, with 9 to 12 inches of that falling during the growing season.

Gardeners along the eastern border below 4,500 feet can expect a growing season of 130 to 150 days. The area from the eastern border to the foothills at elevations of 4,500 to 6,000 feet usually has growing seasons of 100 to 130 days, while elevations of 6,000 to 7,000 feet can experience seasons ranging from 80 to 100 days. Shorter seasons of about 80 days or fewer prevail above 7,000 feet. In some areas frost can occur *every night*. Both hail and wind can cause problems.

The lowlands of eastern Wyoming have some very fertile moist and dry soils but low precipitation and low temperatures limit their usefulness. You can modify these with careful irrigation and season extenders and you will have a great garden.

Putting It All Together

Gardening becomes increasingly more challenging the higher the elevation, and the cool summer nights, short growing seasons, and poor soils make gardening at elevations above 7,000 to 8,000 feet *very* difficult. Site characteristics vary so widely that you must understand your specific garden conditions, based upon the soils, precipitation, and climatic conditions within a few hundred yards of your garden. Pay close attention to your location and choose your varieties wisely. And remember, following some good neighborly advice will go a long way toward making *you* a successful gardener.

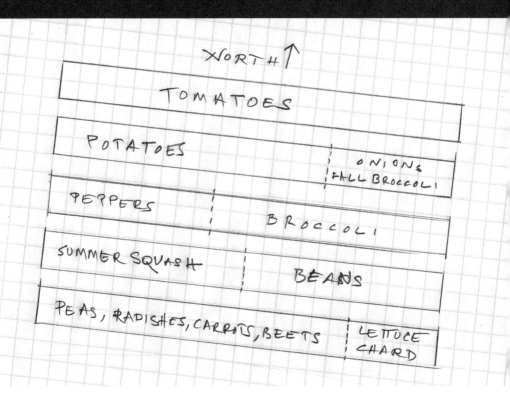

Chapter Two

PLANNING YOUR GARDEN

There's an old saying that goes something like this: a failure to plan is a plan to fail. It may not seem like much, but developing a garden plan will go a long way toward creating a successful vegetable gardening experience. (And in case there is any doubt, success means veggies to eat!)

Begin by scanning the new seed catalogs to see what you might like to plant. Then, ask yourself a few questions, and be brutally honest about the time you have to invest in vegetable gardening, how much financial investment you want to make, and your interests. Remember, you will become a better gardener in time but it's tempting to bite off more than you can chew in the beginning!

How Big is Big Enough?

How big of a garden is enough for you? If you're new to gardening (or even if you're not), there is no shame in starting on a scale that's manageable to fit within your life. First, plant only what you like! If you plan to preserve your vegetables, then plant more. A one-quarter acre garden (10,000 square feet) will feed a family of five for a year. If you include potatoes, cucurbits, or other space hogs, then you'll need additional space. If your time is limited, then perhaps a garden of 2,500 square feet or even 625 square feet (25 x 25 feet) is a better fit. Some beginning gardeners consider a 10 x 10 foot garden a good size. Perhaps the most commonly sized vegetable garden is 25 x 25 feet. But with a garden this size plant only those vegetables that are the most space-efficient, such as beans, root crops, crucifers (broccoli, cabbage, and so forth), onion and garlic, and the leafy crops such as Swiss chard, lettuce, and spinach. Avoid space-hogs such as pumpkin, squash, potato, and corn. If you must have cucurbits, train them to grow on a trellis, plant the bush type, or plant them at the edges of the garden and let them sprawl onto the lawn.

Once you identify the vegetables you think you want to grow, check the approximate yields per length of row that are included in the profiles of individual vegetables later in the book to help determine the garden size.

Location, Location, Location

Where you plant your garden is more important than *what* you plant in it. If you choose the wrong site it won't matter what you plant. Select a spot that receives full sun for at least eight hours each day. If this is not possible, then pick a site that gets the most sun and plant leafy vegetables.

Plants That Produce in Light Shade*

Beet	Cabbage	Carrot	Green onion
Kale	Leek	Lettuce	Mustard
Radish	Spinach	Swiss chard	Turnip

(*Light shade can be that cast by buildings, fences, trellises, and tall garden plants.)

The site should be well away from trees and easy to water. A tree's roots can extend at least 1½ times the spread of its branches, and believe us, you don't want to lug a hose any farther than you must. Another consideration is exposure; southern exposure is the warmest and produces the earliest crops. However, soil on a site with southern exposure will dry faster than soil facing other exposures. Warm-season vegetables ripen earlier when planted near the south side of a building or fence. Northern exposures are moister but too cold for a good garden, so never plant within ten feet of the north side of a one-story building. Move the garden even farther away from taller buildings. Western exposures are nearly as warm as southern exposures but plants there may be exposed to strong prevailing winds.

Elevation is of primary importance in the selection of vegetable varieties for your garden. It is nearly impossible for a 110-day corn to ripen fully in a 110-day season, so at higher elevations plant the varieties that require fewer days to maturity. In general, cool-season crops perform best at higher elevations since they generally require shorter growing seasons and fewer days until harvest. Almost all cool-season vegetables are grown for their vegetative parts (leaves, roots, stems, petioles, and immature buds). Cool-season vegetables have smaller root systems and tops than warm-season ones, are frost-hardy, and their seeds germinate at cooler soil temperatures. Their shallow root systems respond to lower levels of nitrogen and phosphorus. Some are biennials, such as cabbage, that are prone to premature seed stalk formation ("bolting") upon exposure to prolonged cool weather. Bolting renders an otherwise edible portion of a vegetable unpalatable. Warm-season vegetables such as tomatoes, peppers, and squash tend to be large plants with large root systems and require a longer season and higher temperatures to mature. They are generally grown for their fruit. Peas are an exception, being a cool-season vegetable grown for its seeds, as is New Zealand spinach, a warm-season vegetable grown for its leaves.

Elevation

If you garden below 5,000 feet elevation you can easily grow all of the cool-season and many of the warm-season vegetables that require fewer days to harvest. For example, we garden just below 5,000 feet and can easily harvest transplanted tomatoes that have less than a 68-day season and corn with less than a 70-day season. At about 6,000 feet you will have to be a bit more selective since you can expect a frost nearly every Memorial Day. Plant only those warm-season vegetables that need very few days to harvest, such as cherry and grape tomatoes and tomatoes of Siberian origins. All will have seasons fewer than sixty-five days. It will be tough to grow cucurbits, eggplant, and okra at this elevation, but it can be done by modifying a garden's microclimate. Above 7,000 feet choose only varieties with absolutely the fewest numbers of days to harvest and strongly consider season extenders to create warmer microclimates. One season extender option is to plant against a south-facing wall with protection from wind. Root vegetables, peas, onions, garlic, shallots, potatoes, leafy vegetables, and the crucifers should perform nicely for you. You will have a tough go getting eggplant, peppers, corn, tomatoes, and the cucurbits to mature. In all cases and especially at higher elevations, encourage rapid growth with a good fertilizer that is high in phosphorus, a nutrient that encourages strong growth in cool soils. Go easy on the nitrogen, which delays maturity and ripening. See the chapter on season extenders for more helpful hints to growing warm-season crops at higher elevations.

A gentle slope of not more than 1 percent (1 inch drop every 8 feet) provides good air circulation and allows cold air to flow down and away from the garden. If the slope faces south, the soil will warm faster in spring, allowing earlier planting. Buildings and trees located at the bottom of a slope impede airflow and contribute to the formation of a frost pocket. Gardens sited in low areas and affected by frost pockets are more likely to suffer frost damage and their soils may be cold, wet, and poorly drained.

If you are considering planting next spring in an area that is now lawn, kill the grass before you till it under. You can spray the future garden area with a non-residual broad-spectrum herbicide such as glyphosate (commonly sold as Roundup®), or cover the area with black polyethylene (plastic) weighted down. Leave the plastic in place for the entire growing season to kill the grass. At the end of summer, turn under the dead grass to add valuable organic matter to your soil.

Most of us cannot choose the best soil type for our garden, and many of us must garden in thin, infertile soils. But if you have

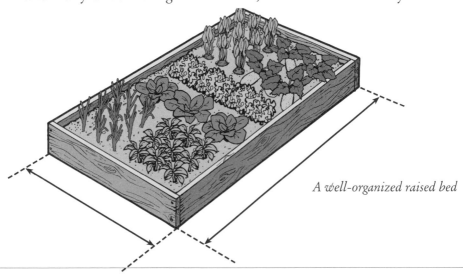

A well-organized raised bed

a choice, then plant in a sandy or silt loam. These combine both good water-holding capacity with good drainage and are light enough to allow good root penetration. We'll share more about soils later.

Space Savers

Some of us just don't have the space to plant a large garden, but you can make the most of what you have by using space-saving techniques.

Raised Beds

Raised beds are usually about 6 to 9 inches deep with soil held in place by 2- x 8- or 2- x 10-inch lumber. The soil in them is easier to improve with liberal additions of organic matter and can be brought to a fine tilth (lots of good, fluffy particles in the soil) by thorough preparation. Soil in raised beds warms up earlier in spring than soil in a conventional garden, especially if the bed is sloped about 1 to 5 percent to the south. You'll learn more about raised beds in the chapter "Getting the Most From Your Garden."

Trellises

Cucurbits and indeterminate tomatoes like to sprawl, but you can train them to run up a trellis to save space. This "vertical cropping" saves lots of space. A trellis can be built with a wooden frame and poultry fencing and set on posts at a 45° angle. Cucurbits will climb up a trellis but you will have to tie tomato stems in place. A trellis made of heavy twine or wire strung between sturdy wooden posts is an excellent way to train tall peas, pole beans, cucumbers, and even tomatoes. The vertical orientation may be a little too much for the vine crops that bear heavier fruit, such as winter squash and pumpkins, so some gardeners make good use of old brassieres, nylon stockings, and onion bags by supporting the fruit in them and tying them to the trellis to take the weight off the fruit stem. It looks odd, but it works.

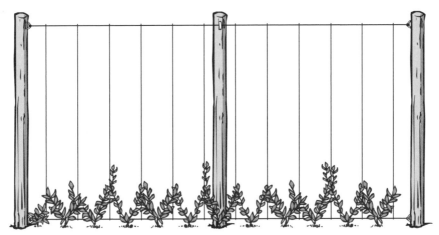

A trellis for peas, beans, and cucumbers

Broadcast Sowing

Most of us plant vegetables in rows, but the walkways between the rows take up a lot of space. To save space, consider broadcasting seeds in one row up to four feet wide. It will be tougher to weed but you will be able to harvest an abundance of quick-growing crops such as spinach, Swiss chard, leaf lettuce, and radish.

Putting Your Plan on Paper

You don't have to be a Picasso, but draw your garden plan on paper before the planting season. Include the varieties, crop succession (a new vegetable to follow the one in place), the amount of space you plan to allow for each vegetable, row length and spacing, and the planting dates. Group perennial vegetables such as rhubarb, horseradish, and asparagus on one side of the garden so they will be out of the way of the tiller. Plant vegetables that need more growing days, such as parsnip, tomato, melon, and winter squash, on another side of the garden, and short-season crops, such as carrot, radish, and leaf lettuce, on yet another side. Try to group plants that have similar cultural requirements and that are susceptible to the same pests. For example, group the crucifers (cabbage, broccoli, cauliflower, and so forth) together, the root vegetables together, and the cucurbits together. Plant tall plants like corn on the north side of the garden so they won't unduly shade the rest of the garden.

It is a relatively minor consideration, but try to plant in rows running north to south to allow the best distribution of sunlight. Plant corn in small blocks of several rows each, rather than in a few long rows, to permit better pollination and greater yields.

Sow fast-maturing, short-season vegetables such as leaf lettuce and radishes in short rows at two-week intervals. This allows an extended harvest season so that you don't end up with ten bushels of radishes in a single harvest! Consider intercropping; that is, planting fast-maturing vegetables such as radishes and leaf lettuce between rows of long-season ones such as tomatoes and peppers. The radishes utilize the empty space when the tomatoes are small. By the time the tomato plants need the extra space, the radishes will have been harvested.

Cool-season vegetables with special considerations

Cool-season vegetables that mature quickly

Leaf lettuce, Spinach, Mustard, Radish, Turnip, Kohlrabi, Peas

---

Cool-season vegetables that do poorly in hot weather; transplant for early ripening or plant for fall harvest

Butterhead lettuce, Cabbage, Cauliflower, Broccoli,
Brussels sprouts, Celery, Celeriac

Cool-season vegetables requiring a long season

Beet, Carrot, Parsnip, Salsify, Horseradish, Swiss chard, Kale,
Endive, Onion, Leek, Garlic, Shallot, Potato

Warm-season vegetables with special considerations

*Warm-season vegetables with shorter seasons that can be directly
sown to the garden at lower elevations*

Bean, Sweet corn, Okra, Cucumber, Squash

Warm-season vegetables with long seasons that should be transplanted to the garden

Tomato, Eggplant, Muskmelon, Pepper, Watermelon

If you follow the simple steps that we have outlined in this chapter to plan before planting your garden, you will be on your way to a rewarding experience!

Chapter Three

GETTING THE MOST FROM YOUR GARDEN

Americans love efficiency, and if you give us an inch, we'll want a mile. But sometimes there is a good reason for that, especially if you want to get the absolute most out of your garden. You can use various systems such as interplanting, also known as inter-cropping, and companion planting. By rotating your vegetables, you can avoid nutrient depletion, diseases, and (added bonus) you'll confuse overwintering insects. And if your season is long enough, you can succession plant another edible vegetable or a green manure to keep the weeds at bay. It's all part of being proactive and using what you have in the most efficient ways possible.

Companion Planting

The term "companion planting" encompasses so many concepts that it's nearly meaningless unless it's defined. Some concepts are scientifically sound and effective; others run the gamut of pseudoscience from metaphysical to downright silly. In the latter category are concepts that anthropomorphize plants; that is, they give human traits to plants.

Sweet peppers and okra are thought to be a good combination.

For example, saying that plants A and B should be planted together because A "loves" B has no basis in reality. Judging which plants should be planted together based upon their "vibrations" and "rhythm" is equally unscientific. Using the idea of sensitive crystallization, wherein extracts of plants A and B are mixed, allowed to evaporate, and the patterns of their residual crystals studied to see if the plants are compatible, is based on metaphysics, not on science. The various companion plant associations are based on a combination of observation, anecdotal evidence, science, pseudoscience, and folklore, and their validity is difficult to establish.

But—there are some methods of companion planting that are scientifically valid and should be observed by all gardeners.

Trap cropping uses one vegetable to attract insects away from another. For example, radishes planted near carrots attract wireworms and root maggots away from the carrots. Kale attracts harlequin cabbage bugs away from cabbage and intercropped patty pan squash attracts pickleworms away from cucumbers. Beans attract armyworms away from tomatoes; collards attract the diamondback moth away from cabbage. Needless to say that the trap crop, having done its job, will be pretty much useless. Perhaps we should call it the sacrifice crop?

Some plants release a compound from their roots that may suppress or enhance the growth of nearby plants. Black walnut releases a compound called *juglone* that inhibits the growth of many plants, while African marigolds release a compound called *thiopene* that repels nematodes. (Note that the African marigold, botanical name *Tagetes erecta*, is not the marigold found commonly in flower beds. This is the large-flowered marigold also referred to as the American marigold. While they may be planted in the garden, the marigolds you purchase at the garden center are often a mix of different species, such as *T. erecta*, *T. patula*, *T. tenuifolia*, or hybrids. Not all of these have been shown to have nematocidic properties. Researchers refer specifically to *T. erecta* having those properties. So, you'll have to ask specifically for the African marigold or plant seeds of that species.)

Nurse cropping is the use of one plant sown directly in a row or in very close proximity to another plant. For example, parsnip and carrot seeds are notoriously slow to germinate. Between the times they are sown and the times the seedlings emerge the soil may crust, preventing many of the weaker parsnip and carrot seedlings from emerging. In that time weeds may also emerge, and it will be difficult to hoe between the rows if you don't know where the rows are. But if you mix radish seeds with the parsnip and carrot seeds the radish seeds will germinate quickly, break through the soil crust, and mark the rows. In addition to serving as a nurse crop, the radishes will attract some insect pests away from the parsnips and when you harvest the radishes you'll be able to thin the rows of parsnips and carrots.

Intermingling tall, full-sun plants with smaller, shade-tolerant plants makes good use of space. This is also a form of nurse cropping. The "Three Sisters" scheme of planting pole beans to climb on corn stalks and planting squash vines between the corn has many benefits. The beans use the stalks as "bean poles" to reach greater amounts of sunlight while the decaying bean roots liberate nitrogen for subsequent use by the corn. (The beans are living, of course, when they climb, but beans and other legumes do not release very much nitrogen into the soil for use by other plants until their tissues die. A few roots of the beans may die during the year and give up their nitrogen, and a bit of nitrogen may leak from the root nodules, but the real benefit to other plants comes when the entire plant dies and is incorporated into the soil. Legumes are good and enrich the soil enormously, but mostly after they die.) The squash vines cover the soil and reduce weed growth and their prickly stems are reputed to deter raccoons from eating the corn.

Intercropping means to plant some plants between rows of others. For example, plant radishes between rows of tomatoes. The radishes will use the space well and will be harvested before the tomatoes need the extra room. The same is true for short-season leaf lettuce planted between rows of longer season crops such as cabbage and tomato. Always intercrop whenever possible to get the maximum yields and biodiversity from your garden. But with any increase in productivity you will have to pay close attention to stepping up your watering and fertilizing regimes to support the extra growth on what would otherwise be bare ground.

Finally, planting many vegetables in a small space creates greater biodiversity and encourages a healthy population of pollinating insects. Should a pest outbreak occur on one vegetable crop, you would have others that wouldn't be attacked.

Rotation cropping means you avoid planting the same or similar vegetables in the same location in successive years; you mix it up. For example, if you plant spinach in the same spot every year, spinach pests will build up in that location. Also, because certain plants make greater use of some nutrients, planting the same crop in the same spot year after year depletes that soil of certain nutrients. Think of it this way, if your child only eats peanut butter and jelly sandwiches, you will run out of these items sooner, while the meat and potatoes remain untouched. In a similar manner, beets and carrots are heavy users of potassium; planting them in the same spot year after year reduces soil potassium levels but leaves levels of other nutrients such as nitrogen and phosphorus relatively high. Corn uses relatively high amounts of nitrogen but uses phosphorus and potassium in lesser amounts. So planting corn where beets were planted the year before makes good sense.

Guidelines for Good Rotation Practices

Do not follow a vegetable with another that's in the same family. For example, do not plant cabbage where broccoli was planted the year before since they both belong to the Mustard family. Tomatoes and peppers are in the same Nightshade family and should not follow each other. If you plant cabbage on the south side of the garden one year, plant it on the north side of the garden the next year and on the east side of the garden the year after that.

Mix things up. Plant a root vegetable where a fruit such as peppers or tomatoes or a leafy vegetable such as lettuce or Swiss chard was planted the year before. An exception would be to avoid following Swiss chard or spinach by beets since all three belong to the Goosefoot family. Follow heavy feeders by light feeders, such as planting lettuce after corn. Follow shallow-rooted plants by those that are deep rooted.

If you wait two years before you replant the same vegetable in the same spot it had been growing, that is called a two-year rotation; if you wait five years, then it's a five-year rotation. Try to practice at least three-year rotations, although even longer rotations are better. For example, in year 1 we plant spinach, which is a shallow-rooted, leafy vegetable in the Goosefoot family. In year 2 we plant carrots, a moderate to deeply rooted root vegetable in the Parsley family, in the same spot. In year 3, we plant tomatoes in that spot. Tomatoes are a deep-rooted fruit in the Nightshade family. In year 4 we plant spinach in that spot once more, ending a three-year rotation. In this plan we rotated by family, root system, and edible part.

Succession cropping means to follow one vegetable crop by another in the same season. It requires more watering and fertilizer but will also increase your season's yields. After one vegetable crop is harvested, till the soil and plant another in its place right away, allowing you to get two harvests where one would normally be grown. However, you must consider how much of the growing season remains, how many days to harvest a second vegetable crop requires, and the climatic conditions under which that second crop will mature. Not all combinations work in all gardens. For example, turnips following onions will probably have enough time to mature under the cooling conditions of late summer and early fall. However, eggplants following onions  would probably not work since eggplants need a long season and warm days to mature. In our garden, we harvest onions about August 2 and can expect a frost by mid-September. We have about one month left after harvesting onions in which a second crop can mature. For us, transplanted kale works well, as does spinach, because both will produce a good crop within a month or so and both will also tolerate light frosts, thus extending their seasons for an additional two weeks or more. Try following bush beans by leaf lettuce, spinach, or turnips to mature in the fall; spring radishes can be followed by bush beans and onions and again followed by a fall crop of spinach or turnips. This is where a knowledge of warm- and cool-season crops can be put to good use as succession cropping also refers to planting at intervals throughout the season, such as planting at two-week intervals during seasons appropriate to the plant.

Relay cropping is a combination between succession cropping and intercropping. For example, you can plant corn seeds or tomato plants beneath the foliage of early cabbage plants. The cabbage leaves will protect the seedlings and transplants from a late frost and the cabbage head will be harvested before the relay crops need the extra space.

Shorter-season Vegetables That May Follow or Be Followed in Succession

Bush bean, Kohlrabi, Radish

Beet, Leaf lettuce, Spinach

Cauliflower, Onion, Turnip greens (spring)

Carrot, Peas

Vegetables for Fall Planting That May Follow Earlier Vegetables

Beet, Kohlrabi, Radish

Kale, Leaf lettuce, Turnip (late)

Vegetables for Intercropping

Bush bean, Lettuce, Onion sets, Radish, New Zealand Spinach

Beet, Mustard, Pumpkin, Spinach, Squash

Fallowing means to allow a portion of the garden to remain unplanted for a season. The soil may be left bare or, even better, it may be planted in a green manure crop. This idea of letting the land rest dates at least to Roman times and was part of the standard planting practices throughout the Middle Ages. It allows the soil to soak up moisture when not planted with a green manure crop and, if planted, allows organic matter turned under to fully decompose before the following season. It also removes the land from production for a season (and therefore is not practiced where space is limited).

Preparing the Land

Preparing the garden for planting is essential. Most gardeners simply use a rototiller or spade to loosen the soil to a maximum depth of about eight inches, which also turns under organic material and soil amendments for plant growth. However, repeatedly spading or tilling to the same depth every season can result in formation of a bottom hardpan, which limits the penetration of water and roots to greater depths, reducing the amount of nutrients available to plants. In the case  of root vegetables such as carrots and parsnips, a shallow hardpan means their roots may be stumpy or forked. Till to different depths each year and, if a hardpan is present, break it up with a pickax or a subsoil or chisel plow.

Rototilling prepares and fluffs the soil and does a good job of mixing and incorporating fertilizers and organic materials. However, there is some concern that it tends to "overaerate" the soil, hastens organic matter decomposition, and forces a gardener to keep a sharp eye on adding amendments. Many gardeners use rototillers for cultivating between rows. This is a poor practice as the tiller will dig too deeply, destroying many of the surface feeder roots. It's better to cultivate by scraping the soil surface with a hoe, not by tilling it.

Double Digging

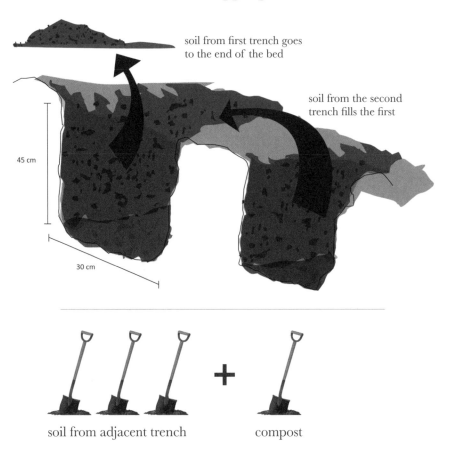

soil from first trench goes to the end of the bed

soil from the second trench fills the first

45 cm

30 cm

soil from adjacent trench   +   compost

Double-digging is a labor-intensive process designed to loosen the subsoil, and is often used to prepare raised beds. Here's how to do it: Start at one end of a garden row and turn up a strip of soil a foot or so wide to create a trench. Remove only the topsoil and toss it out of the way. Next, dig and break up the subsoil at the bottom of the trench but leave it in place. Work well-aged manure or compost into the subsoil. Then, spade the next strip and throw the topsoil from it onto the amended subsoil in the previous trench. Continue in this fashion until the entire garden is double-dug. When you reach the end, use the first topsoil you tossed aside to fill in the last trench.

Raised beds are quite useful in Rocky Mountain gardens but they do need more time and energy to construct and maintain than a regular garden. However, they can be filled with good topsoil and compost to replace any existing poor, wet, or very dry soil. They allow cultivating and harvesting from at least a foot off the ground, making these chores easier for elderly or physically challenged gardeners. Since gardeners don't walk in them, the soil of a raised bed is easier to dig and it warms faster in spring, allowing for somewhat earlier planting. Surrounding raised beds with mulch allows easier access after watering, and raised beds have a tidy look about them that makes them fit nicely into suburban and urban landscapes. But there are some downsides to raised beds: you cannot easily use a rototiller in smaller beds and they usually require more frequent watering than an inground garden.

Raised beds can be constructed with many materials. Completely dried railroad ties are an easy border, as are landscape timbers. Cement blocks are another type of construction material but they are not attractive. Perhaps the most commonly used material for constructing the walls of raised beds is 2- x 8-inch or 2- x 10-inch lumber; screw the boards into posts at the four corners to make a square or rectangular bed. Be careful you do not get carried away with the size of the bed as you should be able to reach the center of the bed from the outside walls. Therefore, make the beds no wider than about four feet, or twice whatever your length of reach is. If you have a problem with moles or pocket gophers fasten a layer of half-inch mesh hardware cloth to the bottom of the bed before you fill it.

If the underlying soil is good, it is not necessary to fill the bed to the top of the frame. Use good soil but think twice about purchasing it. A 10- x 4-foot raised bed with 2- x 10-inch sides requires about 30 to 35 cubic feet of material and that will get pretty pricey at the local garden center. Rather, build up your own soil year by year and mix in a few purchased amendments. Use compost and some topsoil from your existing garden, some coarse sand, and some fertilizer. Over time your "made" soil will mellow. Be sure to add plenty of organic matter to the raised bed each year, but not so much as to hamper plant growth. The various ingredients will blend together over time into a more homogenous mass. Check out soil amendments in the soil chapter (p. 72).

Raised beds can also serve as mini-greenhouses if you cover them with a "hoop" of 2- x 4-inch mesh welded wire and fasten polyethylene or spun-bonded fabric to it. Leave the ends open since spring temperatures in some areas may rise to 80° or 90°F, "cooking" your early crops. You can also arrange the covering so it can be rolled off over the hoops to take advantage of good weather. Plant any of the cucurbits at one end of the bed so they can trail out onto the surrounding area as they grow.

The vegetable garden is a dynamic place, with different plants growing in different places at the same time or in succession, water and nutrients being added and depleted—life. Using different systems such as nurse cropping, intercropping, and rotation will help keep all of these dynamics in balance and mutually beneficial. Not only does it make good sense, it marks the difference between average gardeners and good gardeners.

Chapter Four

STARTING AT THE BEGINNING: SEEDS

Home gardeners are lucky. In addition to being a cost-effective way to garden, a vast world of different and unusual vegetables is open to you once you begin to grow from seeds. You have a choice between growing vegetables from seed inside, as transplants, or direct seeding to the garden, but any of these methods is usually very satisfying and oddly personal. It's a way to connect to your garden, and by extension to the earth itself, in the cycle of life.

Going Shopping!

Supermarkets and garden centers carry a limited, usually inexpensive selection of widely adapted varieties. But why settle for run-of-the-mill of anything? You have many ways to purchase high-quality seeds. Search the seed catalogs and websites for the ones you *really* want. Some large companies offer varieties adapted to a wide range of conditions; some offer varieties that do better in the Pacific Northwest or in the Deep South. You, as a Rocky Mountain gardener, need varieties best suited to our special conditions. Choose the right ones and remember that seeds, no matter how expensive, are your least expensive investment. Seed catalogs and seed packets give you lots of information. But don't worry—we will tell you how to work your way through it.

Hybrid & Nonhybrid Seeds

Hybrid seeds, most of which are the result of purposeful breeding by humans, have been around for a long time. The first hybrid tomato, 'Mikado', was released by the Rice Seed Company in 1880 and commercial hybrid corn made its debut in 1921. By the end of World War II, almost all farmers planted hybrid corn. Hybridization of other vegetables soon followed. First generation hybrids, called "F_1" for "first filial generation," are usually more vigorous than their parents; produce larger, more uniform crops that may ripen in a shorter season; and often have resistance to multiple pests. Because their production and development is costly, hybrid seeds usually fetch a slightly higher price than those of standard, open-pollinated varieties, but this is a small price to pay for all of the benefits of hybrids. One downside is that hybrid seeds will not produce plants that will grow "true to type" in the next generation. So, if you save seeds from the fruit of the hybrid 'Early Girl' tomato they *will* produce tomato plants but they *will not* produce 'Early Girl' tomatoes; rather, the tomato plants will revert to one of the parental types that was used to create the 'Early Girl' variety.

Many gardeners prefer to plant the standard, nonhybrid varieties because they have some unfounded fear of the "new" hybrids, or they simply like the charm of planting something "old-fashioned." Others may feel strongly about maintaining and preserving genetic diversity, thereby avoiding genetically identical plants, all of which are susceptible to the same pests.

Open-pollinated, nonhybrid varieties are the old standards. They often have less pest resistance and less uniformity than the hybrids, and are not as "pretty," but they do have character. They will come true-to-type; that is, seeds saved from an open-pollinated variety will produce plants nearly identical to the parents. So you can save their seeds for the next year's crop. While definitions vary, heirlooms have been around a long time, usually at least fifty years, have documented histories, often have colorful names, are open pollinated, and reproduce true-to-type.

Variety Characteristics

Read the descriptions of varieties carefully. "Determinate" varieties, as found in beans and tomatoes, produce plants that are compact and that ripen over a short period of time. These are useful on windy sites and when you want to freeze or preserve a lot at once. "Indeterminate" varieties produce large, sprawling plants

that ripen over a longer period of time. These work better on protected sites and where you don't intend to have a single canning day but wish to eat a little at a time over the season.

Some varieties of peas and other vegetables are better used for processing, some are better for eating at harvest, and some store better than others. And many varieties have various strains; think of these as "subvarieties" that have certain beneficial characteristics that distinguish them from the parent variety, though these characteristics are not great enough to be considered a new variety. For example, 'Kentucky Wonder' rust resistant strain is a subvariety of 'Kentucky Wonder' bean that has resistance to the rust fungus. It is otherwise identical to its parental strain and will produce beans that are indistinguishable from the parent type except for their resistance to the fungus. Selecting certain strains allows us to fine-tune varieties for our conditions.

Some varieties are regionally adapted and some are adapted to larger areas of the country. For example, 'Vantage Point', a late-maturing green cabbage, performs well in gardens from Texas to Canada, while 'Red Express', a red cabbage, is recommended for northern gardens only. Heirloom varieties have been selected through the generations because of their adaptability to local environments; therefore, they may not be adapted to wide areas of the country.

Remember the designation AAS—it's like a seal of approval. The All-America Selections (AAS) program began in 1932 and tests a large number of vegetables and flowers annually throughout the United States, then publishes a list of what the organization considers the best introductions for that year.

Days to Harvest

All seed packets and most catalogs list a particular vegetable's "days to harvest." If the seed is usually sown directly to the garden, such as carrot, the number refers to the average number of days from sowing to harvest. If the plants are usually transplanted, such as tomato, then the number refers to the average number of days from transplant to harvest. It does not include the number of days required to produce the transplant. For example, 'Jetstar' is a 72-day tomato, which means it requires, on average, 72 days to mature from transplant to harvest. Days to harvest is not a precise number but an *average* number of days in an *average* year, on an *average* soil, and in an *average* location. Further, it is not as simple as figuring that a 120-day season should accommodate a 90-day sweet corn. Because our Rocky Mountain weather is cool in the spring, the actual growing season for aboveground crops is almost always shorter than the published one. You may have 120 days between frosts, but cool-season crops don't grow much at temperatures below 45°F and warm-season vegetables need at least 50°F to begin their growth. Factor in our cool nights, which slows growth of warm-season vegetables, and you really have a shorter effective growing season than you think. For example, a 63-day corn requires about 90 days to ripen south of Bozeman, Montana. This consideration is most important with aboveground vegetables that are exposed to frosts. However, root vegetables like parsnip and carrot are not only hardy but are protected from cold autumn weather by the soil, so there is no trick to growing a 120-day parsnip in a 90-day growing season. If this is a little confusing, just remember that aboveground vegetables are more strongly dependent on the length of the growing season than the soil-protected root vegetables.

Reading Between the Lines: Seed Packets

By law, seed packets *must* state the percentage of germination of the seeds they contain and the date the germination was tested. This ensures that you are purchasing good, viable seeds for the season. Germination standards are set by the federal government and, although they vary among vegetables, most seed packets must state at least 60 percent germination to be legally sold in interstate commerce.

Packets must also provide certain other information. The kind, variety, and hybrid/non-hybrid designation must appear on the packet, along with the name of the seed company, the lot number, and whether or not the seed has been treated with some sort of pesticide.

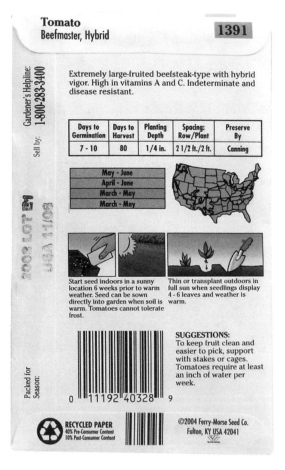

Some seeds are treated with a pesticide to protect them during germination. Fungicide-treated seed often has better "come up," especially in cold, damp soils where germination is slowed and diseases flourish. Treated seed are brightly dyed to distinguish them from non-treated seed. Many gardeners prefer organic methods over seed treatments, choosing instead to wait until the soil warms to avoid seed rots. But to other gardeners, treated seed is highly beneficial in helping to establish a good crop. The choice is yours.

Many companies offer both certified organic and nonorganic seeds. Organic seeds are often more expensive than traditionally produced seeds and will not necessarily produce better. But, many people prefer to "go organic." Let your personal viewpoint be your guide.

Alternatives to Seeds

The small size of some seeds, such as carrot and celery, makes accurate planting difficult and thinning a big chore. Some seed companies coat these seeds with clay or other materials to make them larger and therefore easier to space when planting. These are sold as "pelleted" seeds. They are expensive but they do make planting easier. So also do seed tapes on which seeds are already positioned at the proper spacing. Simply lay the tape in place and all your plants will be correctly spaced—no thinning required. The tape readily decomposes in the garden.

Resistance and Genetic Codes

Many varieties are resistant—but not immune—to various insects and diseases. These traits are given in a code following the variety name. For example, 'Superduper' **VFN** tomato is resistant to the fungal diseases **V**erticillium and **F**usarium and to **N**ematodes. See the vegetable profile on sweet corn for codes that refer to corn's genetic traits for sugar production and retention. Since not all locations harbor all pests, more resistance codes do not necessarily mean a better variety for you. It's not necessary to pay extra for resistance you don't need. Contact your local agricultural county extension office to find out the diseases and pests that are prevalent in your area. But to give you an idea, the following is a short list of resistance codes and what they mean. Most seed catalogs have even more extensive lists.

Resistance Codes and Their Meanings

Resistance Code	Meaning
F	Fusarium resistant
MDM	Maize dwarf mosaic virus
N	Nematode resistant
NCLB	Northern corn leaf blight
St	Common smut
Sw	Stewart's bacterial wilt
V	Verticillium resistant

Resistant varieties are a boon to gardeners, particularly where vegetables have been grown for a long time and pests have increased to destructive levels. Gardeners preferring organic methods should plant resistant varieties to avoid chemical controls. Nearly all hybrids carry some resistant traits, though some non-hybrid varieties may also have some resistance to certain diseases and insects, as well.

National, Regional, and Specialty Catalogs

There are many large seed companies that market to a national audience, carrying varieties that produce good crops from Florida to Washington. There are also smaller companies that market to regional audiences and offer regionally adapted varieties. Finally, there are specialty catalogs that offer only one commodity, such as tomatoes or garlic. These are wonderful sources for unusual varieties, but remember that many of those varieties may not be adapted to our region. Read the variety descriptions in a catalog prior to making your selection.

Separating Opinion from Fact

Beware the advertisers who blur fiction and fact in order to push their product. The variety description should actually tell you something; look for facts. Beware of statements like: "This is the earliest-maturing carrot we have ever seen." Maybe they've seen only one? Rather, look for statements like, "This beet ripens on average ten days earlier than 'Early Wonder'." "This miraculous variety was produced by world-famous breeders at a leading university" says nothing. First, there are no miracles in gardening, and second, why not name the breeders and the university? A more factual statement might be, "This very high-yielding, deep orange carrot was developed by Drs. L. Smith and W. Jones at Montana State University."

Seed companies are generally reputable and offer high-quality products. But there are shysters out there ready to sell you oceanfront property in Cheyenne. The "topepperato," at first blush a single plant that produces tomatoes, peppers, and potatoes, does not exist. If it did, every vegetable grower in the world would plant it. Rather, the advertisement actually offers all three of these commodities in one *planting*, not in one *plant*. You simply plant the seed potato and the tomato and pepper seedlings in one hole and they all grow together. Sometimes the ads work the other way, offering an old variety as a high-priced novelty. Blue potatoes, so-called black corn, and black tomatoes have been around for centuries. They are not new so why pay extra for them? Be skeptical of high-priced fertilizers that provide "30 vital nutrients." Plants need only sixteen or so elements for growth, so why pay more to give them what they don't need? Beware of words such as "magic," "miraculous," "amazing," and "breakthrough," the use of picture-perfect vegetable photos, and the like. In short, ignore the hype and look for the facts.

Harvesting and Saving Seeds

Through the early 1950s many gardeners saved seeds from their vegetables year after year. We recall allowing cucumbers and tomatoes to rot in order to extract their seeds. During the 1950s and 1960s inexpensive, high-quality hybrid seed became widely available and folks simply purchased new seeds each year. But in the 1970s, forward-thinking gardeners began to realize that we were losing genetic diversity, flavor, and vegetable "character" as the old varieties such as 'Bonnie Best' tomato and 'White Cob Cory' corn were fast disappearing. So a movement to save seeds from favorite varieties began once more. Today, many gardeners enjoy maintaining the old lines and once more taste the flavors of a long-ago time. There is a certain charm in eating the same variety of beet that Thomas Jefferson ate. Saving your own seeds is not difficult but it does take time and planning. Try it, but you must play by the rules.

First, don't bother saving seeds from hybrid (F_1) varieties, as they won't come true in the next (F_2) generation. Save seeds only from open-pollinated varieties. Most older varieties, like 'Champion' radish and 'Bellstar' tomato, are open-pollinated. Open-pollinated can further be divided into three categories: cross-pollinated, partially cross-pollinated, and self-pollinated.

Cross-pollinated and partially cross-pollinated vegetables are those that are pollinated by other varieties of the same kind of vegetable; spinach is cross-pollinated. If you plant 'Winter Bloomsdale' spinach in isolation then the seed it produces will continue to produce 'Winter Bloomsdale' in following years. But if you plant different varieties of spinach in your garden in the same year, say 'Winter Bloomsdale' and 'Olympia', they will cross-pollinate and the seed you save will produce an off-type the following year. That's fine if you want to experiment, but if you want to grow the same variety consistently, you must isolate it from other varieties of the same kind of plant. Following is a table of some commonly planted cross-pollinating or partially cross-pollinating vegetables and their means of pollination.

Pollination of Selected Vegetables

Pollinated by Insects	Parsley
Asparagus	Parsnip
Broccoli	Pepper
Brussels sprouts	Pumpkin
Cabbage	Radish
Carrot	Rutabaga
Cauliflower	Squash
Celery	Turnip
Cucumber	**Pollinated by Wind**
Endive	Beet
Kale	Swiss chard
Kohlrabi	Corn
Melon	Spinach
Onion	

Isolation is often difficult. Commercial growers may separate fields of different varieties by as much as five miles, but home growers can't do this. Either avoid planting multiple varieties of the same vegetable in the same year; plant varieties of the same kind of vegetable with different maturity dates; or, if you have a large garden, separate different varieties by at least 250 yards. The simplest plan for a beginning gardener is to pick one variety you think you'll like of any vegetable and plant just that one. Once you know the ropes, you can experiment more. Vegetables in the family of crucifers—broccoli, cabbage, and so forth—all inter-cross, so you will have to isolate them from each other as well.

But wait—there's more! Cucurbits (members of the pumpkin and squash family) belonging to the same *species* will cross, resulting in seeds that will produce off-types. It is not simply a matter of separating pumpkins from squash, as there is no botanical difference between the two. Rather, you must know the species to which each variety belongs in order to separate them effectively. Any varieties within the same species will cross pollinate. For example, 'Jack o'Lantern' pumpkin and 'Acorn' squash belong to *Cucurbita pepo* and will cross-pollinate. Varieties

belonging to *C. pepo*, *C. moschata*, and *C. mixta* will cross with
each other. For example, zucchini will cross with 'Butternut'
squash and 'Green Striped Cushaw' pumpkin. Varieties belonging to *C. moschata* and *C. maxima* will also cross with each other,
such as 'Kentucky Field Pumpkin' and 'Big Max' pumpkin.
Watermelon (*Citrullus lanatus*) belongs to a genus different from
the squashes, pumpkins, and muskmelons and will not cross with
any of them. Cucumbers (*Cucumis sativus*) and muskmelons
(*Cucumis melo*), although they share a genus, differ in species and
will not cross with each other or with the squashes and pumpkins.
The chart on page 302 under Winter Squash contains a partial list
of varieties within each species for the plant nerd in all of us.

Self-pollinating vegetables include peas, bean, and lettuce. They
do not have to be isolated from each other, so go ahead and plant
as many varieties as you like.

Harvesting Seeds

Saving seeds from plants grown as annuals is straightforward,
but the biennials, which produce seed during their *second* year,
require a little bit of special care because you must babysit them
over the winter. The following plants are biennials: beet, cabbage,
carrot, cauliflower, celery, collards, late varieties of endive, kale,
leek, onion, parsley, parsnip, rutabaga, and Swiss chard. Root vegetables also require special attention since you must harvest them
in their first year to determine which to save. Dig them in the fall
and select those with the most desirable characteristics (such as
large roots and minimal zoning). Remove the tops and replant the
roots as they were growing previously. The following season they
will produce a seed stalk from which you can harvest the seeds.

**Harvesting seeds borne in pods (beans, peas, crucifers, and
so forth):** Pick mature pods and dry them until they turn brown,
then shell and store the seeds in a paper envelope in a cool, dry

place. Before storing crucifer seeds, soak them in 122°F water (use a thermometer) for 25 minutes (cabbage) or 18 minutes (broccoli, Brussels sprouts, and cauliflower) to destroy seed-borne diseases. Dry seeds after soaking and store as described.

Harvesting seeds borne on a flowerhead (lettuce, endive, parsley, and so forth): Cut the seed heads just before they dry. Dry them in a paper bag and shake or rub the seeds to separate them from the stalk. Store them in a cool, dry place.

Harvesting seeds borne in fleshy fruit (tomato, cucumber, squash, and so forth): Harvest the fully ripe fruit of tomatoes and cucumbers and squeeze the pulp and seeds into a glass container. Add water and let the mixture ferment for several days at room temperature, stirring occasionally. Good seeds will settle to the bottom; non-viable seeds will float. Pour off the pulp, non-viable seeds, and water and spread the good seeds in a single layer on a paper towel to dry. Store them in a paper envelope in a cool, dry place. Scrape out the seeds of squash, melon, pumpkins, eggplants, and peppers and spread them onto a paper towel to dry. Store them as described.

Saving Seeds

Most seeds stored well in a cool, dry place will still be viable for *five years* or more. Check out the following table to get an idea of how long you could keep seeds before their germination falls below federal guidelines. Even after that you can plant the old seeds successfully by simply sowing a bit more thickly.

Seed Storage Limits

One year

Sweet corn

Two years

Parsley, Leek, Onion, Parsnip

Three years

Asparagus, Bean, Carrot, Peas

Four years

Beet, Swiss chard, Mustard, Pepper, Pumpkin, Tomato

Five years

Broccoli, Brussels sprouts, Cabbage, Cauliflower, Celery, Chinese cabbage, Collards, Cucumber, Eggplant, Endive, Kale, Kohlrabi, Lettuce, Muskmelon, Radish, Rutabaga, Spinach, Squash, Turnip, Watermelon

(Source: Adapted from Harrington and Minges, 1954.)

Checking Germination

You can check the germination of old seeds by using what's called the "ragdoll test." Count out a number of seeds and place them on a paper towel. The more you use the more accurate your results; we test at least twenty seeds. Fold the paper towel so that the seeds will not fall out, moisten it, squeeze out any excess water, and place it in a jar that you will place on a warm windowsill. After a week, remove and unfold the towel and count how many seeds have germinated. Slow-germinating seeds, such as those of parsnip, may take two or three weeks before you can make an accurate assessment. Count the number that have germinated and determine the percentage. If it is 50 percent or greater go ahead and use the seeds for this year's crop. If germination has dropped below 50 percent, then use your judgment. But what do you have to lose? Just plant more seeds!

Chapter Five

STARTING TRANSPLANTS

Even though this book is for those new to vegetable gardening as well as for those who have some experience, we want you to know that growing your own transplants is well within the capability of the newcomers. You can do it! Gardeners transplant started plants for many different reasons. One is to get a jump on the season, since some plants, such as tomatoes and peppers, cannot be successfully direct-seeded in most of our region. Also, some cool-season vegetables such as spring cabbage are set out relatively early in the season to make good growth during cool weather. But probably the main reason for growing your own transplants is that this allows you to sow the varieties *you* want and to grow excellent, inexpensive plants.

Just Say No

Purchasing started plants limits you to relatively few varieties and sometimes to inferior plants that are being sold at stages of their development that are improper for setting out. The best transplants, sometimes called "sets," should be about six inches tall, stocky, pest free, have good green color, and be at the proper stage of development when transplanted to the garden.

Some crops are more easily transplanted than others due to their ability to rapidly regenerate root tips that may be damaged during the transplant process, but even those requiring extra care may be transplanted, provided they are grown in peat pots, or by other methods that do not require the removal of the pot.

Relative Ease of Transplant

Easy	Moderate	Needs Special Care
Beet	Celery	Cucumber
Broccoli	Eggplant	Muskmelon
Brussels sprouts	Onion	Okra
Cabbage	Pepper	Squash
Cauliflower		Sweet corn
Lettuce		Watermelon
Swiss chard		
Tomato		

(Source: Maynard and Hochmuth, 1997.)

Look for the following when purchasing transplants:
- stocky plants 6 to 8 inches tall
- plants that are not crowded
- no yellowing of bottom leaves
- no flowers or fruit present
- leaves that are dark green (not hardened) or gray-green with pink veins (hardened)

There is little point transplanting plants such as peas, beet, Swiss chard, spinach, or carrot as they are relatively short-season crops that mature easily in our region even when they're direct seeded. Sweet corn is also not usually transplanted since there are enough early ripening varieties to allow successful direct seeding.

Containers

Containers for growing transplants vary widely. Styrofoam coffee cups, egg cartons, flower pots, peat pots, peat pellets, multi-plant containers like cell packs, or plastic flats are all used. Use the larger sizes so that plants will not be crowded. A rule of thumb is to allow about 6 to 9 square inches of growing space per plant. A 3-inch diameter pot will provide one plant with about 7 square inches of space. Plants in peat pots or peat pellets may be set into the garden as an intact unit, but be sure that the lip of the peat pot is completely buried as an exposed edge can wick moisture away from the roots. Remove transplants from plastic pots and Styrofoam cups before transplanting. If the rootball is massive and the roots crowded, gently break the ball apart or make several light scoring cuts along the edge of the rootball before planting. This stimulates new root formation.

Growing Media

Growing media must supply good drainage and yet have adequate water-holding capacity; be free of harmful substances, including pests and weed seeds; and be inexpensive and available. For years gardeners used topsoil amended with sand and peat moss that was pasteurized in the kitchen oven. You could make your own using the following ingredients: 1 bushel sphagnum moss, 1 bushel horticultural vermiculite (not building grade), 1

Growing media that have been used, left to right: compost, COIR, vermiculite, peat, perlite, and sand

pound ground limestone, 4 ounces superphosphate, 2 ounces calcium nitrate, 7 ounces calcium sulfate, 1 ounce trace elements, and 2 grams chelated iron, such as Sequestrene 330 Fe. It's less expensive to purchase your media but some gardeners like to have an extra level of control or involvement regarding the quality of ingredients and make their own. One cubic foot of media will fill about 275 2½-square-inch peat pots; or 60 4-inch round peat pots; or 20 cell packs measuring about 5 x 8 x 2¾ inches. Many of the nutrients added to the media by the manufacturer are used by plants during their early stages of growth. Therefore, you will have to add more fertilizer as the plants grow. A plant will tell you if it needs more nutrients because the foliage will turn yellow-green or purple. Dissolve two level tablespoons of 20-20-20 or equivalent high phosphorous fertilizer in one gallon of water and apply this weekly during regular watering.

Sowing

Water the planting media thoroughly the night before sowing. If you use flats, sow enough seeds to obtain about eight plants per inch of row; if you use peat pots, sow two or three seeds per pot. Plant most vegetable seeds about ¼ inch deep. If media is dry after seeding, water it but do not soak it. Bottom watering will avoid disturbing newly sown seeds.

When seedlings emerge after a week or two they will require light and a slightly lower temperature than that used during germination. This is most relevant if you grow the transplants in your home and becomes a moot point if you use a cold frame or hotbed for the plants. Don't worry if you have no way to regulate the temperature; chances are your plants will grow fine.

Some gardeners place heating pads beneath the flats or pots to increase rootzone temperatures, thereby increasing the growth rate. This is useful but not necessary. Carefully monitor the air temperature at which the sets are grown. A high temperature can cause plants to become leggy, especially in low light; too low a temperature slows growth, induces premature seedstalk formation (bolting) in crucifers, and causes the first fruits of tomato plants to be rough and unattractive. Plants grow best if nighttime temperatures are 5 to 10°F cooler than daytime temperatures.

No matter what some books and magazine articles say, the south window in our region in March and April often does not supply sufficient light for good transplant growth. Supplement or replace natural, early-season sunlight with fluorescent and/or incandescent lights, or with special grow lights. The fluorescent lights are especially high in blue wavelengths while incandescent lights are high in red wavelengths, the two spectral bands plants need most for best growth. Use one or two 40-watt incandescent bulbs along with four or five 40-watt fluorescent bulbs and keep them on for about twelve hours each day, placing them only a few inches above the tops of the seedlings. Incandescent bulbs give off a lot of heat so monitor the temperature of the plant canopy closely and move the incandescent bulbs farther from the foliage if the air gets too hot.

Thin plants when they are about an inch tall and still in the cotyledon stage, that is, before the first true leaves emerge. Moisten the media before thinning and, if the plants removed during this operation are to be themselves transplanted, fill new pots and moisten that media before "spotting out" or "pricking off" operations begin. Punch a hole in the new media with a pencil, then gently tease out the plants to be transplanted with a plant label or tweezers and transfer them to the pencil hole in the new media. Hold the plants by their cotyledons only to avoid crushing their stems. Press roots firmly in place and water the pots or flats when they are full. Extra seedlings crowded in peat pots should be pinched out or cut out with scissors and discarded as they will transplant poorly without a rootball.

Thin plants grown in flats to stand at least one-half inch apart after the first thinning. As the plants grow, thin them repeatedly so that, by the last thinning, they are standing a few inches apart in all directions, allowing about 6 to 9 square inches per plant.

Watering

To determine when to water your transplants, take a bit of media from the top one-half inch and squeeze it between your thumb and forefinger. If water runs out of it freely the media is moist enough. Overwatering promotes weak growth and damping-off. Always use water kept at room temperature.

Time

A common mistake is to start your transplants too early in the season. The large plants that result suffer greater transplant shock and will yield poorly. Transplant tomatoes, peppers, and eggplants to the garden before they are ready to bloom. Remove early-set fruit at the time of transplant to improve later fruit development. Set cucurbits in the garden when their leaves are about two inches across. Follow the guidelines in the facing table when starting your transplants. For example, cucumbers require about four to five weeks to grow to transplant size. If you set them in the garden on June 1, then you should start them in late April or early May.

Approximate Length of Germination and Approximate Time Needed for Transplant to Develop to Transplant Size

(The actual time needed will vary by temperature, fertility, and light conditions.)

Vegetable	Germination (days)	Growth to transplant size (weeks)
Broccoli	3–4	4–6
Brussels sprouts	3–4	4–6
Cabbage	3–4	4–6
Cauliflower	3–4	4–6
Celery	14–21	10–12
Cucumber	6–10	4–5
Eggplant	7–14	8
Lettuce	4–10	3–4
Muskmelon	4–8	4
Onion	10	9
Pepper	5–7	8
Pumpkin / Winter squash	6–10	4–5
Tomato	4–9	5–6
Watermelon	3–12	4

Transplants may also be successfully grown in hot beds and cold frames; see chapter 10.

Hardening-off

Plants that have spent their entire life in a protected environment where they wanted for nothing are poorly adapted to outdoor life in the garden, so before setting them out you need to acclimate them, or harden them to the outdoors. Hardening-off involves a process where growth slows and the plant tissues toughen to better enable them to withstand drought, wind, and cold. The process takes about two weeks. When they have reached the proper size, move the transplants outdoors during warmer days and bring them in at night, gradually increasing the length of time they spend outdoors until they remain outdoors day and night for a week before transplanting. During this time decrease

watering to provide only enough to keep the plants from wilting. This reduction in water induces the plant to thicken the waxy
cuticle layer of its leaves and stems, giving it more protection
from drought and wind. If the transplants were grown in flats, cut
the media into small blocks containing a single plant. "Blocking"
temporarily reduces the total functional root surface of the plants
but causes a proliferation in root branching, which in a short time
increases the total root surface substantially. Do not block cucurbits or other plants that are difficult to transplant. For the first
week of hardening, give plants partial shade. Thereafter, provide
them with full sunlight. The stems and leaf veins of well-hardened
plants will normally turn purple. Last, withhold fertilizer during
the hardening process to force the plant to decrease its vegetative
growth, making the stem more woody and the plants stockier in
order to better resist wind-whipping in the garden.

There are different levels of hardening off; some plants tolerate
only a small amount of hardening, some a great degree of hardening, and some no hardening at all. Consider the following before
you start the hardening process:

Broccoli and cabbage can be hardened to withstand a frost, but
repeated chilling of young transplants at 50°F or lower can cause
plants to bolt after planting in the garden.

Brussels sprouts and cauliflower can be hardened to withstand
a frost, but inadequate water and crowding young plants
can cause the stems to become woody and the buds or curd to
develop poorly. Grow both species in individual peat pots to
avoid crowding.

Lettuce and onions are easy to grow and can be hardened to
tolerate light frosts.

Cucurbits should be started in individual containers and their
roots disturbed as little as possible during transplanting. They
cannot be hardened to withstand even light frosts. Do not thin

Take care when hardening-off transplants for the garden. Some vegetable plants can withstand the frosts better than others.

plants by pulling some as this may damage roots of remaining plants. Pinch or snip out excess plants, leaving their roots intact.

Peppers can be hardened only slightly, but be sure to keep the temperature above 50°F at all times during the process.

Tomatoes can be hardened slightly at temperatures above 50°F before their first flower cluster opens. Overhardening will delay establishment and cause rough fruit on the early clusters. Container-grown plants usually produce fruit earlier than plants grown in flats.

Eggplants cannot be hardened as the process will result in low-quality fruit.

If you relish the idea of getting a jump on nature by starting your garden while there is snow on the ground, then growing your own transplants is for you! It gives you the ultimate ability to control when you can get out to the garden.

The following table outlines symptoms and corrective measures for some transplant disorders.

Disorders Affecting Transplants

Description	Possible Causes	Correction
Leggy, spindly plants	Not enough light	Use full-spectrum lights or a combination of fluorescent and incandescent lighting.
	Excessive watering	Do not allow transplants to sit in water. Maintain moist but not wet media.
	Excessive fertilizer	Apply according to label directions. Reduce concentration.
	Plants are too close together	Provide each seedling with enough room to allow for stocky growth.
Dwarf plants	Look for symptoms of nutrient deficiency (below).	Apply fertilizers often, and in low concentrations.
Dwarf plants with discolored leaves Stems and undersides of leaves may be reddish. Leaves may be small. Roots may be stunted.	Phosphorus deficiency	Apply a high phosphorus starter solution according to label directions.
Lack of green color in leaves and stems. Slow growth.	Nitrogen deficiency	Apply nitrogen fertilizer solution according to label directions.

Description	Possible Causes	Correction
Dwarf plants with discolored leaves and discolored roots Plants may wilt in bright sunlight. Lower leaves turn yellow and drop.	Too much fertilizer	Leach excess fertilizer by running clean water through the media.
Dwarf plants with discolored leaves and discolored roots	Too long/too hot sterilization of media	After sterilization of media, soak or leach the soil.
Dwarf plants with no root discoloration	Temperatures too low Growth is slowed	Maintain proper air and soil temperatures.
Rotting and collapse of the stems near soil surface	Damping off. Fungal organisms in media attack germinating seeds and young plants.	Do not use garden soil that has not been sterilized. Wash all reused pots in soap and water. Rinse with bleach solution, then water.
Slow root growth	Soil mixture problems, poor drainage, low fertility, high fertility, low temperatures, herbicide residue in soil mix	Provide adequate drainage, a steady supply of nutrients, adequate moisture, and appropriate temperatures.
Algae and moss growth on media surface	High moisture content of media. Poor media mix, poor aeration	Water in the morning. Increase air movement around plants. Add coarse sand to loosen media.

(Source: Fletcher, 1975.)

Chapter Six

PLANTING

It's time. You understand the challenges facing you, you've planned your garden, purchased seeds or started transplants, and now it's time. Once you've read this chapter and looked up your favorite vegetables' planting requirements in the vegetable section, it'll be time to go down to the garden!

Getting Your Hands Dirty

Prepare the seedbed after the soil has dried sufficiently to work (when it no longer sticks to gardening tools), turning over the top eight inches to incorporate any fertilizers and organic matter that you've added and to remove weeds and stones. Then bring the soil surface to a fine, smooth texture by raking and leveling with a steel garden rake. If you don't take this step to create a fine texture, small seeds will be buried beneath the clods. Mark the rows, leaving enough space between them to accommodate the mature spread of your plants. (This is when your garden plan on paper really helps!) Row orientation doesn't matter a great deal.

Vegetables that produce weak seedlings, such as beet, carrot, parsnip, and onion, are damaged by soil crusting and are very susceptible to competition from weeds. After sowing, cover the rows with vermiculite or sand to prevent crusting or plant a nurse crop of radishes with these seeds.

Spring Fever

Every plant has a preferred soil temperature for its best growth, so don't be in a hurry to plant. Spring fever can be deadly (to plants—not to you!). Crops planted too early will take a long time to grow and those same crops planted even a week or two later into warmer soil will catch up with those planted earlier. Years ago, English gardeners used to determine if the soil temperature was warm enough for planting by dropping their drawers and sitting on the soil's surface. If the temperature felt comfortable, then the soil temperature was right. Maybe you can just use your wrist, at the risk of offending the neighbors otherwise (or use a soil thermometer—yawn).

The following table gives the ideal soil temperature for vegetable seed germination and for seedlings to emerge from the soil. Soil temperature for germination is measured about two inches below the soil's surface; you can purchase a soil thermometer to check temperature or simply use any spare thermometer you have if using the Seat Method doesn't appeal to you.

Optimum Soil Temperature for Direct-seeded Germination and Seedling Growth

Vegetable	Optimum soil temperature for seed germination (°F)	Approximate number of days for seedlings to emerge
Celery, Spinach	70	4–7
Asparagus, Lettuce, Onion, Peas	75	2–13
Bean, Carrot, Cauliflower	80	5–6
Beet, Cabbage, Eggplant, Swiss chard, Pepper, Radish, Tomato, Turnip	85	1–8
Muskmelon, Pumpkin	90	3
Corn, Cucumber, Okra, Squash, Watermelon	95	3–6

(Source: Adapted from Maynard and Hochmuth, 1997.)

It's All Relative: Frost Dates

You can determine when to plant the garden in spring by noting the average date of *last* frost for your area. Fall plantings can be based on the average date of *first* frost. Be aware, however, that you are dealing with *average* dates. Experienced gardeners know that each of these dates can vary by two weeks sooner or later, depending upon yearly and local conditions. Use the following table as a guide, but base your actual time of planting on how the season "feels" to you. If you are new to vegetable gardening, spy on your more experienced gardening neighbors, or better still, get to know them and ask their advice. They know your local growing conditions better than any other resource. After gardening for several years you will know intuitively when the time is right.

Planting Times Based On Hardiness and Average Last Frost Date

Hardy Vegetables (4–6 weeks before last frost)	Half-Hardy Vegetables (2–3 weeks before last frost)	Tender Vegetables (just after last frost)	Very Tender Vegetables (2 weeks after last frost)
Kale	Beet	Snap bean	Cucumber
Lettuce	Carrot	New Zealand	Muskmelon
Collards	Swiss chard	spinach	Okra
Kohlrabi	Mustard	Summer squash	Pumpkin
Peas	Parsnip	Corn	Winter squash
Onion	Radish	Tomato	Watermelon
Rutabaga	Cauliflower		Eggplant
Turnip	Chinese cabbage		Pepper
Salsify	Broccoli		
Spinach	Cabbage		
Asparagus	Celery		
Horseradish	Celeriac		
Rhubarb	Endive		
	Potato		

(Source: Adapted from Knott, 1935.)

Because tender and very tender vegetables grow the most during warm weather, try to plant them as early as possible without jumping the gun. If you plant them too late they may spend the last third of their lives trying to grow to maturity when the weather is too cool.

With our short seasons you will find it difficult to harvest a fall crop from a succession planting. Still, by selecting the right cool-season crop, which must tolerate both the heat of summer planting and the cool of maturing during the fall, you can have great success. Beets, collards, kale, lettuce, mustard, spinach, and turnips can all produce a healthy fall harvest if they're planted six to eight weeks before the average date of the first fall frost.

How Low Can You Go?

Many gardeners plant seeds too deeply. The only source of energy a seedling has until it emerges from the soil surface is what is stored in its seed. The smaller a seed, the less stored energy; hence the less deeply the seed should be planted. In general, plant small seeds like Swiss chard, carrot, lettuce, and beet about ¼ to ½ inch deep and larger seeds like squash, corn, bean, and peas about 1 to 2 inches deep. If the soil is heavy, plant a little less deeply to take advantage of warmer surface temperatures. If it is sandy, hot, or dry, plant a little more deeply to take advantage of cooler, moister soil. Cover the seed with fine soil and tamp it firmly to provide good seed-to-soil contact. Seeds of the cucurbits are traditionally planted in what is called a "hill." This does not refer to a mound but rather to planting several seeds in a group with each group planted a number of feet apart. In fact, mounding can dry the soil excessively. Once the seedlings are up all but two are removed, or thinned out. If closely planted, their roots may be intertwined; *pinch* out the plants to be removed rather than pulling them out and risk disturbing the roots of remaining plants.

Sowing too thickly is also common, for it is very difficult to spread small seeds like carrots thinly enough. You can mix small seeds with sand, or use a salt-shaker to keep from overseeding. The "seed" of beet and Swiss chard are actually the dried fruits, which contain several seeds, so it is impossible *not* to overseed. Seedlings of seeds that have been sown too thickly will be thinned when they are an inch or so tall, and then again when they are somewhat taller in order to provide enough room for the plants to develop and mature. Failure to thin adequately results in stunted, stressed plants that will develop undersized plants and roots, or no fruit at all. Directions for thinning are given under individual vegetables.

Off to a Good Start

A cup of soluble fertilizer high in phosphorus or a handful of wet, composted manure in the bottom of each hole along with plenty of water will help transplants get off to a fast start. A cloudy, windless afternoon is an ideal time to transplant.

In general, water vegetable transplants about an hour or so before transplanting, then plant them as deeply as they grew in their container. An exception is a leggy tomato plant. If you are faced with such plants, set their rootballs about 3 or 4 inches deep then

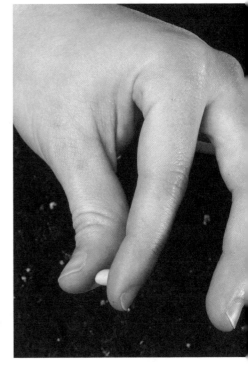

lay the plant's stem along a small trench for a few more inches, finally allowing the top six inches or so of the plant to stand upright above the soil surface. You may have to prop it straight up with a small stick temporarily. Remove all foliage from parts that will be buried. This method effectively shortens the height of the transplant aboveground, reducing wind whipping and moisture loss, and allows the formation of an extensive root system because roots will form all along the tomato plant stem. Unfortunately, this planting system does not work as well with other vegetable transplants.

The Fun Part

The garden is in. Take a deep breath and watch the miracle of your seeds sprouting, beans climbing, and pea tendrils clinging to the trellis. Care for your garden as we'll show you, and prepare for a bountiful harvest. This is the fun part.

Chapter Seven

WHAT'S IN A NAME? SOIL

Good gardens depend upon having good soil. For some lucky home gardeners, their sites have perfectly good soil to begin with and they will have to amend very little. But for the rest of us, it may take a year or even longer to amend poor soils in order to get the garden site in shape. But here's the good news: like plastic surgery, you can create what nature doesn't give you.

What *is* Soil?

All soils are differing mixtures of living organisms, air, water, sand, silt, clay, and organic matter. In an ideal world, we'd all have ideal soil, meaning air would fill about 25 percent of the spaces between soil particles ("pore" spaces) and water another 25 percent. This proportion allows healthy root growth, which is essential to healthy plants. But as the proportions of air and water change, the soil can become too dry or too wet. Organic matter, which makes up about 1 to 5 percent of the volume, is the "glue" that binds soil components into larger particles, which in turn create larger spaces between the pores of the soil and hence, create fluffier soil. The remaining 45 percent or so of the soil volume is composed of various proportions of minerals (sand, silt, and clay). These components give a soil its texture.

IDEAL SOIL

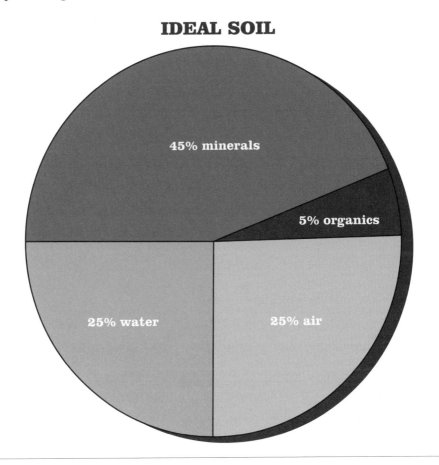

There are pros and cons to each of these minerals. For example, sand particles are relatively large and help make larger pore spaces. As the amount of sand in a soil increases—making it easier for a gardener to work the soil—the water-holding and nutrient-holding capacities decrease. Sandy soils warm faster in spring, allowing you to plant earlier. Conversely, they also dry out faster and you need to pay greater attention to watering.

Soils that also have lots of clay particles have smaller pore spaces, and hold more water and nutrients—but they remain cooler in spring, which can delay planting. They drain more poorly, are tougher to work with, and are easily compacted, further decreasing pore size and restricting the flow of air to plant roots. This reduces the rate of root growth and subsequent topgrowth of vegetables. Silt particles are midway in size between sand and clay.

Soils that are composed of approximately twice as much sand and silt as clay are called "loams" and are, overall, the best garden soils. Loams are further divided into types depending on the amount of mineral particles they contain. Loam that has a slightly higher percentage of sand is called "sandy loam"; that which is slightly higher in clay is termed "clay loam"; and that which is slightly higher in silt is called "silt loam." Sandy loams feel gritty when they're moist while silt loams feel slicker to the touch. Sandy loams and silt loams are the absolute best types of soils to have. And if you haven't got it, you can still make it! (We'll tell you how.)

Know Your Soil Texture

You've heard the saying that "knowledge is power." Well, it's true. To help determine the type of soil you have, send a soil sample to a testing laboratory for analysis. Contact your local agriculture extension office or check online to locate a soil testing laboratory. Among the items in the final report will be soil texture. But it is more fun (and less expensive) to do a simple test yourself (though this home test will not tell you everything that a soil analysis will). Fill a glass or clear plastic jar halfway with a soil sample from your garden (or the area you plan to make into your garden). Then fill the rest of the jar with water to which a little powdered dishwasher detergent has been added. Put the cap on the jar and shake vigorously, then set the jar aside. The different types of soil particles will settle out in layers, the heavier sand first, then the silt, and finally the clay. (The clay remains in suspension for a long time and may take months to settle out. Until then the water will look cloudy.) With the proportions of sand and silt only, you can use the soil triangle to determine its texture.

Any organic components will float. Look at the combined thicknesses of each mineral fraction and estimate the percentage of individual elements. For example, if the sand layer appears to represent about 25 percent of the total soil, then you can assume your soil is about 25 percent sand. Estimate one other of the two mineral portions (silt would be good, since it will settle out faster) and compare the two percentages to the soil triangle. For example, let's suppose our soil is 40 percent silt and 40 percent sand. Look at the soil triangle and find the lines for each; where they intersect is in the loam soil section of the soil triangle. If the percentages were 70 percent silt and 20 percent sand, then we would have a silt loam soil.

This is important: you must first know your soil texture in order to know what materials to add to improve it.

Organic Matter

All garden soils need organic matter, the "glue" that bonds smaller soil particles into larger particles. This bonding increases pore space and the ability of the soil to maintain good air- and water-holding capacities. Organic matter also "lightens" soils high

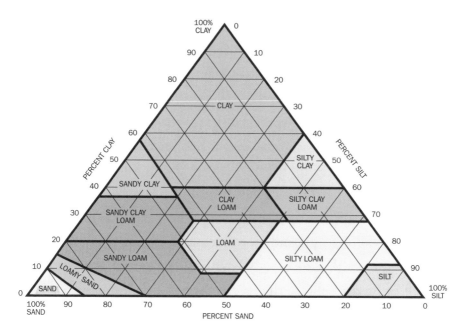

SOIL TEXTURE TRIANGLE

(Source: Soil Science Society of America)

in silt and clay ("heavy" soils) and makes sandy ("light") soils more water absorbent. The increased aeration it provides increases bacterial action, which liberates more nutrients from the organic material during decomposition. In addition, organic matter reduces the loss of nutrients through leaching. In short, organic matter improves soil tilth and improves plant growth.

Most soils contain less than 5 percent organic matter. You can add organic matter to your soil through the use of manures and compost. These can also be supplemented with other organic soil amendments. But applying too much organic matter is just as bad as not applying enough. Excessive amounts of fresh manure can "burn" plants; compacted layers of organic matter interfere with penetration of air and water into the soil; and nitrogen used during the decomposition process can affect the amount available for plant use, resulting in too little nitrogen.

Whatever type you use, incorporate the organic material *into* the soil at rates of about 25 to 50 percent by soil volume. That is, spread a layer of organic material 3 to 4 inches deep over the entire garden and till it into the top 6 to 8 inches or so of soil. But even as little as a ½-inch layer of compost can improve your garden. However, sprinkling organic matter over the garden like commercial fertilizer does no good whatsoever. If your organic material is especially woody, such as corn stalks and rotted sawdust, sprinkle 1 to 2 pounds of nitrogen per 1,000 square feet (20 to 40 pounds of 5-10-10) over the material before you incorporate it into the soil. This will help with decomposition. Organic matter is decomposed by soil microbes over a period of 6 to 12 months and must be replenished annually to maintain good tilth.

Have your soil tested professionally every three years or so. Good times to test your soil are in fall after harvest and in spring before planting. Remove the top two inches of soil in several spots in the garden, as it may contain litter that will affect the test. Then, take a soil sample 4 to 6 inches below the surface. Take several cups of soil from different parts of the garden, mix them in a bucket, and take a cup of the combined soil for testing. Submit the sample to one of many soil test labs around the region and for a modest price you should receive a fairly complete and understandable soil analysis, which you can use to improve your garden. Contact your local county extension office to obtain a list of local labs.

Reading Between the Lines

All fertilizer packages have labels that give you lots of information. For example, all labels display three numbers separated by hyphens. This set of numbers is called the fertilizer analysis or grade. One common garden fertilizer is 5-10-10. The first number (5) displays the percentage of elemental nitrogen the fertilizer contains; the second number (10) shows the percentage of phosphorus pentoxide; and the third number (10) shows the percentage of potassium oxide, or potash. The remaining percentage of the ingredients is a carrier used to evenly disperse the nutrients. Commercially available bagged composted cow manure may have an analysis of 1-1-1, meaning it contains 1 percent nitrogen, 1 percent phosphorus pentoxide, and 1 percent potash. (These are represented by the letters "NPK" found on a fertilizer bag, standing for **Nitrogen, Phosphorus, K**(Potassium).) You can immediately see that the cow manure fertilizer is far less concentrated than the commercial fertilizer. That means you would have to use more of it to supply the same amounts of nutrients.

WHAT FERTILIZER NUMBERS MEAN

NITROGEN   PHOSPHOROUS   POTASSIUM

5   10   10

TOTAL NITROGEN.................................5.00%
  100% of Total Nitrogen Soluble in Water
  100% Inorganic derived from Sulphate of
  Ammonia, Ammonium Nitrate & Phosphate

PHOSPHORIC ACID.............................10.00%
  100% of Total Nitrogen Soluble in Water
  100% Inorganic derived from Sulphate of
  Ammonia, Ammonium Nitrate & Phosphate

SOLUBLE POTASH...............................10.00%
  100% of Total Nitrogen Soluble in Water
  100% Inorganic derived from Sulphate of
  Ammonia, Ammonium Nitrate & Phosphate

The proportion of the numbers in the analysis is called the "ratio." For example, a 5-10-10 analysis has a ratio of 1-2-2. This is important when dealing with various kinds of vegetables. For example, leafy crops benefit from fertilizers with slightly more nitrogen than phosphorus or potash. In that case, a fertilizer with a ratio of 2-1-1 (an analysis of 10-5-5) may be more appropriate.

The nitrogen in fertilizers may be in a rapid-release or slow-release form. Slow-release nitrogen fertilizers like Osmocote® release nitrogen over a long period of time and, since we are dealing with such short growing seasons in many of our areas, are probably *not* the right choice for most vegetable gardeners in the Rockies. Organic fertilizers like manure and blood meal also release nitrogen to the soil over a relatively long period of time. This is because they depend upon soil microorganisms to transform their relatively large organic molecules into smaller molecules that plant roots can absorb. However, by the time the nutrients in organic fertilizers can be used by a plant, they are in precisely the same form as the nutrients found in commercial fertilizers. But, because the microbial action takes some time, organic fertilizers are said to be "slow-acting" or "slow-release" and therefore less apt to burn crops. Microbial activity increases as soil temperature increases, so activity is relatively slow in the cold soils of early spring. If you use organic fertilizers exclusively then your plants may suffer from early season nutrient deficiencies, particularly nitrogen and phosphorus. Fertilizers that burn plants do so because of their concentrated salt content, which dehydrates plant tissues. Because commercial fertilizers are highly concentrated, with higher salt contents, they can rapidly dehydrate a plant if they come into direct contact with the plant's stem, foliage, or roots. But so can manure gathered from feedlots where salts concentrate.

All types of fertilizers have their pros and cons; no one type is right for all situations. If you are a purist organic gardener, then use the liquid organic fertilizers when soils are cool. If you are not a purist, then use a commercial fertilizer in cool soils and either commercial or organic fertilizer as soils warm in summer. Be sure when you apply a summer organic fertilizer there is still enough time in the season for the materials to break down and release nutrients to the plants.

Nutrient Needs and Sources

We all think we know the differences between "organic" and "inorganic" materials, but they are not clearly defined. To a chemist, an organic substance contains carbon, but to the gardener an organic substance may or may not contain carbon. Rather, it's

A smorgasbord of amendments and fertilizers await you at the garden center.

generally a compound that was derived from a once-living organism or is found naturally. For example, manure, compost, and blood meal all contain carbon and were derived from once-living creatures. However, sulfur, gypsum, and rock phosphate do not contain carbon and were not once a part of a living organism, but all are considered "organic" compounds suitable for use in an organic garden. So the term "organic" has more than one meaning. Most folks who define themselves as organic gardeners use only approved organic fertilizers; that is, those that are not highly concentrated and processed and are natural.

Whatever the source and whatever your philosophy, vegetables need 16 or 17 essential nutrients to remain healthy. Carbon (C), hydrogen (H), and oxygen (O) from air and water are three used by plants in large amounts. In fact, about 90 percent of a plant is made up of these three nutrients. Plants absorb the remaining 13 or 14 nutrients from the soil. The remaining major nutrients include nitrogen (N), phosphorus (P), potassium (K), sulfur (S), calcium (Ca), and magnesium (Mg) and are used in relatively large amounts by plants. The first three, expressed in the three numbers of a typical fertilizer analysis, are the ones most often lacking in garden soils. The remaining nutrients—manganese (Mn), iron (Fe), zinc (Zn), boron (B), molybdenum (Mo), copper (Cu), and chlorine (Cl)—are used by plants in small amounts and are called minor nutrients. Cobalt (Co) and nickel (Ni) are needed by some plants and not by others and their necessity in a vegetable garden has not been established. Most minor nutrients are available in soils in amounts sufficient for plant growth, but some, like boron, may be limited. Do not regularly add the minor nutrients to your soil unless you are sure they are needed, as there is a very fine line between their deficiency and toxicity.

Since vegetables remove some nutrients from the soil each year as they are harvested, those nutrients must be replenished annually to maintain productivity. You can do so by fertilizing with a complete inorganic fertilizer such as 5-10-10. Broadcast the fertilizer at the rate of about 20 pounds per 1,000 square feet just before planting, and till it in. This will get plants off to a quick start. As the growing season progresses, the nutrients added before planting may

A dash of fertilizer helps to replenish nutrients used by previous plants.

become depleted or immobilized in the soil. To keep long-season plants growing vigorously, spread more fertilizer in a band about eight inches from the base of the plants; this is called "sidedressing." A half-handful of fertilizer spread completely around individual plants such as cabbage and tomatoes should be sufficient. If you are fertilizing row plants like parsnips or beets, spread enough fertilizer along the row so that it looks like a light dusting of snow. Five pounds of 5-10-10 per 100 square feet, or a handful per 10 feet of row, should be just about right. Usually 1 or 2 sidedressings per season for long-season plants are enough. Inorganic or so-called "commercial" fertilizers are concentrated and inexpensive but they contain no organic matter, a valuable constituent in all garden soils.

Foliar fertilizers are useful for supplying minor nutrients. They are easy to use, but because of this you can get into trouble by applying them too frequently. Usually high in nitrogen, overapplication of these fertilizers tends to promote excessive leaf and stem growth and delay ripening. The result can be 20-foot-tall tomato plants with hundreds of small, green fruits that do not ripen. Take it easy when using foliar fertilizers.

Organic fertilizers are bulky and less concentrated than inorganic fertilizers and hence have to be added in larger amounts. However, they sometimes contain large amounts of valuable organic matter. The table on the facing page lists some organic fertilizers and the amounts that should be added to the garden per application. Do not use pet or other carnivore manures as they may harbor diseases and parasites. Also, try to spread manures and compost on the garden in the fall, and till them in. "Cold" manures are usually high in moisture and decompose slowly; "hot" manures decompose rapidly and can cause severe burn when used directly on plants.

Common Organic Fertilizers

(All analyses are approximate.)

Material	Analysis	*Pounds to add per 1,000 square feet of garden	Notes
Blood meal (dried blood)	13-0.9-0.8	10	Expensive, strong odor; may attract predators
Cottonseed meal	7-3-1.5	50	Expensive; may be unavailable
Cow manure (dry)	1.5-2-1.2	200	Expensive
Cow manure (fresh)	0.5-0.2-0.5	500	Bulky; odor; cold manure; compost fresh manure
Chicken manure (dry)	4.5-3.5-2	100	Odor when wet; may cause excessive vegetative growth
Chicken manure (fresh)	1.5-1-0.5	200	Ammonia can burn young plants; may cause excessive vegetative growth; hot manure
Compost	2-1-1	60	Apply a layer up to 4 inches deep
Feather meal	12-0-0	10	Nitrogen slowly available; hard to find
Fish meal	10-3.8-0	15	Nitrogen and Phosphorus slowly available; odor; may attract predators
Greensand (Glauconite)	0-1-7	150–300	Potassium slowly available; high in micronutrients; apply to gardens every 3–4 years

Common Organic Fertilizers

(All analyses are approximate.)

Material	Analysis	*Pounds to add per 1,000 square feet of garden	Notes
Horse manure (fresh)	0.7-0.3-0.5	500	Bulky; heavy weed seed load; hot manure
Pig manure (fresh)	0.7-0.6-0.7	500	Odor; bulky; cold manure
Rabbit manure (fresh)	2-1.3-1.2	150	May be available in insufficient quantities; hot manure
Sheep manure (fresh)	1.4-0.7-1.5	300	Easy to handle; may cause excessive vegetative growth; hot manure
Sheep manure (dry)	4.2-2.5-6.0	100	May cause excessive vegetative growth
Steamed bone meal	2-12-0	15	Expensive; may require several years for phosphorus to become available to plants in alkaline soils
Rock phosphate	0-30-0	150–300	Dusty; 33% calcium; phosphorus nearly unavailable in soils above pH 6; hard rock phosphate contains about 33% P_2O_5; colloidal rock phosphate about 22% P_2O_5; apply to gardens every 3–4 years
Wood ashes	0-1-5	20	23% calcium; raises soil pH over time

(*One bushel of manure weighs about 50 pounds. For manures, apply about 4 to 5 wheelbarrow loads per square rod (272 square feet) of garden. Apply an additional 2 pounds of phosphorus (20 pounds of 5-10-10 or 15 pounds of steamed bone meal) per 1,000 square feet when using any fresh manure. Suggested rates of application are

Common Inorganic Fertilizers

(All analyses are approximate.)

Material	Analysis	Pounds to add per 1,000 square feet of garden	Notes
Mixed fertilizers	(5-10-10, 10-10-10, 16-16-16, etc.)	9–18	Best applied broadcast before planting, in bands at planting, or as sidedressing
Monoammonium phosphate	11-48-0	8–10	One of the best fertilizers to apply in bands at planting
Ammonium phosphate	16-20-0	4–8	Excellent for sidedressing
Superphosphate	0-20-0	5–8 banded; 8–16 broadcast	Excellent source of phosphorus; broadcast and turn under when using large amounts of manure.
Treble superphosphate	0-45-0	4–6 banded; 5–10 broadcast	All phosphorus sources should be placed close to the root zone since phosphorus does not move much in the soil.

approximate and intended as guides only.)

Buyer Beware

Many books, catalogs, and garden centers sell fertilizers packaged as "Asparagus Food" or "Tomato Food" or "Carrot Food." These are marketing ploys and many times the various "foods" do not differ significantly in analysis among themselves. Yet they often sell for high prices and you will accumulate untold numbers of bags of the different foods at needless expense. Leave the specialty foods on the shelves and purchase a bag of inexpensive 5-10-10, or a bag of blood meal for your garden.

How to Calculate Fertilizer Equivalencies

Books or magazine articles will often advise you to apply a certain fertilizer or its equivalent. What does that mean and how do you calculate equivalencies? Let's take two fertilizers, say a bag of 5-10-10 and a bag of 10-6-4. Both have nitrogen in rapid release form and contain no special micronutrients or organic matter. In other words, they both contain only N, P, and K. When we use the term "equivalent" without qualification we refer to equivalent amounts of nitrogen, since that is the nutrient used in greatest amounts and the one that is lost rapidly to leaching or volatiliza-tion. Since a bag of 5-10-10 contains half the amount of nitrogen as a bag of 10-6-4, we would have to apply twice as much to get an equivalent amount of nitrogen. Now, let's say that the bag of 5-10-10 weighs 25 pounds and sells for $10 and the bag of 10-6-4 weighs 25 pounds and sells for $15. The bag of 10-6-4 supplies twice the nitrogen as the bag of 5-10-10 but sells for less than double the price, so the nitrogen in the 10-6-4 is less expensive than the nitro-gen in the 5-10-10. The 10-6-4 fertilizer is the better value.

Fertilizer Equivalents

Most granular commercial fertilizers weigh about one pound per pint of material. The following table gives you the amount to apply when recommendations are made in pounds or tons per acre.

Per Acre	Per 1,000 square feet	Per 100 square feet	Per 1 square yard
100 lbs.	2½ lbs. (2½ pints)	¼ lb. (½ cup)	½ oz. (2½ tsp.)
2,000 lbs. (1 ton)	50 lbs.	5 lbs. (5 pints)	½ lb. (1 cup)

Let's continue with equivalencies. You read a recommenda-tion that one pound of *actual* nitrogen be applied per 1,000 square feet of garden. How much 5-10-10 must you spread to apply one pound of *actual* nitrogen? Divide the percentage of nitrogen as a whole number into 100: $100 \div 5 = 20$. Therefore, you must spread twenty pounds of 5-10-10 to apply one pound of actual nitrogen. Now, say your neighbor gives you a bag of ammonium sulfate with an analysis of 21-0-0. How much of that must you spread

Mixed fertilizer being measured before planting

to apply one pound of actual nitrogen? Doing the math, we get $100 \div 21 = 4.76$, which we can round to five pounds. We might also have rounded 21 to 20 to simplify the arithmetic since it is a waste of time to deal with a quarter pound of fertilizer over 1,000 square feet.

Fertilizer equivalencies usually require more thought than these examples. For example, say you have some 5-10-10 and some cow manure. You want to fertilize 1,000 square feet of garden. How much cow manure must you apply to get the equivalent amount of nitrogen to the 5-10-10? We know that twenty pounds of 5-10-10 will supply one pound of actual nitrogen. According to the table, dry cow manure contains about 1.5 percent nitrogen. Therefore, we must apply 66.6 pounds of the dry cow manure ($100 \div 1.5 = 66.6$) to supply one pound of actual nitrogen. However, the 5-10-10 and the cow manure are not equivalent since the cow manure also adds slow-release nitrogen and organic matter to the soil, whereas the 5-10-10 does not. It's fine if you consider only the nitrogen, but the organic matter is very important for the health of the soil. You can figure equivalencies in the same manner on the phosphorus and potassium as well.

Equivalent Amounts

Fertilizer recommendations are often given in pounds per acre; but most of us do not have an acre of garden. To calculate smaller amounts, consider that most mixed, commercial fertilizers weigh about one pound per pint of fertilizer, a cup of material will weigh about eight ounces, and a teaspoonful of material will weigh about ¾ ounce. The following table indicates how much fertilizer should be applied to fifty feet of row with different spacings between rows when the amount is given in pounds per acre.

Fertilizer Math

(Ounces of fertilizer to apply per 50 feet of row at various distances between rows when the total fertilizer amount is expressed in pounds per acre.)

DISTANCES BETWEEN ROWS

Lbs./acre	12 ins.	18 ins.	24 ins.	30 ins.	36 ins.	42 ins.	100 sq. ins.
100	2	3	4	5	6	7	4
150	3	4.5	6	7.5	9	10.5	6
200	4	6	8	10	12	14	8
300	6	9	12	15	18	21	12
400	8	12	16	20	24	28	16
500	10	15	20	25	30	35	20
600	12	18	24	30	36	42	24

(Source: Tate, 1964.)

Getting Vitamins into Your Veggies

Luckily, you don't have to trick your vegetables into eating their one-a-day vitamin, but plants need nutrients just like we do. These descriptions of the major nutrients explain how each contributes to plant growth and what to look for if they are deficient or present in excessive amounts. Following the name of the nutrient is its chemical symbol.

Nitrogen (N): Nitrogen strongly promotes vegetative growth of leaves, stems, and roots; leafy plants like spinach require it in large amounts. Nitrogen compounds in inorganic fertilizers are readily available to plants but those in organic fertilizers must be broken down by microbial action before plants can use them. The ammonium form of nitrogen is volatile and easily lost to the atmosphere but does not easily leach into the soil. Bacteria convert it to the nonvolatile nitrate form, which does leach easily. In compacted soils bacteria convert nitrates back into atmospheric nitrogen, making it unavailable to plants. Bacteria use nitrogen to decay organic matter. The more organic matter you add to the soil, the more nitrogen the bacteria must use and the less nitrogen will be available for plant growth. In fact, about half the nitrogen in manure volatilizes (changes into vapor) and is lost into the atmosphere. About half the nitrogen applied in commercial fertilizers is used by microbes to decompose soil organic matter and therefore is unavailable to plants. So, plants have only about half the nitrogen you apply available to them. Legumes such as peas and beans have root nodules containing bacteria that "fix" atmospheric nitrogen into a form that plants can use. Peas fix almost two pounds of nitrogen per 1,000 square feet and beans, about half that amount. These soil-enriching crops must be tilled under and their tissues allowed to decay in order for most of that nitrogen to be released for use by other plants.

Plants suffering from a nitrogen deficiency look stunted and have fibrous, stiff stems and small yellow leaves that drop early. Yellowing appears first on the older leaves. Flower and fruit production may be scarce and fruit size small.

With the overuse of foliar fertilizers, it is sometimes more common to experience an excess of nitrogen. This is most easily seen as luxuriant growth and the overproduction of fruit on plants such as tomatoes, resulting in many small, green tomatoes that fail to ripen. Ripening is generally delayed on all crops and foliage and stem growth can be rampant, with stems tending to lack stiffness. Plant tissues will be soft and perhaps more prone to pest infestations and drought.

Phosphorus (P): Phosphorus promotes root, flower, fruit, and seed development and stiffens plant stems. Much of the phosphorus in soil is chemically "bound" and not available for plant growth, especially in soil with pH above 7. It does not move easily in the soil and so fertilizers containing phosphorus should be tilled into the top 4 to 6 inches to be nearer a plant's root zone.

A deficiency of phosphorus delays growth and maturity and causes stems to become thin, short, and purple. The purple color also develops on the undersides of the leaves, eventually progressing throughout the entire leaf, which may also become a dull, blue-green color. Leaves of some plants may develop a bronze coloration. Fruit on phosphorus-deficient plants may be highly colored, soft, and sour with poor storage quality. The number of potato tubers may be reduced. Early season transplants, especially tomatoes, often display purple stems and leaves due to the relative unavailability of phosphorus in cold spring soils.

Potassium (K): Potassium stimulates general vigor of a plant. It promotes root growth and is used by root crops such as parsnips and beets in relatively large quantities.

A potassium deficiency results in development of a gray or

buff-colored area near the margins of older leaves. Eventually, the entire margin appears burned and the leaves may roll. Potassium-deficient plants are stunted, with poor development of flowers and fruit.

Calcium (Ca): This nutrient helps build strong cell walls. When stressed for water-some plants may not be able to absorb sufficient calcium, even if it's available, resulting in blossom end rot in tomatoes and peppers, cavity spot in parsnips, black heart in celery, and cabbage tipburn. Further, excess potassium can interfere with a plant's ability to absorb calcium, thereby creating an artificial deficiency of calcium.

Magnesium (Mg): This nutrient is necessary for the production of chlorophyll, the green pigment that facilitates photosynthesis. Soil organic matter and clay particles keep magnesium readily available for plant use.

A magnesium deficiency causes yellowing between the veins on older leaves and premature leaf drop. The leaves also sometimes take on a brilliant reddish to orange tint. Symptoms often show in midsummer when the stress of a crop load, heat, and drought is most severe. This nutrient may become deficient in acidic, sandy soils or if excessive calcium or potassium is added to the soil.

Sulfur (S): Vegetables need sulfur to make certain proteins. These give radishes, crucifers, onions, garlic, and so forth their characteristic pungency. Sulfur deficiency is rare.

Minor Nutrients: These are seldom deficient in the garden. Where they are deficient soils are usually very low or very high in organic matter or have a very high pH. They may also be deficient in coarse-textured or highly weathered soils. A very high soil pH is usually the main culprit, so take measures to keep your soil as close to neutral pH as you can. Of all the minor nutrients, boron and iron are most often deficient in our soils.

Boron (B): Damage from boron deficiency usually shows as black, sunken spots with dead or water-soaked areas. This is called "brown rot" in turnips and rutabagas, "hollow stem" in celery, and "canker" in beets. Flowering can be reduced and fruit appear rough and spotted. The stems of crucifers and celery become brittle, cracked, and hollow. Boron is most often deficient in asparagus, bulb and root vegetables, crucifers, and tomatoes. Apply boron only as directed by a soil-testing lab as excess boron will sterilize your soil.

Iron (Fe): Iron deficiency is often the result of soil iron being chemically unavailable for plant use due to our high soil pH. It causes severe yellowing of the newest leaves on a plant, resulting in poor shoot growth and poor fruit production. Deficiency of this nutrient is actually more commonly found on fruit plants and ornamentals but still can affect vegetables.

There is a fine line between deficiency and excess of micronutrients. Never add these to the soil unless a soil test indicates they are deficient.

Types of Fertilizers

Fertilizers also come in various physical forms. Granular fertilizers are most common. The dry granules are easily spread, easily stored, and freezing is not a concern. Liquid fertilizers should not be allowed to freeze and may separate if they get old, losing their fertilizer value. These are usually mixed with water and applied to the soil or directly to the plant foliage. The term "soluble fertilizer" is a misnomer, as all fertilizers are soluble. The term is applied to dry fertilizer that is to be mixed with water to form a liquid that is then sprayed directly onto foliage or applied to the soil (as are liquid fertilizers). Since this type of fertilizer is stored in dry form, freezing is not a consideration. Many organic fertilizers are liquid (fish emulsion), dry granular (rock phosphate), or powder (blood meal).

All fertilizers must be dissolved in water before their nutrients can enter plant roots. If you apply granular fertilizer to the soil when there's no rain in sight and no plans to irrigate, it does no good at all; it just sits there. Because the process takes some time, dry fertilizers may not affect plant growth for a week or two after application. While dry fertilizers depend upon rain or irrigation to become effective, a gardener must dissolve liquid fertilizers and soluble fertilizers before application, which allow them to work very fast to stimulate plant growth. Nutrients sprayed on the foliage enter the plant rapidly and effect a change in a matter of days. However, because these foliar fertilizers are very handy and act quickly, they are very popular and, in our opinion, often overapplied.

Banding, Sidedressing, or Broadcasting Fertilizer

Soluble fertilizers can be applied to the foliage of a plant with a watering can, a sprayer, or they can be poured onto the soil around a plant. The latter method is safest in that it avoids putting salts directly onto foliage. Dry fertilizers can be **broadcast** before or during garden preparation to raise the general fertility level of the soil. In this case, the correct amount of fertilizer is sprinkled on the garden as you would feed scratch to chickens or spread with mechanical spreaders, then tilled in during soil preparation.

Banding is placement of fertilizer an inch to the side of and an inch below seeds in a row. This places the fertilizer closer to the plant for maximum benefit and minimizes waste.

Sidedressing is placement of fertilizer in a band around a growing plant, as in the case of tomatoes and cabbage, or along the sides of the plants in rows, as with New Zealand spinach and Swiss chard. It is particularly important for long-season crops since the fertilizer added before planting will be lost or used long before the end of a growing season. If you're sidedressing, position the band several inches away from a plant's stem to avoid burning the tissue. And continue the band entirely around a plant. Sidedressing may need to be done two or three times through a season to keep long-season vegetables growing rapidly.

What is pH and What Can I Do About It?

A fertilizer may contain primarily one nutrient, like rock phosphate, or, like sheep manure and 5-10-10, it may contain many nutrients. How available those nutrients are for plant use depends on microbial activity, soil temperature, and the availability of water. It also depends upon how acidic or alkaline the soil is. The degree of acidity or alkalinity is expressed as the pH. The gardening pH scale runs from 1 to 14, with 7 being neutral. Values below 7 mean the soil is acidic and those above 7 mean the soil is alkaline. The scale is logarithmic, so there are multiples of 10 between numbers. For example, a pH of 6 is 10 times more acidic than a pH of 7; a pH of 5 is 100 times (10 x 10) more acidic than a pH of 7. Most vegetable plants do best in soils that are slightly acidic, with a pH ranging from 6 to 7, although they tolerate wider ranges. However, a soil that is far outside that range, say at pH 4 or pH 8, becomes problematic in that some nutrients become chemically bound and unavailable to the plants. Other nutrients may become toxic. So it is important to maintain the soil pH as close to slightly acidic or neutral as possible. In general, soils in areas with higher

The pH Scale

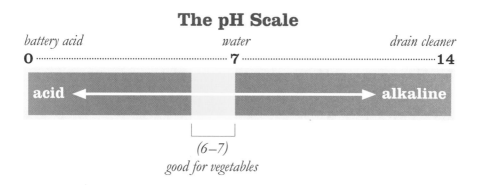

battery acid   water   drain cleaner

0   7   14

acid ← → alkaline

(6–7)
good for vegetables

amounts of rain tend to be more acidic and those in areas with lower amounts of rain are more alkaline. If your soil pH is too low, raise it by tilling in limestone or wood ash; if it is too high, then lower it by tilling in sulfur, ammonium sulfate, iron sulfate, or composted organic material. Low soil pH is not common in the Rocky Mountain region so you may never have to use limestone. Altering soil pH can be difficult in soils that contain compounds that resist pH change. Organic matter will lower pH weakly; vinegar usually not at all, so save the vinegar for cooked spinach and kale.

You may have a lab test your soil pH or you may purchase an inexpensive soil test kit that uses a dye to determine pH. Soil pH meters are also available for purchase, but keep in mind the dye method and the inexpensive pH meters may be accurate only to within one whole pH point.

Pounds of Sulfur to Apply per 1,000 Square Feet to Lower Soil pH to 6.5

Soil pH	Sandy Soil	Loam Soil	Clay Soil
8.5	50	63	75
8.0	30	38	50
7.5	13	20	25
7.0	3	4	8

Pounds of Limestone to Apply per 1,000 Square Feet to Increase Soil pH to 6.5

Soil pH	Sandy Soil	Loam Soil	Clay Soil
6.0	25	50	60
5.5	48	93	115
5.0	65	128	165
4.5	80	160	210

Amendments

Some soil amendments have relatively little fertilizer value but are highly valued for their ability to alter soil structure, in turn altering the workability of the soil and its water-holding and nutrient-holding capacities. Pulverizing or finely grinding amendments increases their surface area, thus speeding decomposition and their subsequent availability for plant use. This is particularly important when using rock powders.

Chemically inorganic soil amendments include sulfur, limestone, gypsum, wood ash, and coarse sand.

Sulfur adds elemental sulfur, an essential nutrient, to the soil but it is primarily used to lower soil pH. Agricultural sulfur (also called prilled sulfur) is preferred and should be applied in early spring before the gardening season begins. The elemental sulfur reacts with rainwater and snowmelt to form sulfurous acid, which lowers the pH. The sulfur portion of ferrous sulfate and ammonium sulfate will also acidify the soil and the compounds add valuable iron and the ammonium form of nitrogen.

Limestone (calcium carbonate) is applied to raise soil pH. Ground limestone contains large amounts of calcium and smaller amounts of magnesium. Dolomitic limestone contains larger amounts of magnesium. If your soil is particularly deficient in magnesium, an unlikely event in our area, use dolomitic limestone.

Gypsum (calcium sulfate) does not substantially alter soil pH but is helpful in amending saline soils. The presence of sodium and other salts in the soil reduces the size of the pore space, making the soil compact, harder to work, and poorly drained. It also can result in water deficits in a plant, restricting plant growth and yield. Gypsum makes the salt more mobile so that it can be flushed out of the soil with a good irrigation of rainwater or hand watering. It will not make soil easier to work unless the difficulty is due to underlying salt problems. Like sulfur and limestone, gypsum should be spread on the soil surface and thoroughly tilled in to do its job. Do not use sheetrock or other construction grade gypsum.

Wood ashes are high in calcium and potash and are used as a substitute for limestone. Because they raise soil pH, use them with caution, applying no more than a five-gallon bucket (20 pounds) of the ashes per 1,000 square feet per year unless your soil is strongly acidic. (This is about the amount of ash you get from burning a cord of wood.) Excessive use of wood ash can result in an overabundance of potassium, which in turn may restrict calcium uptake by the plant. A lack of calcium can increase the incidence of blossom end rot in tomatoes, squash, and peppers.

Chemically organic amendments are generally of low analysis, are bulky, and are primarily of benefit in adding valuable organic matter, improving soil texture, and overall soil health. Improving soil texture is something commercial fertilizers cannot do.

Compost is decayed organic matter. It loosens heavy soils and improves root penetration and water infiltration. You can build a compost pile or you can simply till organic material directly into the garden soil and let it rot in place (although do not bury diseased plant material or weeds that have gone to seed). A compost pile is something new gardeners want to build as a rite of passage into the gardening world. The building is simple, but the process in the Rocky Mountains can be time consuming. Our cold nights, short seasons, and dry climate conspire to slow the rotting process and the final product may take a year or more to achieve. But don't give up! *Eventually*, you should have some "black gold" to use in your garden. But if our climate and cultural conditions conspire against you, you can always purchase what you need.

Sod, grass clippings, hay, straw, kitchen scraps, leaves, and even shredded newspaper and cardboard can be composted. Materials such as wood shavings and wood chips can be used, but they rot

The compost pile is a rite of passage on your way to obtaining that "black gold."

very slowly. Do *not* use meat scraps, eggs (although eggshells are okay), fish, animal carcasses, fat, or pet manure in the pile as all add strong odors, may attract varmints, and the manure might carry parasites. Do not use diseased plants or noxious weeds such as spotted knapweed or field bindweed. Grass clippings from lawns treated with a broadleaved herbicide such as 2,4-D may carry that compound into the compost pile. It will be slow to decay and can harm the garden when the compost is spread on, so know if the source of the lawn clippings has been treated.

There are a few rules to remember in order to build a successful compost pile.

The woodier the material, the higher its carbon content and the slower it decomposes.

The greener and more succulent the material, the higher its

nitrogen content and the more rapidly it decomposes.

The finer the materials, the faster they decompose.

Optimum composting occurs when the material in the pile contains about 30 parts carbon to 1 part nitrogen. This is called the carbon to nitrogen (C:N) ratio. If the C:N ratio is greater than 30:1 you will have to add nitrogen to help the microorganisms break down the compost.

Carbon to Nitrogen Ratios for Common Materials

High Nitrogen ("Green") Materials	Carbon to Nitrogen (C:N) ratio*
Vegetable waste	12–20:1
Grass clippings	20:1
Cow manure	12–25:1
Horse manure	25:1
Poultry manure	10:1
Poultry manure with litter	13–18:1
Pig manure	5–7:1
High Carbon ("Brown") materials	
Dead leaves	30–80:1
Corn stalks	60:1
Straw	40–100:1
Tree bark	100–130:1
Paper	150–200:1
Wood chips and sawdust	100–500:1

(*C:N ratio varies depending upon the amount of bedding in manures and upon the woodiness of plant material.)

Locate the compost pile near the garden. Some gardeners build a cage out of poultry wire or even bales of straw to contain the material. Some simply pile the material. However you do it, the pile must be *at least* 3 feet wide and 3 feet high in order to work properly; small piles do not heat sufficiently to maintain the process. Piles 3 feet high and 5 feet wide are popular.

The standard method for making compost produces finished

compost in a summer; the static method may take a year or more to produce compost but your involvement will be quite low; and the rapid method creates compost in as little as six weeks but requires relatively high involvement, requiring you to turn it every 3 or 4 days until internal temperatures drop.

The Standard Pile Method

Gather sufficient green and brown materials to make the pile; shred or chip most material that is too coarse (bigger than about 2 x 2 inches). Keep some larger pieces, such as corncobs and small branches, to help aerate the pile. Spread a 6-inch layer of coarse, high-carbon material on the ground, then add a 6-inch layer of green material. If green material is limited, sprinkle about 2 ounces of actual nitrogen per bushel of brown material to add enough extra nitrogen. These 2 ounces can be supplied by adding 7 ounces of ammonium nitrate, 16 ounces of calcium nitrate, 5.2 ounces of urea, 20 ounces of dried blood, or 24 ounces of fish meal. Mix the fertilizers with the organic materials as they are added to the pile. Water each layer to wet the material, testing the moisture by squeezing a handful of material; it should feel like a moist (not wet) sponge. Continue to add layers of brown and green material until the pile is complete. Several days later the internal temperature should reach 110°F. Turn the pile after a week, checking the moisture and moving any coarser, drier outer layers toward the center. An easy way to do this is to simply move the pile from one location to another. Mix the pile again a week later, following the same process. By this time the internal temperature should be between 120 to 140°F and steam should be rising from the pile in the cool of the morning. Mix the pile again after another week. Decomposition should have begun, the internal temperature should have dropped to about 110°F, and the pile may have shrunk to half its original size. By the fourth week the material should look dark and crumbly and have a good, earthy smell. Its internal temperature will drop even more. Wait another week or two, then filter your compost through a screen and use the finer material on the garden. Coarse material that did not break down can be added to the next pile.

The Static Method
(AKA The Laid-back Gardener's Method)

This method requires more time to create good compost. You need not pay close attention to mixing materials in the proper ratio and only minimal attention is paid to moisture levels. Build the pile as materials become available but do try to chop and mix the materials before adding them. Allow the materials to break down at their own rate, with little or no turning. After six months you should be able to find some compost near the bottom of the pile. This method is very slow but requires little of your time or effort.

The Rapid Method
(AKA The Impatient Gardener's Method)

If you're in a hurry, this labor-intensive method will require you to have three bins. Build the pile in the first bin as described for the standard method, paying close attention to shredding the materials, mixing the proper amounts of brown and green materials, and adding nitrogen, should that be needed. Move the pile to the second bin after three days, and be sure to check for proper moisture level. Do not add any new material to this batch. Rather, add to the first bin to start your next batch. Temperatures near the center of the pile should reach about 160°F, killing diseases and weed seeds. If the temperature exceeds 160°F, the microbes responsible for decomposition will themselves be killed. If the temperature does rise too high, mix the pile. After two weeks of regular turning, the temperature in the second bin will drop and the compost will be brown, crumbly, and have an earthy aroma. Move the first batch to the third bin from where you can screen the compost and use it where you wish, returning any coarser materials to the first pile.

The organic materials and the soil have all the microbes you need to do the job and use of commercial activators or compost starters is not necessary.

Instead of, or in addition to, composting you should plant a cover crop in unused portions of your garden during the growing season or during winter to hold the soil against erosion and to reduce the amount of weed growth. When these cover crops are tilled under they become "green manure." It is always a good idea to use green manures to build soil organic matter.

You may also add organic matter directly to your garden soil without first composting it. Spread straw, peat moss, leaves, and other material directly on the soil surface and turn them under. Alternatively you may dig a trench in an unused portion of the garden and fill it with organic material as it becomes available, backfilling the trench as you go. This is easy and effective, requires little time, and keeps the garden neat and tidy all season long.

Soil is the not-so-secret element to gardening success. Monitoring and maintaining the proper levels of soil nutrients and organic matter is an ongoing process, but doing so will go far in ensuring you have the best vegetable garden possible. Too little or too much of either can cause big problems and more work for you. So remember—an ounce of prevention is worth a pound of the cure (literally!).

Cover Crops or Green Manures

Type	Legume	Ounces of seed to sow per 100 square feet	When to Sow	When to Turn Under	Effects	Notes
Alfalfa	Yes	0.5	Spring	Fall or following spring	Fixes 150–250 lbs. N/acre/yr.	Roots break hard soil and bring trace nutrients to the surface; needs warm temperatures for germination; sow by August 10 at high elevations; can become weedy
Barley	No	4	Spring, Fall	Spring, Fall	Adds organic matter	Tolerates drought; not as hardy as rye
Buckwheat	No	2.5	Spring, Summer	Summer, Fall	Mellows soil	Occupies part of the garden during season; grows quickly; not hardy; attracts bees
Oats	No	4	Spring, Fall	Summer, Spring	Improves soil aggregation	Not hardy
Rye	No	4	Fall	Spring	Adds organic matter	Very winter hardy
Winter wheat	No	4	Fall	Spring	Improves soil aggregation	Same as barley

Chapter Eight

WATERING

Watering is easy, right? All you do is aim the hose and voila! But, providing the *right* amount of water is one of the greatest challenges a Rocky Mountain gardener faces and many folks have trouble determining how much water is enough.

Most vegetable plants are about 90 percent water so they need to have plenty. But too much waterlogs the soil, ruins its structure, and compounds your problems. Excess water delays plant maturity, attracts pests, and causes fruit skin to crack. Mature plants and those with extensive leaf surfaces need more water than young plants and plants with shallow root systems need more frequent watering than those that are deep rooted. Insufficient water stunts and stresses all plants, leads to poor tipfill in corn, and to poor flower set in tomatoes.

The higher the air temperature, the more water plants need. Windy conditions increase water need because wind accelerates transpiration (water loss from the plant) and soil water evaporation. Early cool-season crops, which do much of their growing during cool weather, need less water than those that produce in the heat of summer. For example, vegetable plants need about 1 inch of water per week in Bozeman, Montana, in April and early May. This requirement increases to about 1½ inches per week by late May and early June, 2 inches per week from mid-June to early July, and 2 to 2½ inches per week from mid-July to mid-August. Water needs decrease later in the season, from about 1½ inches in mid-August to early September to about 1 inch of water per week through the first frost. These figures are highly variable according to location, with areas in eastern Montana requiring up to three inches of water per week in the heat of summer. Use pan evaporation figures from your local weather bureau or set up a test in your garden to determine how much water you really must apply to replace that used by your garden plants.

Here's how: Place a wide-surfaced container, such as a 9x13-inch cake pan, in the garden exposed to full sunlight. With an indelible ink pen mark one-inch intervals down the inside wall of the container, then fill it with water so that the water line rests on a mark. Check the water level after one week. If the level has gone down to the next lower mark then evaporation loss for that week was about one inch. Pan evaporation fairly closely mimics water use by your plants, so you should apply about one inch of water (or whatever the loss was) to the garden to compensate.

What does one inch of water mean? It means enough water so that, if none of it drained away, it would make a puddle one inch deep. To apply one inch of water over 1,000 square feet requires about 623 gallons, which weigh about 5,200 pounds. Applying two inches of water over 1,000 square feet requires 1,246 gallons (twice as much!); the point is, this is a lot of water. But lots of soil organic matter and the use of mulches increase water-holding capacity and substantially reduce the need for frequent watering.

How Much is Enough?

There are a couple of ways to figure if you are applying sufficient water. You can measure how much water your outside faucet emits in one minute. The one at our house discharges about ten gallons per minute. Therefore, it would take a little over one hour to apply one inch of water to 1,000 square feet (60 minutes x 10 gallons = 600 gallons, or nearly enough to cover 1,000 square feet with 1 inch of water). Another way is to place empty shallow cans (such as tuna fish cans) about the garden beneath overhead sprinklers or soaker hoses; when they are full of water you have applied about one inch. Since overhead sprinklers do not distribute water evenly over the soil surface, place those cans at various distances from the sprinkler head. An approximate distribution pattern will provide 1 inch of water at a distance of 8 or so feet from the sprinkler, 3 inches of water at a distance of 4 feet, and 4 inches of water at 2 feet.

Soil that's just a little too wet will stick together.

The easiest way to determine if you have watered enough is to squeeze a little bit of soil in your hands. If it will not form a ball, it is too dry; if it forms a ball that will not crumble with a firm touch, it is too wet. If it forms a loose ball that breaks with the slightest touch, then you are probably okay. Dig a hole in the garden and feel the soil on its sides. Moist soil feels cool. If the soil is moist to a depth of a couple of feet, you have watered enough. Your garden is in trouble if the soil is not damp to that depth. In fact, shallow-rooted crops such as cabbage, which have most of their roots in the upper 18 to 24 inches of soil, suffer if the top inch or two of soil is bone dry.

When to Water

When cucurbits wilt in the heat of day and recover at night, they are at the stage of incipient wilt. *Water immediately*. Waiting

Don't let your new plants wilt. Early or incipient wilting may cause long-term damage to your harvest.

even a few days may place them in a permanent wilt condition. Even after plants suffering from incipient wilt recover, yield may be reduced by as much as 30 percent. Water is more critical during certain stages of plant growth. Be sure to supply enough water when your crop is beginning to form a plant and when the portion you are interested in eating is developing.

How to Water

Water newly seeded beds lightly but frequently. There's no need to water deeply when there are no roots. *But,* don't just sprinkle established crops. When you water established crops, water deeply so the upper one to two feet of soil is dampened. This promotes deeper root development. Water more deeply as the vegetables' root systems grow more deeply into the soil; the more deeply you water the less frequently you will have to water. Water when the air temperature is rising and the air is calm; from 7 to 9 a.m. is a good time. Too much water evaporates or is blown away from the plants if it's applied in midday. Overhead sprinklers are popular but they waste water; it's better to use soaker hoses that apply water directly to the soil. You don't water the weeds with soaker hoses! Always water the soil, not the plants' foliage. Depending upon the species, very little to no water is absorbed through the leaves; water placed there only evaporates.

If You Do Nothing Else

Watering is an easy thing to do, but whether you use a soaker hose or enjoy hand watering—be sure it gets done. The single most important task that you can accomplish in the garden is providing the right amount of water. Without water, plants cannot absorb nutrients from the soil, cannot make food from sunlight, and they cannot grow.

Critical Watering Stages

Vegetable	Growth stage when watering is critical
All vegetables, particularly summer and fall plantings	Germination
Asparagus	Fern development
Beans, peas	Flowering, development of pods
Beet, carrot, radish, rutabaga, turnip	Root enlargement
Broccoli, cabbage, cauliflower, lettuce	Head development
Cucumber, eggplant, melon, pepper, squash, tomato	Flowering, fruit set, and development
Garlic, onion	Bulb enlargement
Potato	Tuber enlargement
Sweet corn	Tasseling and ear development

(Source: Adapted from Splittstoesser, 1979.)

Broccoli and other head-forming vegetables will need your attention to watering as heads develop.

Chapter Nine

FIGHTING THE GOOD FIGHT: WEEDS AND PESTS

How to define a weed?
Ah, let us count the ways.

Like many things, weeds are a matter of perspective because a weed is simply a plant out of place. Volunteer tomatoes in your cabbage patch are weeds. Weeds can take many forms: like prickly lettuce, a weed may be unsightly; like purslane, very tough to control; or like red-root pigweed, they can be tall and gangly, shading other plants. Most are vigorous and difficult to control, harbor insects and diseases, and compete with vegetables for sunlight, water, and nutrients—that's why we call 'em weeds. They have no place in the garden and you will have to control them— one way or another—before they go to seed. Just *one* plant of common purslane can produce more than 100,000 seeds that can remain viable in the soil for 20 years. (Seeds of black mustard can remain viable for more than 40 years!) So, let one weed go to seed and you could compound your problems manyfold.

Fighting the Good Fight

One way to help keep a garden weed-free is to watch what you put into it. Fresh manure, particularly horse manure, will be infested with weed seeds. Be sure all manure is composted or well-aged before you add it into the garden. Do not substitute grass hay for clean straw in the garden (for any reason) as this hay may contain weed and grass seedheads. If you do have weeds that have gone to seed before you can pull them, don't compost them or till them under but get them out of the garden altogether.

Rototilling the garden in autumn can bury some weed seeds, preventing them from germinating, while uncovering others that will be exposed to winter conditions and hopefully killed out-right. Oregon studies have suggested that tilling at night discourages some weed seeds from germinating. Summer annuals such as lambsquarter and pigweed are most affected by night tillage. Try it on a moonlit night and see if it works for you. In a few weeks, a gardener will see a reduction—or not—of weeds. A fall cover crop can smother winter annual weeds and will serve as a great green manure crop when it's turned under in spring. Summer cover crops such as buckwheat also help to smother weeds as well as add organic matter to the soil.

The low-tech way still works! Cultivating with a sharpened hoe destroys most weeds. Hoes should be used with a scraping motion, not a chopping motion. You only have to *scrape* the soil surface to sever the weed stems—disturbing the soil as little as two inches deep can destroy the surface feeder roots of your vegetable plants. Not only does hoeing destroy weeds but it conserves soil moisture, decreases surface water runoff, and slows the upward migration of moisture from lower soil levels. Cultivate as soon as you see weeds emerge,

Barley is one of those cover crops that can help the condition of your soil.

preferably when the soil is dry; cultivating wet soil ruins its structure, causing it to become compacted. If you wait until the tall weeds are grown you will be tempted to pull them. *Don't!* Tall weeds have roots that are intertwined with those of nearby vegetables and pulling them could damage those vegetables' root-systems. If a tall weed is too tough to sever with a hoe, cut it off with pruning shears and leave the roots in place until the vegetables are harvested. Then, get rid of it!

We often see ads where a smiling gardener is using a rototiller to cultivate between rows of vegetables. Listen up: this is a bad idea. Using a rototiller destroys surface roots and most feeder roots between the rows, truncating a plant's root system, which severely and negatively affects its ability to search for water and nutrients. Use a rototiller *only* for tilling a garden *before* planting.

Much About Mulches

You've all heard that mulches are good, but here's why. Mulching conserves soil moisture by up to 50 percent compared to bare soil, keeps ripening fruits and vegetables off the ground, and reduces the chance of fruits and vegetables rotting. Mulches may cool or warm the soil, depending upon the type of mulch used; add organic matter when they're turned under; and prevent weed seeds from germinating. You want to get a head start; before applying a mulch remove all weeds and moisten the soil.

Organic mulches cool the soil and delay the soil from warming in spring. For that reason they should not be applied until early summer when soil has warmed sufficiently for rapid root growth. Apply about six inches of organic mulch for the best weed control. As the bottom layers of mulch begin to rot, vegetable roots grow into them, establishing a dense network of feeder roots in order to better forage for water and nutrients. Soil microbes use nitrogen to break down the organic mulch, so add about two pounds of 5-10-10 or its equivalent per 100 square feet of mulched area.  Like all mulches, organic mulches moderate soil temperature, conserve soil moisture, and suppress some weed growth. But most organic mulches will not adequately control grasses, perennial weeds, or established annual weeds.

Clean straw makes a good mulch and keeps the soil cool and moist. We think soft oat straw makes a better mulch than the stiffer rye or wheat straw. Barley straw is good and its barbs prevent the wind from moving it around. You will need about a ton of straw to mulch a 1,000-square-foot garden. Weed-free legume hay breaks down rapidly, requires no additional nitrogen, and is particularly good for use on slow-growing crops such as peppers because it releases its nutrients fairly rapidly. Chopped leaves make a great mulch, though some weeds will find their way through them. You can chop leaves by running over them with a mower or by putting them through a chipper/shredder. Grass clippings from lawns where no herbicides have been applied work well, though be sure to let them dry for a day before you put them on the garden; wet clippings can mat, ferment, and damage young seedlings. Compost and well-aged manure make great mulches, as does peat moss. Unfortunately, peat moss is pretty expensive, can be blown about by wind, and may crust over, preventing water from penetrating into the root zone. To prevent this, mix peat moss with other materials such as leaves or straw. Shredded newspapers soaked in water also make a satisfactory mulch. Like peat moss, however, these too can crust over, so it's better to mix them with straw before applying. Wood chips and sawdust have no place as mulch in the vegetable garden. Because both are high in carbon, microbes require a lot of nitrogen to break them down. In every case where we have seen sawdust used as mulch in a vegetable garden the vegetables have suffered from severe nitrogen deficiency.

Inorganic mulches, particularly the plastics, are becoming more popular. All plastic mulches come in sheets of various colors and widths. Check online at http://plasticulture.cas.psu.edu/P-Mulch.html as a source of information. They warm or cool the soil, depending upon their color; are weed-free; reduce fluctuations in soil temperatures; increase earlier ripening (earliness) and total yields, particularly in warm-season crops; and prevent some grasses and other difficult-to-manage weeds from emerging. They are lightweight, inexpensive, and easy to apply. Plastic mulch can be used between rows of vegetables such as beets and carrots, or transplants such as cabbage and tomatoes can be set in holes cut through the mulch. Their downside is that they add no organic matter to the soil and normally must be removed at the end of each growing season.

Three mil (0.003 inch thick) or 1.5 mil (0.0015 inch thick) sheets of black polyethylene block sunlight to prevent weed seeds from germinating. Most references also state that it warms the soil. In our Bozeman trials we found that it does not warm the soil substantially but rather warms the air trapped between the soil surface and the underside of the plastic. By conserving soil moisture and preventing weed growth the black plastic promotes strong root growth, which in turn can lead to vegetables maturing earlier than vegetables planted in bare soil.

Recently, colored plastic mulches have come onto the market. Perhaps the most noteworthy of these are the red plastic mulches. Like the black plastic mulches, these conserve soil moisture. Unlike the black plastic, they warm the soil and strongly promote growth and maturity of some plants, particularly tomatoes and peppers. Unlike black plastic they do not totally prevent weed growth; some weeds germinate beneath them but their growth is etiolated (spindly) and weak, preventing them from causing major interference with growth of your vegetables.

Clear plastic mulch warms the soil up to 8 to 10°F more than other plastic mulches and is preferred for heat-lovers such as melons and on early plantings of cucumbers, peppers, tomatoes, squashes, and sweet corn. The clear plastic can hasten harvest by a week or so and leads to higher yields. Unfortunately, clear plastic allows weed seeds to germinate, sometimes leading to heavy weed growth beneath the plastic. Be sure that the temperature beneath the clear plastic does not rise above 90°F during bright summer days.

Other inorganic mulches include white plastic, which may repel some insects but has little effect on soil temperature. Aluminum foil used as a mulch *will* repel some insects such as aphids but it also keeps the soil up to 10°F cooler than bare soil. With our short growing seasons this is probably not a good option.

New "designer" mulches are constantly being released, including photodegradable and wavelength selective products. Visit your local garden center to see what's new.

More Ways to Fight Weeds

Some vegetable plants produce so much foliage that they shade the soil around them, minimizing germination and growth of many weeds. The cucurbits, beans, corn, potato, and tomato are effective shade crops. Plants that produce little foliage, such as lettuce, carrot, and onion, are not. Keep your soil weed free early in the season and the foliage of shade vegetables will keep it mostly free from weeds later.

Herbicides kill plants, and non-selective herbicides kill *all* plants, so take care to apply them accurately. Most herbicides have no place in the home garden. However, some new organically acceptable herbicides show promise as being safe and effective for home use. These include some soap-based products and some essential oils. Recent research has shown that both clove oil and cinnamon oil at concentrations of 1 to 5 percent in water effectively controlled some small grass plants. All of these herbicides kill only the tissue they contact so it is important to achieve good coverage, with use of a surfactant highly recommended. Because they have no residual effect, they have to be applied repeatedly as weeds emerge.

Corn gluten meal has been highly touted as a pre-emergent herbicide; that is, one that is applied before a weed seed germinates. The effectiveness of this expensive product in controlling a broad range of weeds is still being evaluated.

If the products described do not provide effective control and you are sore from hoeing, you may have to resort to an herbicide such as glyphosate, especially for control of tough weeds such as quackgrass. This product is commonly sold under several trade names, including Roundup®. Upon being absorbed into a plant, glyphosate interferes with protein synthesis, killing the plant. It is strongly adsorbed by soil particles and so runoff is inconsequential, and its very low toxicity means it poses little threat to the health of the gardener. In fact, glyphosate binds to soil so fast that you could actually plant seeds right after using the product, but that is not recommended. Soil microbes degrade the compound, which has a half-life of only forty-seven days. Used according to label directions, this product is safe and effective for control of a large number of weed species. It is non-selective and thus will kill any green tissue to which it is applied. Follow all label directions and use with care.

Another herbicide that is becoming widely used by home-owners is trifluralin, sold under names such as Treflan®, Advance®, and Passport®. This product must be applied before weed seeds germinate. It gives effective control of grasses and some broadleaf weeds by inhibiting cell division in shoots and roots of seedlings. The active compound is strongly adsorbed by soil particles, particularly soil organic matter, and it has a field half-life of about forty-five days during which time it is slowly degraded by soil microbes and by sunlight. Like glyphosate it has a very low toxicity and poses little threat to humans when used according to label directions.

Read all label instructions when using any pesticide, and be sure to follow them carefully, wearing all of the recommended protective clothing and using equipment as directed. Read that sentence again.

Water can be used as a management tool. Weeds need water to grow, so effective water management may help suppress them. Subsurface irrigation with a buried soaker hose will minimize the amount of surface moisture available to weeds.

Pests and weeds and gardens go hand in hand—so get used to it. Controls involve a variety of options, but always begin with the least harmful as your first line of defense. You don't always need to work down the list to a pesticide, but its use is an option.

In addition to weeds, vegetables may be damaged by various pests including insects and disease, but damage also may be caused by the environment, inadequate or excessive levels of nutrients, and soil issues. Check out this table for some common problems, their possible causes, and what you can do about it.

Controls for Common Problems

Symptom	Possible Cause / Possible Control
Wilt	Lack of water / Water
	Excess water / Stop watering
	Disease / Use resistant varieties; crop rotation; fungicide sprays
	Damage to stem or roots / Protect next time; control insects
Spots on leaves and stems	Fertilizer burn / Follow label directions
	Pesticide burn / Follow label directions
	Disease / Use resistant varieties; fungicide sprays; crop rotation
	Nutrient deficiency / Determine deficiency and correct
Weak growth	Shade / Eliminate shade
	Excess water / Stop watering; improve drainage
	Crowding / Thin
	Excess Nitrogen / Reduce fertilizer
	Disease / Use resistant varieties; crop rotation; fungicide sprays
	Root damage / Determine source and correct

Controls for Common Problems

Symptom	Possible Cause / Possible Control
Leaf curl	Wilt / Use resistant varieties; rotate crops; remove diseased plant
	Virus / Remove diseased plant; control insects
	Aphids / Control insects
Leaf roll	Drought / Water
	Virus / Remove diseased plant; use resistant varieties
Stunted growth; yellow foliage	Insufficient water / Water
	Excess water / Don't water
	Poor drainage / Improve drainage
	Improper soil pH / Correct soil pH
	Compacted soil / Amend soil
	Insufficient fertility / Fertilize
	Disease / Use resistant varieties; remove diseased plants; apply fungicide
	Virus / Use resistant varieties; remove diseased plants
	Nutrient imbalance / Correct imbalance
Poor germination	Insufficient time / Wait
	Too hot; cold / Wait
	Too wet; dry / Adjust watering
	Bird damage / Control birds; wait
	Seed maggots / Use treated seeds
	Old seeds / Use viable seeds
Young plants die	Damping off / Use a fungicide; sprinkle sand over seeded row
	Fertilizer burn / Follow label directions
Leaves have holes	Slugs / Trap
	Insects / Use insecticide; hand pick
	Hail / Row cover protection

Controls for Common Problems

Symptom	Possible Cause / Possible Control
Leaves dried out	Wind damage / Construct or grow windbreak
	Mildew / Use fungicide next time; improve air circulation
Twisted; deformed growth	Herbicide damage / Follow directions on the label; don't use herbicide-treated lawn clippings; examine sources of manure for herbicide contamination
	Virus / Remove diseased plant
	Nutrient deficiency / Correct deficiency
Fruit blossom end rot on eggplant, tomato, pepper, and squash	Improper soil pH / Correct – See Chapter 7
	Insufficient calcium / Add calcium to soil; calcium nitrate sprays
	Compacted soil / Amend – See Chapter 7
	Root damage / Be careful next time
	Soil water imbalance / Mulch; apply water evenly and consistently
	Fruit rot / Use fungicide; remove affected fruit
Poor fruit set	Too cold; too hot / Wait
	Excess nitrogen / Follow directions
	Poor pollination / Insufficient bees; weather too hot, too cold, or too windy
	Immature plants / Wait

First Line of Defense

You've heard it before—location, location, location. Locate the garden in an area that has good air circulation and is in full sunlight. Well-drained soil is critical; poorly drained soil promotes seed rots, damping off, and restricted root systems leading to weakened plants. Water only in the morning, as wet foliage at night may increase the incidence of mildew.

Common Insect Pests and the Damage They Cause

Damage	Insect	Plants attacked
Many small green or black sucking insects, usually on the undersides of the leaves; may cause leaf curl	Aphid	Many
Young plants cut down at night at soil level	Cutworm	Beans, corn, tomato, pepper, eggplant, and crucifer transplants
Wedge-shaped insects that suck sap, and hop when disturbed	Leafhoppers	Beans, lettuce
Chewed leaves, silvery trail of dried slime visible in the morning	Slugs	Plants with heavy foliage near the soil
Weak plants, maybe wilted, lateral roots absent	Cabbage maggots; onion maggots	Crucifers, onion
Holes in leaves eaten by inch-long green worms	Cabbage worm; cabbage looper	Crucifers
Numerous pinholes in leaves	Fleabeetles	Crucifers, eggplant, pepper, potato, tomato, kohlrabi, radish, kale
Silks cut at ear, large worm eats corn kernels; holes chewed into okra pods	Corn earworm	Corn, okra
Worms tunnel in corn ears and stalk	Corn borer	Corn
All parts of plant chewed	Cucumber beetles	Cucurbits

Common Insect Pests and the Damage They Cause

Damage	Insect	Plants attacked
Brown or white tunnels in leaves, small maggot in tunnels	Leaf miners	Beet, chard, spinach
Plants defoliated by black-striped beetles or red-brown larvae	Colorado potato beetle	Potato, eggplant
Vines suddenly wilt, holes in stem near soil line	Squash vine borer	Squash
Leaves eaten by large green worm with reddish horn	Hornworm	Tomato

Keep the garden and surrounding area clean and neat. Compost, turn under, burn, or otherwise dispose of plant debris right after harvest. Do *not* compost diseased plant material; any material infected with the soilborne pathogens *Verticillium* and *Fusarium* should be removed from the property and never turned under or composted. Keep the garden weed free. Weeds compete with your vegetables for water and are hosts for diseases and insects. For example, lambsquarter harbors leaf miners, which ruin spinach, beet greens, and Swiss chard, and pokeweed is a host for tobacco mosaic virus, which attacks tomatoes, potatoes, and peppers. Do not even allow smokers or tobacco chewers into the garden, for their tobacco can also carry the tobacco mosaic virus. Last, do not walk through the garden when it is wet. You may brush against a diseased leaf, picking up fungal spores, then spread the pathogen to a healthy leaf.

Not all pests are present in all locations. When in doubt contact your local county extension office to find out which ones to watch for. The preceding table lists some damage you may see in the garden, the insect possibly causing the damage, and the plants attacked. Use this table to identify the insect you are up against.

Plant only disease-free seeds and transplants. Fungicide-treated seeds are helpful in warding off rots, especially in cold, wet soils. Some crucifer seeds are pre-treated with hot water to control some seed-borne diseases. The catalogs may note whether the seeds have been treated with hot water, but the seed packets generally do not. Using onion sets will avoid onion smut, which attacks only onion seedlings.

Three- or four-year crop rotations are very effective in controlling soilborne diseases. For example, clubroot, a disease that attacks crucifers, and root knot nematode, which attacks many plants, remain viable in soil for up to 3 years, so a 4-year rotation will go a long way toward controlling these problems. Unfortunately, some diseases such as onion smut and potato scab remain viable in the soil for many years and cannot be controlled effectively solely with crop rotation. Root maggots, grubs, and wireworms are especially attracted to root vegetables and crucifers. If you have a lot of these insects in the garden then plant beans, peas, Swiss chard, and spinach, which are vegetables that are not attacked by these insects.

Fall plowing turns under debris and turns up insects that will later be winter killed. Plant a cover crop after plowing and turn that under in spring.

Work with Mother Nature when possible by using trap crops when necessary. Radishes attract wireworms away from carrots and kale attracts harlequin cabbage bugs away from cabbage.

The Second Line of Defense

In spite of all of your hard work defending your garden with the first line of defense, you may have to follow through with the second line. Use tarpaper collars around transplants to control cutworms, being sure the collars extend about one inch below

Tarpaper collars protect young plants from cutworms.

and two inches above the soil line, leaving no more than one inch between the plant stem and the collar. Tarpaper collars that lay flat on the ground and around the stems of young crucifer transplants will protect them from root maggots. (Tarpaper is a heavy paper impregnated with tar available at many lumberyards. As an alternate, you can also use heavy cardboard.) Fit the stem through a slit in the collar. Finally, wood ashes, sharp mason's sand, or diatomaceous earth sprinkled around the stems of young transplants reduces damage from slugs and cutworms. (Sharp mason's sand can also be found at many lumberyards or hardware stores; it's the type of sand that masons use in construction and has sharper edges than river sand.)

Protect young plants from insects by positioning row covers over your garden rows immediately after planting.

Trap slugs by placing shallow bowls of stale beer along the rows or by placing a board between rows of vegetables. The slugs will drown (!) or will take shelter under the board. You'll have to squish them after capture.

Aluminum foil disorients aphids and reduces their feeding damage by

Use bricks to weigh down your row covers.

reflecting sunlight onto the lower sides of the leaves where aphids hide. Unfortunately, in our Rocky Mountain region, we get so much sunlight that the aluminum foil might reflect so much that it could damage the plant tissues.

A strong stream of water knocks some insects off plants. This is especially effective in controlling aphids and mites. Since 1787, gardeners have been spraying warm, soapy water onto their plants. This is effective in controlling damage from some insects. You can buy prepared insecticidal soap; try it on a few plants first to be sure it does no damage. Do not spray in the heat of the day and never use detergents.

Encourage birds by planting fruit plants near the garden. Elderberry, crabapple, and highbush cranberry are good examples. Birds swoop from these onto the insects in the garden and do a nice job of cleaning up the area free of charge. Chickens and geese will do a great job eating not only insects but young weeds, as well. Garden snakes, toads, and bats all help to control garden insect populations.

Hand-picking is inexpensive, easy, and perfectly alright for larger insects like hornworms and Colorado potato beetles. Pick these every day to keep populations and damage low. You can find hornworms clinging to the lower surfaces of the foliage in early morning. Pull them off and step on them. Place other insects into a can of cooking oil.

The Third Line of Defense

Until now we have talked about defensive and very light offensive measures for controlling insects. But as pest populations increase you may have to take more severe measures. Encouraging and even introducing predators and parasites into your garden is the third line of defense. Predators are larger than the insects they control and are not diet-conscious, eating "good" as well as "bad" insects. Nor do they have any allegiance to the gardener, for as soon as their food supply is gone, so are they. Also, introducing these in a windy area is probably a waste of money.

Nearly everyone has a fond spot for praying mantises and think of them as one of the "good guys." But praying mantises are not among the beneficial predators in the following table since these insects are not effective in controlling garden pests. Their preferred food sources are bees, wasps, flies, grasshoppers, and crickets. Except for grasshoppers, these insects are not really destructive to the garden. Further, mantises sit and wait for their prey. They hatch in late summer after most of the damage has been done, and the first to hatch eat those that hatch sub-sequently, so many are destroyed quickly.

Beneficial Insects and Their Prey

Predator	Food source
Lacewing (ant lion)	Aphids, mealybugs, scale, spider mites, insect eggs, other small insects
Ladybug	Aphids, insect eggs, scale, mites
Pirate bug	Aphids, small insects, mites
Damsel bug	Aphids, caterpillars, leafhoppers, mites
Syrphid fly	Aphids
Ichneumon wasps	Cutworms, caterpillars
Tachinid fly	Cutworms, caterpillars, some beetles
Chalcid wasp	Imported cabbage worm
Braconid wasp	Caterpillars, beetles

Some pathogens control insects when used according to directions. One very effective group of pathogens is *Bacillus thuringiensis* (Bt), sold under such trade names as Dipel® and Thuricide®. There are several strains of this *Bacillus* available for use, depending on the target pest. Be sure you use the correct strain for the insect damaging your crop. These bacterial pathogens attack over 400 species of caterpillars but leave other insects and animals unharmed and are very safe for the home garden.

The Fourth Line of Defense

In most years these first three lines of defense will hold the line against total destruction of your garden. But sometimes they fail and you may have to go to your fourth, and last, line of defense. Give up or use a pesticide. The word "pesticide" invokes fear into the hearts of some gardeners but it shouldn't. A pesticide is a substance that kills pests, so *you* were a pesticide when you stepped on that hornworm. Soap and water are pesticides and so is *Bacillus thuringiensis*. We are often asked to recommend nontoxic pesticides. That is an oxymoron since by definition a pesticide kills a pest. Pesticides have their effective use, but misused they can have unfortunate effects such as killing beneficial as well as the nonbeneficial insects. There are relatively innocuous, less toxic pesticides and there are stronger, more toxic pesticides. There are pesticides that are effective on some insects and diseases but ineffective on others. You can choose to use them or not.

Just as there are many types of pests, there are many types of pesticides. Insecticides kill insects, fungicides kill fungal pathogens, rodenticides kill mice and rats, miticides kill mites (which are not insects), and herbicides kill plants.

We can gauge the relative toxicity of a substance by referring to its LD_{50}. This is the amount of a substance needed to kill 50 percent of a test population and is expressed in mg/kg of body weight. The LD_{50} is also given as "oral" or "dermal"; that is, if a dose is administered by mouth or through the skin; and as "acute" or "chronic." Rats are often used as test animals for oral values and rabbits, for dermal values. We commonly discuss toxicity in terms of an acute, oral dose. The smaller the LD_{50} number, the more poisonous the compound. The table on the facing page provides information on some pesticides commonly used in the home garden along with the toxicity of some common household products for comparison.

A word of caution regarding oversimplification: simply because a compound has a high acute oral LD_{50} does *not* mean it is harmless. Carbaryl is a good example of a compound that has a relatively low toxicity to mammals but is highly toxic to some non-target organisms such as bees. Also, do not be fooled into thinking that a pesticide made from plants (botanical) is "naturally" safe. Far from it. Rotenone, made either from the cubé root of South America or the derris root of Africa, is fairly toxic to mammals and highly toxic to fish. Pyrethrum, made from the dried and ground flowers of tropical chrysanthemum, is about as toxic to humans as malathion.

Pesticides are tools, no more or less dangerous than the person using them. Before you use them, stop and think: "Is the damage being done to the garden sufficient to warrant their use? Can I control the damage in another way, perhaps by handpicking or a water spray?" If the answer to the first question is "yes" and the answer to the second "no," then consider using the least toxic pesticide that will do the job.

Toxicity of Common Pesticides and Household Products for Comparison

(LD$_{50}$ values vary slightly among different data sets.)

Substance	Acute, Oral LD$_{50}$ (mg/kg body weight)	Amount ingested by a 150 lb. person to meet the LD$_{50}$	Notes
Nicotine	10	A few drops to 1 tsp.	Very toxic botanical insecticide. "Danger" with skull and crossbones on the label.
Gasoline	150	A few drops to 1 tsp.	
Rotenone	130–1,500	1 tsp. to 1 oz.	Common botanical insecticide. "Warning" may be on the label.
Caffeine	200	1 tsp. to 1 oz.	
Carbaryl	500	1 tsp. to 1 oz.	Low toxicity to mammals but highly toxic to bees. Do not apply to blooming crops. "Caution" may be on the label.
Malathion	1,200	Over 1 oz. to 1 pt. or 1 lb.	"Caution" on the label. Highly toxic to bees. Do not apply to blooming crops.
Ryania	1,200	Over 1 oz. to 1 pt. or 1 lb.	Botanical insecticide
Sabadilla	1,200	Over 1 oz. to 1 pt. or 1 lb.	Botanical insecticide
Aspirin	1,300	Over 1 oz. to 1 pt. or 1 lb.	

Toxicity of Common Pesticides and Household Products for Comparison

(LD$_{50}$ values vary slightly among different data sets.)

Substance	Acute, Oral LD$_{50}$ (mg/kg body weight)	Amount ingested by a 150 lb. person to meet the LD$_{50}$	Notes
Pyrethrum	1,500	Over 1 oz. to 1 pt. or 1 lb.	Common botanical insecticide. No warning word on the label.
Table salt	3,300	Over 1 oz. to 1 pt. or 1 lb.	
Glyphosate	4,300	Over 1 oz. to 1 pt. or 1 lb.	Commonly known as "Roundup®," a non-selective herbicide. No warning word on the label.
Sulfur	>5,000	Over 1 lb. or 1 pt.	All natural fungicide; can be phytotoxic. No warning word on the label.
Captan	9,000	Over 1 lb. or 1 pt.	Common fungicide. No warning word on the label.
Treflan	>10,000	Over 1 lb. or 1 pt.	Common ingredient in some pre-emergence herbicides. No warning word on the label.
Insecticidal soap	16,900	Over 1 lb. or 1 pt.	No warning word on the label.
Bt	Essentially nontoxic to non-target organisms	Over 1 lb. or 1 pt.	No warning word on the label.
Copper, fixed	Essentially nontoxic to non-target organisms	Over 1 lb. or 1 pt.	Fungicide. No warning word on the label.

Read all labels carefully and follow all directions. Here are a few points to consider:

- For pesticides labeled "Caution," wear at least long pants, a long-sleeved shirt, socks, and shoes. For those labeled "Warning," add chemical resistant gloves to your outfit. Pesticides labeled "Dangerous" should *not* be used in the home garden.
- Mix according to the label's directions. Wettable powders (W or WP) and emulsifiable concentrate (E or EC) formulations *must* be mixed with water before application. Follow the recommended concentrations carefully. If 2 tablespoons of wettable powder are recommended to be mixed with 1 gallon of water, don't use 4 tablespoons thinking that the mix will be more effective. It won't be; you will waste your money *and* you'll put more of the compound into the environment than is necessary.
- Do not spray on a windy day. Spraying in early morning is often the best time. Spraying in the heat of the day can cause phytotoxicity with some plant/pesticide combinations. Cucurbits are particularly sensitive to applications of carbaryl when temperatures are above 80°F.
- Direct the pesticide at the target plant, being sure to treat both the upper and lower sides of the leaves.
- Clean sprayers and clothes thoroughly after use, following directions on the pesticide label.
- Store all pesticides in a locked cabinet out of reach of children and pets.
- Dispose of empty containers as directed on the label.

Most new gardens should have very few pests and it's likely you won't need to use any pesticides. After a few years some pests may find your garden but you won't have all of them that we talked about. If you need any help at all begin with the least toxic controls like handpicking and a hard blast from the hose. Weeds

are often the worst pests of the garden and, if left uncontrolled, they will take over the area in short order. Weeds are thieves; they rob plants of water, nutrients, and sunlight and rob you of good harvests. Stay on it—evict them from your garden as soon as you see them. But, take heart! Pest and weed control is not all that difficult and can be managed one bug and one weed at a time.

The following table lists pests and diseases often found on certain vegetables with some suggested controls. This list is not intended to be conclusive, and is accurate as of the date of this publication. Rules and regulations governing pesticide use change constantly. Always check the latest recommendations before using any pesticides.

Vegetable Pests and Diseases and Some Controls

Vegetable	Pest	Description	Control
Asparagus	Rust	Red-black blisters on foliage and stem	Burn diseased material; plant resistant varieties
	Asparagus beetle	Metallic blue-black adults with yellow wing markings and slate gray larvae feed on shoots and foliage	Carbaryl, rotenone, malathion; handpick
Bean	Anthracnose	Dark sunken spots with pink centers on pods; deep-red to black cankers on stems	Use disease-free seeds in a 2- or 3-year rotation and do not cultivate beans when the garden is wet; sanitation
	Bacterial blight	Large brown spots encircled with yellow on leaves; watery spots on pods	Use disease-free seeds in a 3-year rotation and do not cultivate beans when the garden is wet
	Powdery mildew	Very faintly colored spots appear on leaves, eventually turning white and powdery	Sulfur

(Source: Adapted from Maynard and Hochmuth, 1997.)

Vegetable Pests and Diseases and Some Controls

Vegetable	Pest	Description	Control
Bean	White mold	Watersoaked spots on the plant; white cottony mold on pods	Good sanitation with a long rotation
	Aphid	Very small green, black, or pink soft-bodied insect that sucks sap from the plant and may transmit diseases	Wash plants with a strong water spray
	Leafhopper	Green, soft-bodied, wedge-shaped insect that sucks the sap and causes plant distortion	Carbaryl or handpick
	Tarnished plant bug	Brown, oval, flat bugs with a triangle marking at their rear suck plant sap	Handpick
Beet	Cercospora	Light brown spots with deep red borders on leaves	Long 3-year or greater rotation; fixed copper

Vegetable Pests and Diseases and Some Controls

Vegetable	Pest	Description	Control
Beet	Leaf miner	Yellowish maggotlike larvae tunnel between the upper and lower surfaces of the leaves, causing white, papery tunnels	Eradicate weeds, especially lambsquarter; trim infested leaves before eating; destroy badly infested leaves; malathion; row covers
Crucifers (broccoli, Brussels sprouts, cabbage, cauliflower, collards, kale, kohlrabi)	Black leg	Girdling of stems at soil line; gray spots speckled with black dots on stems	Sanitation and long rotation; use hot-water treated seeds
	Club root	Leaves that flag on hot days; yellow leaves; large irregular swellings on roots	Maintain soil at pH 7.2 or slightly higher; use disease-free seeds
	Fusarium yellows	Yellow-green leaves; lower leaves drop; plants stunted	Use resistant varieties
	Flea beetle	Very small, dark beetles early in the season make numerous pinholes in leaves during feeding	Carbaryl

(Source: Adapted from Maynard and Hochmuth, 1997.)

Vegetable Pests and Diseases and Some Controls

Vegetable	Pest	Description	Control
Crucifers	Cabbage maggot	Yellowish maggot tunnels into lower stem and roots	Use tarpaper swatches over the soil and around the base of the stem
	Cabbage looper	Green worms 1½ in. long with thin white lines; worms "loop" as they crawl	Carbaryl, malathion, Dipel
	Imported cabbage worm	Thin, velvety green worms 1¼ in. long emerge from egg masses on the undersides of the leaves and eat holes in the head and foliage	See cabbage looper
Carrot	Aster yellows	Bushy purple tops with yellow young leaves; roots become woody and hairy	Control leafhoppers, which carry the pathogen
	Leafhopper	See Bean	See Bean
	Rust fly	Yellow-white maggots tunnel into roots	Long rotation
Celery	Aster yellows	Yellow leaves; brittle and bitter petioles; plants stunted	Use resistant varieties; control leafhoppers and weeds

Vegetable Pests and Diseases and Some Controls

Vegetable	Pest	Description	Control
Celery	Bacterial blight	Bright yellow spots appear on the leaves; center of the spots turn brown	Sanitation; copper fungicides
	Aphid	See Bean	See Bean
	Loopers and other worms	See Crucifers	See Crucifers
Cucurbits (cucumbers, melons, squash, pumpkins)	Anthracnose	Red-black leafspots; brown cankers on stems; oozing sunken spots on fruit	Use resistant varieties in 3- to 4-year rotations
	Bacterial wilt	Vines wilt and die; sap is stringy	Sanitation; control striped cucumber beetles
	Powdery mildew	White, powdery film on leaves; foliage wilts	Use resistant varieties
	Aphid	See Bean	See Bean
	Cucumber beetle	Yellow beetle with 12 black spots on back or with 3 black lines on back; transmits bacterial wilt	Carbaryl; rotenone; handpick
	Squash bug	Flat, brown stinkbug	Carbaryl; handpick with rubber gloves

(Source: Adapted from Maynard and Hochmuth, 1997.)

Vegetable Pests and Diseases and Some Controls

Vegetable	Pest	Description	Control
Cucurbits	Squash vine borer	White caterpillars bore into stem close to where it exits the soil; vines wilt	Slice stem lengthwise through the hole with razor blade
Eggplant	Colorado potato beetle	Oval beetle with 10 black and 10 yellow stripes that lays yellow eggs beneath the leaves; larvae have black spot; both forms destroy leaves	Carbaryl; handpick
	Flea beetle	See Crucifers	See Crucifers
	Aphid	See Bean	See Bean
Endive and Lettuce	Tipburn	Edges of leaves brown and die	Prevent stress; use resistant varieties
	Aphid	See Bean	See Bean
	Flea beetle	See Crucifers	See Crucifers
	Loopers	See Crucifers	See Crucifers
Okra	Aphid	See Bean	See Bean

Vegetable Pests and Diseases and Some Controls

Vegetable	Pest	Description	Control
Onion	Neck rot	Soft brown tissue at neck	Be sure bulbs are cured and dry before storage
	Pink rot	Roots turn pink, shrivel, and die	Use resistant varieties; long rotations; plant disease-free stock
	Smut	Black leaf spots open to reveal black spores	Captan; long rotations
	Maggot	Small maggots bore into bulbs and stems	Long rotations
	Thrips	Very small (1/25 in.) suck sap from plant tissue causing white stippling and brown leaf tips	Long rotations; soap spray; rotenone
Parsnip	Canker	Brown tissue at crown	Mound soil over crown
	Rust fly	See Carrot	See Carrot
Pea	Powdery mildew	White powdery mold on leaves and stems	Use resistant varieties; sulfur
	Wilt	Wilting, yellow leaves; stunted growth	Use resistant varieties; early planting; 3-year rotation

(Source: Adapted from Maynard and Hochmuth, 1997.)

Vegetable Pests and Diseases and Some Controls

Vegetable	Pest	Description	Control
Pea	Aphid	See Bean	See Bean
	Seed maggot	Maggots burrow into seeds	Long rotations
Pepper	Anthracnose	Dark, round spots with black specks on fruit	Captan
	Aphid	See Bean	See Bean
	Flea beetle	See Crucifers	See Crucifers
Potato	Early blight	Dark brown leaf spots; reduced yields	Sanitation
	Late blight	Dead areas on leaves and stems; tubers rot in storage	Sanitation
	Scab	Rough scabby lesions on skin	Use resistant varieties; rotations; sulfur
	Aphid	See Bean	See Bean
	Colorado potato beetle	See Eggplant	See Eggplant
	Flea beetle	See Crucifers	See Crucifers
	Leafhoppers	See Bean	See Bean
Rhubarb	Crown rot	Petioles wilt; browning of the leaf base	Plant in well-drained soil; do not use heavy winter mulch

Vegetable Pests and Diseases and Some Controls

Vegetable	Pest	Description	Control
Rutabaga and Turnip	Club root	See Crucifers	See Crucifers
	Flea beetle	See Crucifers	See Crucifers
	Maggots	See Crucifers	See Crucifers
Spinach	Leaf miner	See Beet	See Beet
Sweet corn	Seed rot	Seed rots in soil	Wait for soil to warm before planting; use treated seeds
	Smut	Large, smooth, white galls form on ears, tassels, and at nodes, breaking open to release greasy black spores	Control corn borer; use resistant varieties; long rotations
	Earworm	Brown, green, or pink larvae feed on silk, kernels, and foliage	Carbaryl; daub silks where they emerge from husks with mineral oil just as they begin to brown
	European corn borer	Caterpillars feed on leaves then bore into the stalk up to the ear	Dipel, carbaryl; handpick worms before they enter the stalk

(Source: Adapted from Maynard and Hochmuth, 1997.)

Vegetable Pests and Diseases and Some Controls

Vegetable	Pest	Description	Control
Tomato	Anthracnose	Sunken spots on fruit enlarge, their centers darken, fruit rots	Sanitation; rotations
	Blossom end rot	Dark brown, leathery sunken spot appears at the blossom end of the fruit, enlarging to cover up to half of the entire fruit	Not pathogenic but a physiologic disorder specifically caused by a lack of calcium in the fruit; keep soil moisture constant; mulch plants
	Early blight	Dark brown spots on leaves; brown cankers on stem; girdling; leathery rotted areas on fruit near stem	Sanitation; rotations
	Fusarium	Yellowing and wilting of the entire plant	Use resistant varieties or long rotations
	Verticillium	Yellow areas on leaves turn brown; plants wilt at midday; leaves drop beginning at plant base	Use resistant varieties or long (7-year) rotations

Vegetable Pests and Diseases and Some Controls

Vegetable	Pest	Description	Control
Tomato	Aphid	See Bean	See Bean
	Colorado potato beetle	See Eggplant	See Eggplant
	Flea beetle	See Crucifers	See Crucifers
	Hornworm	Large 3- to 5-inch green worm with white lines on its side and a distinct reddish horn at its rear	Carbaryl; Dipel; handpick

(Source: Adapted from Maynard and Hochmuth, 1997.)

As interesting as they appear, don't let hornworms get the best of your tomatoes before you do! Pick them off or use Carbaryl® or Dipel® to get rid of them.

Chapter Ten

CHEATING TIME: SEASON EXTENDERS

Season extenders are just what they sound like—techniques or methods that can stretch the growing and harvesting seasons. In our Rocky Mountain region good gardeners must take advantage of every means to lengthen what are relatively short growing seasons. The difference of even a few days can mean the difference between a bountiful harvest and no harvest at all.

Tricking the Calendar

Any season extenders that are smaller than greenhouses are meant to give you a few extra *weeks* of season, not months. Despite claims by a national producer of plant protectors, you cannot plant tomatoes in your garden in Montana in January and expect them to make it simply by using individual plant protectors. Remember that all plants grown beneath plant protectors become tender and may be injured by sun and wind if the protectors are suddenly removed. Therefore, remove them gradually as plants become too large for them.

Individual plant or row covers used early in a season can allow you a few days head start. They help warm the soil underneath them. Hot caps are small, inexpensive cones made of waxed paper and placed over individual transplants. They are meant to be used for one season only and in non-windy locations. Cut a slit in the top for ventilation.

Water jackets resemble double-walled corrugated plastic cones and come in clear, red, and green types. Filled with water and placed over a transplant, these jackets moderate nighttime temperatures and provide good protection from cold and wind. They will not protect plants from deep cold but can provide pretty good protection down to temperatures in the low 20s°F, if the water doesn't freeze and depending upon the species of plant.

Homemade plant protectors include gallon milk jugs with their bottoms and caps removed and even an upside-down 5-gallon

The resourceful Rocky Mountain gardener has a few tricks to allow longer harvests before the heavy frost and snows of winter arrive.

plastic bucket with half its bottom removed for ventilation. Old tires placed around transplants afford some protection against wind and cold as the tires heat up the air surrounding the plant. Unfortunately, they can become mosquito nurseries later in the season if you do not keep them emptied of standing water.

Row covers look like miniature greenhouse tunnels and are made from clear plastic, woven fabric, polyester sheets, and other materials. The sheets are placed over wire hoops that are set along the row at about 4- to 6-foot intervals and their sides are anchored in a soil trench on both sides of the hoops and buried. The ends of the tunnels can be left open for ventilation and the sides can be rolled up during nice weather. These row cover tunnels promote early-season growth by increasing the humidity and temperature around the plants, while protecting them from wind and frost. Unfortunately, they are difficult to keep in place in windy locations. The same is true for the spun bonded materials that are light enough to be placed directly on plants. Called floating row covers, these provide some frost protection but will easily blow away in a strong wind if they're not anchored with rocks. (Row covers also protect plants from some insects.)

Protecting vegetables from a frost by covering with a blanket or sheet is more successful in fall than in spring as the covers trap ground heat stored during the summer; soils in spring have not yet begun to store much ground heat-making this method less successful. Covering vegetables in fall may extend your season by several weeks if an Indian summer follows a light frost.

Cold frames and hot beds were popular in previous generations for starting and hardening transplants and for growing a fall harvest of spinach or lettuce. Depending upon the kind of plants you want to grow and the severity of your area's season, you may be able to harvest fall-planted greens through early winter. Both types of frames are constructed similarly except that a hot bed is a cold frame with an internal source of heat. At one time the heat source was derived from fermenting horse manure but modern frames use electric heating cables or other sources. It is important to be aware of the ventilation and temperature to be sure the interiors of the frames do not overheat. Check out these planting schedules using a cold frame. The best times to plant depend strongly upon local conditions and season.

Approximate Planting Schedule for Sowing Fall and Winter Greens in a Cold Frame

Crop	Approximate Planting Dates	Approximate Harvest Dates
Endive / Escarole	Mid-July	Mid-September to mid-November
Leaf lettuce	Mid-July to early September	Mid-September to mid-November
Radish	Early September to mid-October	October to late November
Spinach	August	Mid-October to late November
Swiss chard	July	October through winter

(Source: Adapted from Coleman, 1999.)

A cold frame is a simple structure best located so that its sashes (a fixed or flexible framework similar in appearance to a window or door) are to the south. A cold frame isn't a rectangle or a square; common dimensions are for the north wall to be twelve inches in height above the soil line and the south wall eight inches in height. These are located the length of a window sash apart, usually 4 to 6 feet. Select rot-resistant wood for construction, or use copper naphthanate-treated lumber. All sides should be banked with soil for insulation. The north side can be set against a building or into a bank for added protection. Old storm windows were once commonly used for sashes but today you can make sashes out of rigid or flexible plastic in any width

A cold frame is a useful tool to help plants weather harsh seasonal changes.

and length you prefer. Be sure their frames fit the cold frame walls tightly. For added protection on cold nights cover the sashes with blankets, sheets of rigid insulation, or straw mats, and be sure to provide very good ventilation during sunny spring days. Place a thermometer inside the frame to monitor temperature; if the air temperature rises above 85°F ventilate by opening the top of the sash. There are devices on the market that will open and close the sash automatically to maintain proper temperature.

Add a source of heat to the cold frame and voila! It's a hot bed. The traditional source of heat used to be fermenting horse manure. If you *have* horses this may work for you (seriously). First, lower the soil level inside the frame by 3 feet. Place fresh manure in a pile next to the hot bed. When it begins to ferment it will steam. Place a 3- to 4-inch layer of the manure in the bottom of the frame, pack it down, then add another layer. About 30 inches of manure total should be enough to warm the hot bed in our cold springs. Close the sashes and monitor the temperature, which may rise to about 130°F. When it has cooled to below 90°F spread about 6 inches of loam soil over the manure. After a week or so the temperature should cool sufficiently for weeds to begin to sprout. Pull the weed seedlings and sow your seeds directly into the soil or into flats placed on the soil's surface.

For the horseless among us, thermostatically controlled electric heating cables placed beneath the soil also work well as long as you have a source of power. The same holds true for placing about eight 25-watt incandescent light bulbs inside the frame. These should be sufficient to heat a 3 x 6-foot section. (Be sure to use safety measures to guard against electrical short circuits or your hot bed might be hot in more ways than one.)

For more information on constructing hot beds and cold frames contact your local county extension office, or download this free Montana State University Extension MontGuide, http://msuextension.org/Publications.

The Rocky Mountain region is known for long, cold winters and short, intense summers. Don't be intimidated! You *can* "fool" Mother Nature out of a few extra weeks of growing season by utilizing season extenders both early and late in the season.

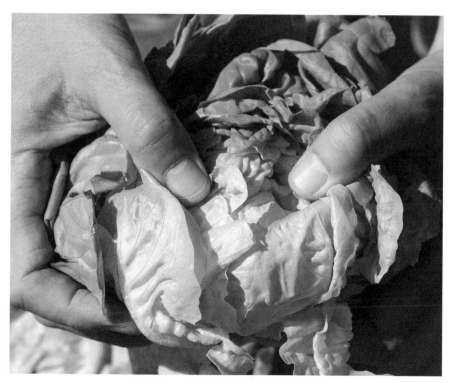

Sowing in a cold frame allows another harvest before winter sets in.

Chapter Eleven

HARVESTING AND STORING

You'll (probably!) enjoy working in your garden all season long but harvesting is the ultimate payoff to reap the benefits of your labors. Harvest when the vegetable has reached its peak flavor (and it's not always when you think) and store it properly. You will literally be able to enjoy the "fruits" of your labor all year long. After all you've gone through, when you finally are at the end of the season, it seems like a miracle.

Is It Soup Yet?

The best time to harvest is not necessarily when a vegetable is ripe but rather when it has reached the stage for best eating. In fact, allowing some crops to ripen fully on the plant reduces yield and quality. For example, cucumbers are picked and eaten when they are at an immature stage; allowing them to mature on the vine will give you big, mushy, yellow, inedible fruit. The developing seeds of the cucumber will signal the plant to stop producing flowers and start ripening the seeds. The same thing holds true for summer squash, beans, peas, and some other vegetables.

The number of days to harvest serves as a very general guide to determining when to harvest, though it may be off by a couple of weeks due to local weather and cultural conditions.

Also, examine your crop and look for the following general characteristics by checking the physical conditions of the edible parts.

Ripeness

Most crops attain their peak eating quality (horticultural maturity) just before they attain full botanical maturity. Corn allowed to ripen fully on the stalk quickly passes its best eating stage (the milk stage) and develops a tough skin around the kernels, finally drying into an ear with hard, starchy, inedible seeds (at least, for people!). Technically, it is at that end stage that the corn is "ripe" but by then it has long passed the best eating stage. Fully ripe summer squash develop a tough rind and generally become unpalatable. Fully ripe peas and beans are dry and their pods are ready to burst open. This is the stage to harvest for shell beans and shell peas to be used in baked beans or pea soup. But snap beans and peas to be cooked and served (as usual) are harvested long before they are ripe, and before their sugars convert to starch. Leafy vegetables allowed to grow for too long become fibrous, yellow, and bitter tasting. So, harvesting at the right time is paramount.

When to Harvest

Characteristic	Vegetable
Full size	Most vegetables
External color	Most vegetables
Separates easily from the plant; good netting development; aromatic	Muskmelon
Compact head	Broccoli, cauliflower
Solidity	Cabbage, head lettuce, Brussels sprouts
Tenderness	Asparagus, corn, peas
Dry foliage	Garlic, horseradish, onion, potato, shallot
Internal structure	Tomato (jelly-like tissue forms around the seeds)
Milk stage	Corn
Orange ground spot; hard rind	Winter squash, pumpkin, watermelon
Moderate size	Carrot, beet, parsnip, radish, salsify, summer squash

(Source: Adapted from Swaider and Ware, 2002.)

Harvesting

This is the good part! And what you've been waiting for. Harvest in the early morning after the dew has dried or in evening when temperatures are cool. Spinach and Swiss chard, however, are quite brittle in the early morning and may break into pieces during harvest; wait until midmorning to harvest these. If your vegetables are warm when they're harvested, remove field heat quickly by submerging them in a sinkful of cold water.

Once you have separated a plant part from the parent plant, you have destroyed its source of water, nutrients, and sugars. What it had in it at that moment of harvest is the most that vegetable will have. The warmer the temperature the faster a vegetable will use up its stored nutrient reserves and the shorter time it will "keep." Sweet corn loses up to one quarter of its sugar in *a couple of hours* at 80°F; peas lose their sugar four times faster at 68°F than at 32°F.

Storage

Some vegetables continue to ripen after harvest and some don't. However, the ripening will involve mostly a change of skin color, softening of the flesh, and perhaps an accumulation of starch or sugar under certain conditions. Ripening usually will not involve much sweetening because produce, once separated from the plant, has little means of manufacturing new sugars. Root vegetables and winter squash convert stored carbohydrates into sugars after harvest. Produce ripened off the plant will usually be lower in quality and less tasty than those ripened intact on the plant, so delay harvest for as long as possible, without delaying too long.

Most cool-season vegetables store well at a temperature just above 32°F. At temperatures below that they freeze and their tissues will begin to rot. Warm-season vegetables such as peppers and cucumbers store best at a temperature around 50°F. If they're stored at lower temperatures they develop chilling damage, which often shows up as pitting and sunken areas on the skin. An exception to this rule for warm-season vegetables is sweet corn. Always store corn as close to 32°F as possible to prevent the sugars from turning to starch. If stored below about 38°F potatoes convert their starch into sugar. If you fry those potatoes they will develop black spots where the sugars caramelized.

Most vegetables contain about 90 to 95 percent water and they will lose water to any air that is dryer, causing them to shrivel. It is therefore important to keep the air in their storage compartment as close to 95 percent relative humidity as possible by sprinkling the produce or compartment periodically with water and/or by storing the produce in plastic bags. Be sure the bags have about one quarter-inch-diameter hole per square foot of surface area for ventilation. Exceptions include winter squash, dry bulb onions, and garlic, which should be stored at about 65 percent relative humidity after curing to reduce rotting.

To maintain high humidity for root vegetables and cabbage some folks store them in a box filled with moist sand placed in an unheated basement kept at about 55°F. Alternatively, you can store them in a refrigerator in zip-style plastic bags with the corners cut off. Removing the corners allows gas exchange and excess moisture to escape. Hang tomato vines with both green and ripening fruit upside down in a cool room. This allows the fruit to continue ripening while extracting some nutrients from the plant itself.

Store only healthy produce in good condition. Vegetables with bruises, rot, spade cuts on root vegetables, or damage caused by insects and disease will rot rapidly and release large quantities of ethylene, the ripening hormone. Root vegetables will become more fibrous as they age so harvest these at a somewhat immature stage if you intend to store them for more than a month.

Ventilation is necessary for long storage. Ripening produce gives off heat as it respires. Called the "heat of respiration" this can build up in enclosed areas and make it difficult to maintain a cool temperature. A refrigerator is able to remove this heat, but some simple cold storages may not. If you can, open a window and run a fan for a few hours to get some fresh air into the storage area. Ventilation will also help remove excess water and ethylene gas given off by ripening vegetables. Ethylene is a natural ripening hormone, and the more ethylene in the atmosphere, the faster any produce will ripen and the faster it will produce more ethylene. Think of it as a snowball going downhill, its size ever increasing. Rotting vegetables, as well as sound apples, bananas, pears, plums, muskmelons, and peaches, in particular, give off large quantities of ethylene; never store these among your produce. The old trick about ripening tomatoes by placing them in a bag with an apple (or banana) uses the ethylene produced by the fruit to hasten the process. The less ethylene there is in the storage the longer the produce will keep. (Interestingly, fluorescent lights, engines, and lighted cigarettes also emit large quantities of ethylene.)

Keep all lights off in storage. Lights can cause heat buildup and also cause some vegetables such as onion, garlic, and potato to turn green. This is potentially serious in potatoes since the greening reaction signals the buildup of the colorless alkaloid solanine, a poison that can give you a bad stomachache if you eat enough of it.

Some vegetables store better than others. In general, cool-season ones keep longer than warm-season ones. Later ripening varieties keep longer than earlier ripening vegetables. American dry bulb onions store better than mild European-type onions; root vegetables store better than fruits. So don't expect cucumbers to store as long as parsnips. If you intend to store a lot of produce select the right species and varieties.

Adding It All Up

The benefits and rewards of growing your own food are so many. Now you know where your food is coming from, you've saved money, you've been able to be out in our great outdoors, you're able to grow so many more types of vegetables than is offered in the groceries, and it tastes so good! So, what's for dinner?

Ideal Vegetable Storage Conditions
& Storage Lifespan

Crop	Storage (°F)	Relative Humidity (%)	Approximate Storage Life
Asparagus	32–35	95	2–3 weeks
Bean (snap)	41–46	90–95	7–10 days
Broccoli	32	90–95	10–14 days
Brussels sprouts	32	90–95	3–5 weeks
Cabbage	32	95–98	1–6 months
Carrot	32	95–100	1–3 months
Cauliflower	32	95–100	3–4 weeks
Celeriac	32	90–95	3–4 months
Celery	32	98–100	1–2 months
Chinese cabbage	32	98–100	2–3 months
Cucumber	50–55	95	10–14 days
Eggplant	50–54	90–95	1 week
Garlic	32	65–70	6–7 months
Kohlrabi	32	90–95	2–4 weeks
Lettuce	32	98–100	2–3 weeks
Muskmelon	46–50	90–95	1–2 weeks
Onion (dry)	32	65–70	1–7 months
Peas	32	95–98	1–2 weeks
Pepper	46–54	90–95	2–3 weeks

Ideal Vegetable Storage Conditions
& Storage Lifespan

Crop	Storage (°F)	Relative Humidity (%)	Approximate Storage Life
Potato	39	90–95	4–8 months
Pumpkin	50–55	50–75	2–3 months
Radish (leaves removed, also known as "topped")	32	90–95	3–4 weeks
Rhubarb	32	95	2–4 weeks
Rutabaga	32	90–95	2–4 months
Salsify	32	90–95	2–4 months
Spinach	32	95–98	10–14 days
Summer squash	45–50	95	1–2 weeks
Sweet corn	32	95–98	5–8 days
Swiss chard	32	90–95	10–14 days
Tomato (mature green)	54–57	90–95	1–3 weeks
Tomato (ripe)	46–50	90–95	4–7 days
Turnip (topped)	32	90–95	4–5 months
Watermelon	46–54	90	2–3 weeks
Winter squash	50–54	60	1–6 months

(Source: Lutz and Hardenburg, 1968.)

Chapter Twelve

OVERVIEW OF THE VEGETABLES

You don't have to be a botanist or a horticulturist, but a little knowledge goes a long way in the vegetable garden. For example, vegetables may be classified according to botanical classification, edible portion of the plant, lifecycle, temperature requirements, or hardiness. Because similarities among plants mean you can treat them in a similar manner this can be really helpful information for the home gardener.

For example, botanically, horseradish, cabbage, turnip, and radish are all members of the Mustard family (*Cruciferae*) and therefore have similar growing requirements. Because cabbage and turnip are members of the same genus, their growing requirements will be even more similar than those for members of different genera, such as radish and horseradish. Looking at classification by edible parts, beet, carrot, and turnip all have edible roots and are classified as root vegetables. Kale, Swiss chard, and lettuce all have edible leaves and are classified as leafy vegetables or greens.

Plants are also classified by their lifecycle (whether they are an annual, biennial, or perennial). If a seed germinates and the plant grows, flowers, and goes to seed within one growing season it is an annual; cucumbers and peas are annual vegetables (meaning they grow, mature, and reproduce within one growing season). Biennials grow only leafy parts their first season and after the chilly winter, develop their flowers and go to seed in the second year; carrots and beets are biennials. Perennials are not killed by winter temperatures and return year after year; asparagus and rhubarb are good examples. Some plants may botanically be termed biennials, such as cabbage and beets, but we grow them as annuals.

One of the most useful methods of classifying vegetables for those of us living in the Rocky Mountains is by temperature requirements and hardiness. This allows us to separate cool-season from warm-season vegetables. Cool-season vegetable seeds germinate at a lower soil temperature, allowing anxious gardeners to get out and plant at earlier dates. The young plants are frost tolerant and hardy. For the most part, cool-season vegetables are smaller plants than warm-season vegetables, and because the plant material above the ground is smaller, their root system is also smaller. We almost always consume the vegetative parts of a cool-season vegetable, including roots, immature flower buds, leaves, and stems. (Peas are an exception.)

Cool-season vegetables can be *annuals* grown as annuals, *biennials* grown as annuals, and *perennials* grown as annuals or perennials. Sound confusing? It really isn't. We harvest biennials during their vegetative period as the plant is making its leaves and roots sweet and full of nutrition to feed the second season's growth.

If we don't harvest biennials the first season, the plant uses all those sugars and nutrients to form flowers and seeds in the second season, thereby making the parts we would normally eat—leaves, roots, and stems—woody and tasteless. Some perennials may not be winter hardy in much of our region. Take artichokes, which are technically perennials. In mild climates (USDA hardiness zone 7 and above), the plant produces year after year, but will winterkill in cooler climates. Now, that doesn't mean you can't transplant an artichoke into your garden and reap the harvest in one year.

Just be sure you set transplants and give them plenty of time and space. Perennials such as asparagus, rhubarb, and horseradish are winter hardy here in the Rockies and will produce year after year without replanting.

Some cool-season biennials are susceptible to bolting (meaning they'll flower or produce seed much earlier than expected) if they're exposed to too much cool weather in their first season.

There are certain temperatures that are optimal for all crops to produce their best growth. Warm-season vegetables grow best between 65 and 85°F, while cool-season vegetables grow best between 55 and 65°F. Within the classifications of cool season and warm season, there are sub-categories of hardy, half-hardy, tender, and very tender plants. These sub-categories are used to define the ability of young plants to withstand frosts and their ability to germinate at low temperatures.

We have divided the vegetables in this book into three categories: cool-season perennials, cool-season annuals, and warm-season annuals. At the beginning of each vegetable profile is a series of quick tips.

Genus, species, and family: It is useful to know the botanical relationships of the various vegetables because those that are closely related often share the same cultural requirements and the same pest problems.

Temperatures: All temperatures are given in degrees Fahrenheit.

Soil temperatures: Sowing seeds at the minimum soil temperature is skirting danger as they may not germinate at all or germinate so slowly as to be highly susceptible to seed rots. Try to sow when soil is in the optimum range for plant growth.

Distance between rows: This is somewhat dependent upon what equipment you use for cultivation. The old recommendations were established for cultivation using horses. If you intend to use a hoe only, you may use closer spacings. The optimum spacings allow for cultivation and for the foliage of mature plants to cover the space between rows, thus crowding out weeds.

Direct seed or transplant: Our season is long enough in most cases to direct seed the named vegetable, but you may also transplant it for especially early harvests.

Ease of transplant: Some plants tolerate transplanting well because they reestablish their root systems rapidly and continue growing soon after. Others are slow to reestablish their root systems and resume growing and thus will suffer great and sometimes fatal setback following transplanting.

Days to maturity: This is not a real number but a composite average for a particular plant in an average soil in an average year under average conditions. It is meant as a relative guide only (but it's the best we've got!).

Depth of root system: Contrary to popular opinion, some vegetables have extraordinarily deep root systems. The deeper the roots the more able the plant is to tolerate dry conditions and to mine subsoil nutrients; the more shallow the root system the more often you will have to irrigate and fertilize to keep plants healthy. A plant with a shallow root system has most of its roots in the top two feet of soil while one with a moderately deep root system has most of its roots in the top four feet of soil. Roots of deep-rooted crops extend to depths of six feet or more. Absolute depth depends upon absence of a hardpan, soil texture, height of the water table, depth of water, oxygen, and nutrient availability.

Need for Nitrogen: Some plants require a lot of nitrogen for the best vegetative growth and crop production and are termed "heavy feeders." These deplete the soil rapidly if supplemental nutrients are not supplied in fairly large quantities. Pay close attention to fertilizing these vegetables.

Average yield: This is highly variable and subject to modification by cultural practices, temperature, variety, and growing season.

Approximate length of the germination period: This figure is highly variable and depends upon the temperature. Generally, lower temperatures lengthen this period, higher temperatures shorten it. Your goal is for seeds to germinate in the shortest amount of time.

Approximate time to grow to transplant size: Again, this is highly dependent upon temperature. Low temperatures prolong the time needed and may result in woody plant material that is slow to recover from transplant shock. Very high temperatures produce soft, spindly plants that don't do well in the garden.

Now that you've read all the basics, let's get into the garden!

THE VEGETABLES

Asparagus

Asparagus officinalis

Family: Liliaceae — Lily

perennial vegetable

Transplant: 1- or 2-year-old crowns

Optimum Range of Soil Temperature for Planting: 75–85°F

Minimum Soil Temperature for Planting: 50°F

Spacing Within Trenched Row: 8–14 inches

Depth of Root System: Deep

Trench depth: 6–8 inches

Distance Between Rows: 3–5 feet

Ease of Transplant: Easy

Consumption of Nitrogen: Low

Average Yield per 10-foot Row: 3 lbs.

Asparagus is a hardy, dioecious herbaceous perennial. It tolerates severe cold when it's dormant and grows best when daytime temperatures average about 80°F and nighttime temperatures fall to about 60°F.

Planting and Care: Prepare the soil using plenty of organic material and till in a fertilizer high in phosphorus and potassium; well-drained, sandy loams are best.

Purchase 1- or 2-year-old disease-free crowns, each containing two or more well-formed clusters of buds. Place the crowns in a trench about 8 inches deep and spread the roots out carefully. Cover them with an inch or two of soil. Continue to fill in the trench as the shoots grow until you have regained the original soil level allowing the top inch or two of the shoot to remain above the soil as you fill the trench. If your soil is heavy clay, plant the

FUN FACTS

The Roman statesman Cato, the author of the early treatise on agriculture called On Farming, *gave directions for its cultivation about 200 B.C. Pliny and Columella spoke highly of it and the emperor Augustus apparently relished the young shoots. Although introduced into the United States very early in our history, it was not planted extensively until about the time of the Civil War.*

crowns only 4 inches deep. Asparagus is susceptible to *Fusarium* so plant in a location that has not been planted previously with asparagus.

Sidedress plants in early spring and again after harvest. Some gardeners recommend topdressing with composted manure after harvest to keep plants vigorous.

Watering is critical while plants are becoming established. By the third season the plants should have developed an extensive root system and thus require less water.

Keeping weeds out of the bed can be a problem as the crowns begin to spread and the rows fill in. Also, some volunteer asparagus seedlings may appear. These will not be as vigorous or productive as the mother plants so consider them weeds and keep them out of the bed.

Older varieties are based on the 'Martha Washington' strain, but lately, breeders have developed a number of all-male or predominantly male varieties. Male plants produce as many as 3 to 5 times more spears than a mixed population of older varieties, where male and female plants will be present in approximately equal proportions.

Recommended Asparagus Varieties

Variety	Comments
Mary Washington	Old standby
Waltham Washington	Old standby
Viking	Male variety
Jersey Centennial	Male variety

Asparagus has a combination of perennial rhizomes and fleshy roots that make up the crown of the plant. The rhizomes grow in a slightly upward pointing manner, which is the reason that old beds have crowns near the surface. Fleshy roots grow about 6 feet outward from the plant and 5 feet deep. Fibrous roots that absorb water and nutrients develop from the fleshy roots and die back each fall.

Spears arise from buds on the crowns and become increasingly woody as they get longer. The rhizome buds will produce only a few shoots unless the early shoots are harvested and new shoots develop as the old are harvested.

The growth of spears is temperature dependent, requiring about five days to produce a 6-inch spear at 53°F but only two days at 78°F. Warm temperatures cause rapid growth and decrease the spear quality, though very cool temperatures cause the spears to become woody and bitter and lowers their quality, as well.

The spears continue to lengthen into shoots up to six feet tall. The ferny foliage produces carbohydrates to replenish those used in overwintering the crowns.

Harvesting: Don't harvest the first season and harvest only lightly in the second season. In the third season, harvest spears for the first 3 weeks only, then extend the length of harvest by 2 weeks each year until you've reached a maximum of 6 to 8 weeks.

—WHAT HAPPENED HERE?—

MY ASPARAGUS IS WOODY – This is due to slow growth. The bed is probably too crowded or conditions were droughty.

MY PLANTS HAVE RUSTY SPOTS – Asparagus rust is the most common cause of failure in asparagus beds. Destroy the existing bed and plant rust resistant varieties in a new location.

MY ASPARAGUS TASTES BITTER – The weather is probably too warm. Quit harvesting.

Spears developing later should be left to produce leaves to make carbohydrates that will be stored in the roots. Stop harvesting immediately if you see pencil-thick spears, for this is a sign the crowns' supply of nutrition is nearly depleted.

The best spears are 6 to 10 inches long with tight tip scales. The scales open sooner during warm weather, so you will have to harvest every day.

If you cut the spears about an inch below the soil line the portion of the spear that was below ground will be white and tough, so trim it off. If you snap the spears at the soil line you'll eliminate the tough white base and have less trimming.

Let all later shoots develop fully and overwinter, removing them before growth begins in spring.

Beet

Beta vulgaris
Family: Chenopodiaceae — Goosefoot

Direct Seed or Transplant: Either, but it's usually direct seeded
Optimum Range of Soil Temperature for Germination: 50–85°F
Minimum Soil Temperature for Germination: 40°F
Optimum Range of Soil Temperature for Planting: 60–65°F
Minimum Soil Temperature for Planting: 40°F
Seed Planting Depth: ½–1 inch
Seed Spacing Within Row: 1 inch
Depth of Root System: Moderate
Thinned Spacing Within Row: 2–4 inches
Distance Between Rows: 12–30 inches
Ease of Transplant: Easy
Consumption of Nitrogen: Moderate
Days to Maturity: 56–70
Average Yield per 10-foot Row: 10 lbs. roots / 4 lbs. greens

cool-season vegetable

Beets are grown for their roots and for their tasty greens. They are easy to grow from seed and easy to transplant. But what you

probably don't know is that the "seeds" in the packets are actually clusters of seeds within a shriveled fruit!

Planting and Care: As seeds germinate, the resulting plants don't come up all at once. The weak seedlings cannot push through crusted soil, so be on guard! Plant radish seeds as a nurse crop. Thin young plants when their roots and tops are large enough to eat. Succession planting may be used in regions with longer seasons, through the spring and again in late summer for a fall crop.

In a 10-foot row, you can expect somewhere in the neighborhood of ten pounds of roots and four pounds of greens, if the leaf miners don't get them. In fact, some varieties are grown only for their greens. 'Bulls Blood' is an heirloom variety with—you guessed it—blood-red foliage; what a beautiful addition to everyone's salad bowl!

Beets are biennials grown as annuals, forming a rosette of leaves and thick taproot the first year and a flower stalk the second. Because of this two-year growth pattern, sudden, drastic changes in the weather or low temperatures (40 to 50°F) for more than a couple of weeks while seedlings are small will cause the plants to flower and set seed (bolt). Prolonged high temperatures result in zoning and low sugar content in the roots. Zoning is undesirable in some varieties, but not all. In fact, many gardeners plant 'Chioggia' beets for the beautiful, candy-striped zones. Beet roots will develop poor color if dry periods are followed by heavy rains.

Good, deep loamy soils produce the best beets. Heavy soils

produce asymmetrical roots. Beets must grow rapidly to develop the best quality and they respond well to organic matter. Apply well composted manure as well as preplant fertilizer and sidedress about 4 to 6 weeks after planting. Take care not to apply too much nitrogen, however—that will force excessive topgrowth and faded root color (unless you are growing *for* greens).

Beet greens look ragged when the beets are grown in low pH soils. In fact, early gardeners used them as indicator plants for acid soils. Test your soil for boron also, since beets are sensitive to low levels of this nutrient.

Few pests attack beets. Leaf miners are among the most troublesome insects, eating the juicy tissues between the leaves' upper and lower sides, rendering the greens unfit to eat without trimming. Boron deficiency shows up as internal browning. Corky black spots appear in the root, and the young leaves resemble straps and sometimes turn a deep red. Boron deficiency is often a problem in dry conditions and neutral or alkaline soils.

Harvesting: When the roots have reached about 1½ inches in diameter, harvest them and store them just above 32°F. If you plan to eat the greens (tops), remove and store them separately. When you remove the leaves, leave an inch or so of the stem attached to the beet roots to prevent them from "bleeding" and drying out.

FUN FACTS

Since the very ancient Greeks and Romans did not mention beets in their writings, they are probably of fairly recent origin. The Roman author and naturalist Pliny recommended that people eat a roasted beet to sweeten their breaths and the Greeks offered them in silver bowls to Apollo. Beets were used as medicine in the second century A.D. and eaten as food by the third century. Roman gardeners selected both red- and white-rooted types for the table. Beets were first grown for cattle feed in northern Europe. Then, around 1400 A.D., the author of an English cookbook mentions beets grown for the table and they soon became widely grown in Europe, beginning in Germany by 1558. They were known as "Roman beets" in England in 1576, suggesting they came from Italy. They were being grown in the United States by 1800.

——WHAT HAPPENED HERE?——

IT LOOKS LIKE THERE IS INTERNAL BROWNING – High pH soils combined with hot, dry conditions can cause boron deficiency. Test your soil before next year's planting. Don't supplement with boron without a professional recommendation as you can sterilize the soil.

I HAVE BROWN AREAS IN THE LEAVES – Leaf miners lay their eggs in leaf tissues. The young maggot–like leaf miners tunnel between the upper and lower sides, leaving dead, brown tissue behind. Remove badly damaged leaves and destroy them. If you want to eat the leaves, simply snip out the slightly damaged areas. Exclude the adult leaf miner by using a row cover at planting.

I HAVE TOUGH, WOODY BEETS – Conditions that cause growth to slow can cause woodiness. If you forgot to thin, or planted too thickly, the beets will compete with each other for water and nutrients. Very hot weather also causes woody beets.

THERE ARE SEED STALKS ON MY BEET PLANTS – Beets are biennials and can be fooled into producing their flower and seed stalk the first year by an extended cold snap soon after you've seeded. When this happens, the plant's reserves go toward developing seeds, not toward developing sugars in the roots. Pull the beets up and plant again if it isn't too late. Beets that mature in the heat of summer will be poor quality.

Recommended Beet Varieties

Variety	Days to Maturity	Comments
Bull's Blood	35 for baby leaves	Heirloom; grown mostly for tops
Chioggia	55	Heirloom; attractive red-and-white striped zoning
Detroit Dark Red	45–70	Heirloom; widely used
Early Wonder	45	Heirloom; arguably one of the earliest
Red Ace	50	Little to no zoning; widely adapted
Golden	55	Heirloom; green leaves, yellow stems, gold root interior

Broccoli

Brassica oleracea (Italica group)

Family: Cruciferae (or Brassicaceae) — Mustard

Direct Seed or Transplant: Transplant
Optimum Range of Soil Temperature for Planting: 60–65°F
Minimum Soil Temperature for Planting: 40°F
Depth of Root System: Shallow
Transplant Spacing Within Row: 12–24 inches
Distance Between Rows: 18–36 inches
Ease of Transplant: Easy
Consumption of Nitrogen: High
Days to Maturity: 55–78
Average Yield per 10-foot Row: 7½ lb.
Grow your own transplants:
Optimum Range of Soil Temperature for Germination: 65–70°F
Approximate Length of Germination Period: 3–4 days
Approximate Time to Grow to Transplant Size: 4–6 weeks

cool-season vegetable

Broccoli tolerates light frost, which improves its flavor, but it bolts during hot summers, doing best at temperatures between 57 to 68°F. Slightly higher temperatures produce leafy heads that bolt quickly, while temperatures above 77°F cause plants to form no heads at all.

Planting and Care: Transplant broccoli in early spring or direct seed later to mature in fall. In either case you should plan to harvest the heads before or after the heat of summer. In our region, with its short growing seasons, broccoli is usually transplanted as a spring crop. Transplant younger plants (6 to 8 weeks), as older transplants of both broccoli and cauliflower may form tiny, poor quality heads if

FUN FACTS

There are two types of broccoli: heading broccoli is actually a late cauliflower, while sprouting broccoli forms a central head made up of several smaller heads. American gardeners are more familiar with the latter.

Scientists believe that our common broccoli arose as a mutation of wild cabbage growing along the European coasts. Pliny mentions its culture but the issue is confused since the same Latin name cyma *is applied both to broccoli and cauliflower. Both green and purple-colored broccoli were introduced into England in 1724 where they were called "sprout colli-flower" and "Italian asparagus." Broccoli was introduced into the United States about 1800 but remained obscure until soldiers returning from Europe after World War I began to ask for it. California farmers of Italian origin or descent shipped the first commercially grown broccoli East in 1920 and the vegetable has continued to gain popularity ever since.*

Recommended Broccoli Varieties

Variety	Days to Maturity	Comments
Goliath	53	Early; produces many sideshoots
Premium Crop	58	AAS Selection; main season; bolt resistant
Packman	50	Early; widely adapted
Windsor	56	Heat tolerant; widely adapted

exposed to temperatures below 50°F.

All crucifers need rich soil with plenty of manure and compost for their best production. Their need for nutrients is high so don't be shy about sidedressing each plant. Since most crucifers have growing requirements similar to those of cabbage, see that vegetable for more details (page 177).

Ask your soil-testing lab to check the levels of boron and molybdenum from your soil analysis as broccoli is very sensitive to deficiencies of these. Never add these nutrients to the soil unless you are sure they are deficient, and never add more than is recommended. In soils below pH 5.5, molybdenum deficiency causes "whiptail," the development of straplike leaves. Boron deficiency causes "browning" wherein the stems develop water-soaked areas, which develop upward into the flower head; individual flowers then become brown.

Harvesting: Cut a tight central head when it is about 3 to 6 inches in diameter, and also cut 8 to 10 inches of stem. If the head is loose and the yellow florets have opened, you waited too long and the broccoli may taste bitter or simply insipid. After the harvest of the central heads, sidedress with a fertilizer relatively high in nitrogen to promote strong development of the lateral shoots. These lateral shoots should be harvested when their heads

————WHAT HAPPENED HERE?————

LEAVES HAVE DEVELOPED IN MY BROCCOLI FLOWERHEADS – This can be caused by too much hot weather. Time planting so the heads mature in cooler weather. Heads in this condition are not desirable but they remain edible.

MY BROCCOLI PLANTS WILTED AND SOME TURNED YELLOW A FEW WEEKS AFTER TRANSPLANTING – Pull up a plant or two and look at the roots. If root maggots are present the side roots will be absent and you'll find the tiny maggots burrowing into the stem. Rotate your crop next year and protect the transplants with row covers or small pieces of tarpaper placed on the soil around the plants' stems.

MY BROCCOLI PLANTS ARE WEAK AND YELLOW BUT THEY DO NOT HAVE ROOT MAGGOTS – If the main root is malformed then clubroot may be the problem. Rotate your crop next year and be sure to plant only treated broccoli seeds.

ARE THE PRETTY WHITE BUTTERFLIES AROUND MY BROCCOLI EATING HOLES IN THE LEAVES? – Cabbage worms are very destructive to all crucifers. Use row covers to prevent the adult butterflies from laying their eggs. Disinfest the broccoli heads prior to eating by soaking them in salt water.

are about 2 inches in diameter. You may use a small handful of 10-5-5 or a larger handful of dried bloodmeal applied in a ring around each plant and about 8 inches from its base.

Brussels Sprouts

Brassica oleracea (Gemmifera group)
Family: Cruciferae (or Brassicaceae) — Mustard

cool-season vegetable

Direct Seed or Transplant: Transplant
Optimum Range of Soil Temperature for Planting: 60–65°F
Minimum Soil Temperature for Planting: 40°F
Depth of Root System: Shallow
Transplant Spacing Within Row:18–24 inches
Distance Between Rows: 24–40 inches
Ease of Transplant: Easy
Consumption of Nitrogen: High
Days to Maturity: 90–100
Average Yield per 10-foot Row: 6 lbs.
Grow your own transplants:
Optimum Range of Soil Temperature for Germination: 65–70°F
Approximate Length of Germination Period: 3–4 days
Approximate Time to Grow to Transplant Size: 4–6 weeks

Brussels sprouts tolerate cold better than some other crucifers, surviving temperatures below 20°F with little damage. Low temperatures mellow and improve the flavor of sprouts and help the

FUN FACTS

Like broccoli, Brussels sprouts also developed from wild cabbage and very quickly became popular in northern Europe. Legend has it that Brussels sprouts were first discovered growing in the fields around Brussels, Belgium, in the 1600s. By 1821 it had become widely popular in Belgium and France. American gardeners were growing it by 1800 and English gardeners by 1854. However, not until the end of World War I did it become widely grown throughout Europe and the United States. Brussels sprouts is a non-heading cabbage grown for its axillary buds and most gardeners agree that the sprouts we grow ourselves taste far superior to the store-bought ones.

plant form tight, compact buds. As with the other crucifers, heat is the bane of tasty Brussels sprouts and will turn them into a loose, soft, and strong-flavored mess.

Planting and Care: Like the other crucifers, Brussels sprouts need rich, fertile soil with plenty of organic matter worked in. Because it is a long-season crop, sidedress it about a month or so after transplanting to encourage rapid growth. But be careful as too much nitrogen can cause unproductive plants with loose sprouts. See the section on cabbage for more details on cultural requirements (page 177).

You may transplant young plants in late spring for a fall crop, or direct seed in spring for a late fall crop. This plant is usually transplanted in our region due to our short seasons.

Recommended Brussels Sprouts Varieties

Variety	Days to Maturity	Comments
Jade Cross	80	AAS Selection; old standby
Tasty Nuggets	78	Very sweet; very vigorous plants
Oliver	90	Large sprouts that mature quickly

Harvesting: Sprouts will be ready for harvest about 14 weeks after transplanting, but rely upon the plant to indicate when to harvest. When the lower leaves begin to lighten to a yellow-green and the lower sprouts are firm and about an inch or slightly more in diameter, it's time to harvest. If you wait too long after the leaf color begins to yellow, the sprouts will become tough-skinned, loose, and strong-flavored. Remove the leaf by cutting the leaf stalk at its base, then cut the bud from the stem. Begin with the lowest leaf and bud and continue up the stem as each sprout is ready to harvest. The plant will produce new leaves and sprouts at its top as the harvest of the lower buds continues; each plant can potentially produce up to 100 sprouts before the season ends. Remove the leaves at each bud just before harvest because removing them too far in advance will reduce yields and flavor.

If your season is shaping up to be a short one you can borrow a trick from English gardeners to speed harvest. Remove the end bud after the lower sprouts have begun to form. This increases the size of each sprout and may increase total yield on a weight basis, (though doing so will reduce the total number of sprouts).

——WHAT HAPPENED HERE?——

MY PLANTS STOPPED GROWING AND FORMED NO MORE SPROUTS – There are many reasons for this, including lack of water, lack of nutrients, and excessive heat.

THE LOWER SPROUTS ARE LARGE AND COMPACT BUT THE UPPER SPROUTS ARE OF LOWER QUALITY – Don't remove all the leaves at the same time but rather snap each off just before the sprout next to it is ready to harvest. Taking a leaf off too soon lowers the quality of the bud nearest it.

Cabbage

Brassica oleracea (Capitata group)

Family: Cruciferae (or Brassicaceae) — Mustard

Direct Seed or Transplant: Transplant
Optimum Range of Soil Temperature for Planting: 60–65°F
Minimum Soil Temperature for Planting: 40°F
Depth of Root System: Shallow
Transplant Spacing Within Row: 12–24 inches
Distance Between Rows: 24–36 inches
Ease of Transplant: Easy
Consumption of Nitrogen: High
Days to Maturity: 62–120
Average Yield per 10-foot Row: About 6 heads
Grow your own transplants:
Optimum Range of Soil Temperature for Germination: 65–70°F
Approximate Length of Germination Period: 3–4 days
Approximate Time to Grow to Transplant Size: 4–6 weeks

Although well-hardened plants tolerate temperatures in the low 20s, they won't grow well at temperatures below 40°F. Cabbage grows best at temperatures between 60 to 65°F and stops growing above 75°F, so don't plant it to mature in summer heat.

Cabbage is a biennial grown as an annual for its enlarged vegetative bud. The first leaves remain as outer leaves and the head

FUN FACTS

Cabbage has been used for food for more than three thousand years. Prior to that, cabbage was considered to be medicinal only and was worshipped by the Egyptians almost five thousand years ago. The ancient Greeks also esteemed cabbage. These old-style, loose-headed cabbages were introduced by the Romans and Celts two thousand years ago to residents on the coasts of southern England and Brittany, where they became the ancestors of our modern heading varieties.

Cabbages were commonly grown in Europe by 900 A.D. and modern heading types were grown in England by 1536. Most of these firm-headed types were developed in northern Europe; the Savoy type was developed in Italy.

Cabbage was brought to Scotland by Cromwell in 1649 and later made it to North America, being introduced into Virginia by 1669.

grows from the inside out. As the inner leaves are produced and become tightly packed against the outer leaves, the head becomes firm and compact. When moisture is excessive or soil nitrogen levels very high, the primary head will split and several smaller heads will form. The smaller heads resemble Brussels sprouts and are edible.

If cabbages are exposed to temperatures of 40 to 50°F for more than a month or so, or to lower temperatures for less time, the head will split and the plant will bolt. This is primarily a problem with plants that have at least 3 to 4 leaves, or stems thicker than a pencil, at the time of exposure.

Like all crucifers, cabbages need adequate moisture and high fertility with a slightly acid to slightly alkaline soil pH. A pH of 7.5 or slightly higher to control clubroot, along with a four-year rotation and good sanitation, works well for our region. Spring cabbages are usually transplanted to the garden a couple of weeks before the last frost is expected. Use stocky, medium-sized plants. If you plant earlier, use smaller, hardy plants with no more than three leaves to avoid bolting. Don't crowd the plants when transplanting since the closer you space your cabbages, the smaller the mature heads will be (unless you want smaller-sized heads).

Planting and Care: Fall crops are often sown where they will mature. Thin plants to their final in-row spacings (12 to 24 inches) when they are about 2 to 4 inches high and before they become crowded. Direct-seeded cabbage will often mature 2 to 3 weeks earlier than transplants.

Like all crucifers, this vegetable responds well to highly fertile soil; turn under plenty of organic matter. Broadcast a complete fertilizer such as 5-10-10 before you plant and sidedress when plants are about 4 to 6 inches tall. Don't fertilize when the plants begin to mature or use too much nitrogen since both can cause the heads to loosen and split or the leaves to show tipburn.

Although they have extensive but shallow, dense, fibrous root systems, cabbages and other crucifers are poor competitors. Practice good weed control, but stop hoeing as the plants mature. Mulching is a great way to control weeds in crucifer plantings.

Cabbage and other crucifers are relatively drought tolerant, in part due to the heavy waxy coating on their leaves. Nevertheless, be sure they get sufficient water each week and that it is applied with a soaker hose or watering can, since wetting the foliage promotes the spread of black rot and *Alternaria* pathogens. Keep the water supply steady since dry spells followed by heavy watering during head formation may cause the heads to split.

Recommended Cabbage Varieties

Variety	Days to Maturity	Comments
Farao	64	Early green; thrips resistant
Early Copenhagen Market	68	Heirloom; early green; crack resistant
Earliana	60	Heirloom; very early green; 2-lb. heads
Stonehead	60	AAS Selection; midseason green; 4-lb. heads
Salad Delight	50	Extra early red; 3-lb. heads
Red Express	63	Red; resists splitting
Alcosa	72	Blue-green Savoy type; 3-lb. heads

——WHAT HAPPENED HERE?——

MY CABBAGE HEADS SPLIT OPEN – Maintain steady watering and harvest as soon as the heads mature. If the heads begin to crack, stop watering and twist the plant to break some of the roots or use a spade to sever roots on one side of the plant. In warm weather, the heads of early varieties sometimes split a week or so after they mature.

THE CABBAGE HEADS ARE FULL OF HOLES – This is probably due to cabbage worms feeding. Apply *Bacillus thuringiensis* (Bt) as soon as you see white moths around the plants.

THE CABBAGE HEADS ARE SMALL – Did you plant a small–headed variety or space your plants too closely?

Cabbage and the other crucifers can suffer from many nutrient deficiencies. Be sure to have your soil tested regularly. Among these deficiencies is internal tipburn caused by tissue breakdown near the center of the head. The tissue becomes papery and black. Its cause is related to an imbalance in plant calcium and made worse by uneven watering. It's most common on short-season varieties when the water supply is insufficient for rapid growth.

Harvesting: Cut the heads from the plants when they are firm and mature. Leave a few of the older wrapper (outer) leaves on the head. The heads will split if you let them remain on the plants too long after they mature or if temperatures are very high. Late cabbages store the best, holding up for several months; early cabbages keep only a month or two.

Carrot

Daucus carota var. *sativus*

Family: Umbelliferae (or Apiaceae) — Parsley

Direct Seed or Transplant: Direct Seed
Optimum Range of Soil Temperature for Germination: 45–95°F
Minimum Soil Temperature for Germination: 40°F
Seed Planting Depth: ½–1 inch
Seed Spacing Within Row: Sow thinly
Depth of Root System: Moderate
Thinned Spacing Within Row: 1–3 inches
Distance Between Rows: 16–30 inches
Consumption of Nitrogen: Low
Days to Maturity: 50–95
Average Yield per 10-foot Row: 10 lbs.

cool-season vegetable

Carrots are biennials grown as annuals for their large taproot, which can reach diameters up to 2½ inches and lengths up to a foot or more, depending on soils. Variet-ies can have white, yellow, orange, red, purple, or purplish-black roots, with orange being the most popular today.

Planting and Care: Carrots grow best at temperatures between 60 to 65°F; top-growth is stunted and the roots become strongly flavored above 82°F. The roots become long and tapered but develop poor color below 60°F and they grow very little below 50°F.

The shape and color of carrot roots depends upon their genetics, the tempera-tures, and age (young carrots are lighter in color than mature carrots). The roots develop their best color between 60 to 70°F and longest length between 50 to 60°F. The higher the temperature, the shorter the roots. (Drought actually promotes longer roots.)

Light, sandy soils produce early crops and stone-free soils produce the most uniformly shaped roots. Compacted soils cause the roots to grow short and curved. Carrot seeds require a long time to germinate and produce weak seedlings unable to compete with hard soil crusts, so use radishes as a nurse crop.

Plant carrot seeds thinly and you don't have to thin the plants. Thinning may promote nicer roots but it will yield fewer useful roots. You can also avoid much thinning by making your own seed tape. Space seeds within a single fold of toilet paper. Roll it up as you go to maintain seed spacing, and unroll in the garden; the tissue will simply decompose.

Fresh manure applied to carrot beds promotes forked roots,

FUN FACTS

Carrots are native to Europe, Asia, and northern Africa where they have been cultivated for thousands of years. The ancient Greeks and Syrians used wild carrots medicinally. Galen, a second century A.D. Greek, was the first to mention cultivated carrots. Carrot cultivation spread from France and Italy into other parts of Europe, and the crop had become a staple by the thirteenth century. They were introduced into China around 1300 A.D. and were widely grown there and in Japan beginning in the sixteenth century.

The roots of early carrots were purple and the yellow-orange color arose as a mutation. The Dutch further developed orange varieties in the 1600s. They entered the New World by 1565 and were grown in Virginia by 1609. By this time, carrots with purple roots were being superseded by those with yellow roots. Native Americans were fond of carrots and General John Sullivan reported them growing it in central New York in 1779 (whereupon he destroyed their crops as part of the campaign to punish the Iroquois for supporting the British during the Revolutionary War).

Carrots entered into modern folk culture by way of the Hebrides, where young women served them to special friends on Sundays. In Germany, finely chopped and browned roots were used as a substitute for coffee, and the English used red carrot juice to color butter. During World War II, British plant breeders developed carrots with high levels of carotene for their aviators so that they might see better at night.

but composted manure is fine. Carrots must grow rapidly in order to obtain the highest quality, so apply preplant fertilizer and side-dress when the plants are about 4 to 5 weeks old.

Sufficient water is important because if the weather is hot and dry the roots will develop a strong flavor. On the other hand, excessive moisture results in poor color development.

Carrot types are distinguished by their shapes. Nantes type varieties produce cylindrical roots, while the Imperator type produces long, slightly tapering roots. The Chantenay type produces roots that are shaped almost like a toy top and are most useful for growing in heavy or shallow soils.

Recommended Carrot Varieties

Variety	Days to Maturity	Comments
Purple Haze	73	AAS Selection; Imperator type; orange interior with purple skin
Napoli	58	Nantes type; very sweet; 7-in. blunt roots
Scarlet Nantes	68	Heirloom; very sweet; open-pollinated
Early Chantenay	68	Heirloom; 6-in. roots; for heavy soil

Harvesting: Pull carrots when the roots are about 1 to 1½ inches in diameter at the top. The upper part of the carrot "root" is made of stem tissue and turns green when it's exposed to sun. This won't hurt you but it detracts from the root's eye appeal. Mound soil over the crown of the root a couple of weeks before harvest to avoid this greening.

Remove the carrot tops before storing the roots since they pull water and nutrients out of the roots and lead to rapid deterioration.

——WHAT HAPPENED HERE?——

MY CARROT SEEDS PRODUCED A POOR STAND – The soil may have crusted, or the seeds dried out before germination. Use a nurse crop with the carrot seeds next time.

MY CARROTS HAVE MISSHAPEN ROOTS – Root twisting is due to overcrowding. Forked roots are likely caused by stony soil. If the roots are stubby or grew horizontally for a bit, you have a hardpan layer.

THE TOPS OF MY CARROT ROOTS ARE GREEN – The stem tissue at the root's top turned green when exposed to sunlight. Mound soil over them a few weeks before harvest to prevent this.

Cauliflower

Brassica oleracea (Botrytis group)

Family: Cruciferae (or Brassicaceae) — Mustard

cool-season vegetable ❄

Direct Seed or Transplant: Transplant
Optimum Range of Soil Temperature for Planting: 60–65°F
Minimum Soil Temperature for Planting: 45°F
Depth of Root System: Shallow
Transplant Spacing Within Row: 14–24 inches
Distance Between Rows: 24–36 inches
Ease of Transplant: Easy
Consumption of Nitrogen: Moderate to heavy
Days to Maturity: 50–125
Average Yield per 10-foot Row: 9 lbs. or about 6 curds
Grow your own transplants:
Optimum Range of Soil Temperature for Germination: 65–70°F
Approximate Length of Germination Period: 3–4 days
Approximate Time to Grow to Transplant Size: 4–6 weeks

Like the other crucifers, cauliflower grows best in cool, moist weather and it will not tolerate as much cold or as much heat as cabbage. It grows best at temperatures between 57 to 68°F. At temperatures above 68°F the quality of the curds deteriorates and the plants become leafy. At temperatures above 77°F and below 32°F the curd may not form at all.

Planting and Care: While cauliflower can be grown in our region as both a spring and a fall crop, it is grown mostly as a fall crop to avoid summer's heat. You can transplant young plants to the garden or direct seed. Space rows about 30 inches apart and thin plants about 14 to 24 inches apart in the rows.

These plants have high fertility soil requirements doing best in fairly acid soils within the pH range of 5.5 to 6.5. Yields are reduced in soils with pH ranges much above or below this.

Turn under organic matter, broadcast preplant fertilizer, and sidedress the cauliflower when they are several inches tall. Cauliflower has a high magnesium requirement so take care to watch for deficiencies of that nutrient. If plants receive too little nitrogen, they will "button," meaning they form small, inedible curds.

Cauliflower can develop several other nutrient deficiencies.

FUN FACTS

Cauliflower evolved from sprouting broccoli and ultimately from the leafy cabbages of southern Europe and the eastern Mediterranean. While references to broccoli and cauliflower are confused in ancient literature as the same name cyma *was applied to both plants, cauliflower was considered its own plant in eighteenth-century England.*

Whiptail, due to a molybdenum deficiency, shows up when the soil pH is very acid (below 5.5). In our region this could result from amending garden soil with mine tailings. The leaves become straplike and extremely savoyed and plant growth is stunted.

Browning (also known as brown rot or red rot) is caused by boron deficiency and shows as water-soaked areas in the stem and branches of the curd. The curds turn red-brown and become inedible. The foliage thickens, becomes brittle, and curls downward. Have your soil tested for boron and follow the recommendations of the testing agency. Do not guess at the amount of boron to add, as too much can sterilize the soil.

Buttoning results in small, exposed curds. The plants and leaves are stunted. Crowding in the flat, nitrogen deficiency, and any other condition that restricts growth can cause buttoning.

Blindness, the result of no terminal bud forming, is caused by physical damage to the tip.

Cauliflower curds may be white, green, or purple. The purple-curd types are actually hybrids of broccoli and cauliflower that develop the curd shape of cauliflower and the sweet tenderness of broccoli. Called "broccoflower," they require no blanching and the color disappears when the curd is cooked. Another such hybrid produces plants with green curds.

Recommended Cauliflower Varieties

Variety	Days to Maturity	Comments
Early White	52	White-curds; 4 in. diameter curds
Snow Crown	50	AAS Selection; white-curds; good seedling vigor; medium-sized heads
Graffiti	85	Purple-curds; medium vigor
Veronica	78	Lime-green curds; Romanesco type

Protect cauliflower from sunlight (blanch) to get a nice white curd. The leaves of self-blanching varieties naturally curl over the curd and shut out the sunlight. You will have to blanch curds of the other white-curded varieties yourself, which is not at all difficult. Tie the outer leaves over the curd when it is a couple inches in diameter and leave them for a few days before you harvest. Cooler fall weather may require you leave them for up to 10 days. Be sure to check curd development every day, for leaving them tied too long in hot weather can cause the leaves to rot, while in cool weather the curd will flower. Flowering turns the curd fuzzy and brown-gray due to the production of flower parts (stamens and anthers). This is called "riciness." Instead of tying the leaves you may break off several outer leaves and arrange them over the curd. If you don't want to do this but don't want to take the time to tie the leaves either, try gathering several outer leaves over the curd and holding them in place with a toothpick.

Harvesting: Cut the blanched curd from its stem when it is about 6 inches in diameter. Trim the leaves square across the top and about ½ inch above the curd to protect it.

──WHAT HAPPENED HERE?──

MY CAULIFLOWER PRODUCED SMALL HEADS – This could be due to uneven or insufficient watering or, if they are very small (about the size of a quarter), the plant buttoned.

I HAVE OFF–COLOR CURDS – You waited too long to harvest and they became ricey.

MY CURD HAS LEAVES GROWING IN IT – Blame hot weather! Time the planting so the curds ripen earlier or later in the season.

Celeriac

Apium graveolens var. *rapaceum*

Family: Umbelliferae (or Apiaceae) — Parsley

Direct Seed or Transplant: Transplant

Optimum Range of Soil Temperature for Planting: 60–65°F

Minimum Soil Temperature for Planting: 45°F

Depth of Root System: Shallow

Transplant Spacing Within Row: 4–6 inches

Distance Between Rows: 24–36 inches

Ease of Transplant: Moderate

Consumption of Nitrogen: High

Days to Maturity: 100–120

Average Yield per 10-foot Row: 6 lbs.

Grow your own transplants:

Optimum Range of Soil Temperature for Germination: 70°–75°F

Approximate Length of Germination Period: 2–3 weeks

Approximate Time to Grow to Transplant Size: 10–12 weeks

Planting and Care: Grow celeriac as you would celery.

Harvesting: Celeriac is ready when the roots are 3 to 5 inches in diameter. 'Brilliant' and 'Large Smooth Prague' are two good varieties.

FUN FACTS

Also known as turnip-rooted celery, celeriac is a type of celery grown for its celery-flavored tuberous root that grows to about the size of a fist. Although celery roots were eaten before 1536, the first mention of celery grown for its root was in 1613. The plant likely arose in Mediterranean marshes but became highly developed among northern Europeans. It was grown in England in 1752 and made its way into American gardens by 1806.

Celery

Apium graveolens var. *dulce*

Family: Umbelliferae (or Apiaceae) — Parsley

Direct Seed or Transplant: Transplant
Optimum Range of Soil Temperature for Planting: 60°–65°F
Minimum Soil Temperature for Planting: 45°F
Depth of Root System: Shallow
Transplant Spacing Within Row: 6–12 inches
Distance Between Rows: 18–40 inches
Ease of Transplant: Moderate
Consumption of Nitrogen: High
Days to Maturity: 90–125
Average Yield per 10-foot Row: 10 heads
Grow your own transplants:
Optimum Range of Soil Temperature for Germination: 70°–75°F
Approximate Length of Germination Period: 14–21 days
Approximate Time to Grow to Transplant Size: 10–12 weeks

Celery is a biennial grown as an annual, forming a short stem surrounded by leaf stalks (petioles) up to two feet tall.

The plant grows best at temperatures of 60 to 65°F, and young plants will bolt if they're exposed to tem-

peratures between 40 to 50°F for more than ten days. Temperatures in the 70s or higher while the plants are maturing turn the plants stringy and strong-flavored.

Planting and Care: Celery is very exacting in its requirements. Because of its marshy origins it does well in well-drained loam high in organic matter. Soil pH is best between 5.5 and 6.7 and the plant should grow rapidly to avoid stringiness.

FUN FACTS

Homer mentioned celery in the Odyssey *and Hippocrates, Theophrastus, and Pliny spoke of wild celery's medicinal properties. The ancient Greeks rewarded athletes with celery leaves and the Romans seasoned foods with its seeds. It was widely used by Chinese doctors in the fifth century A.D. and is mentioned in a ninth century A.D. European work. At that time, it was still gathered wild from swamplands from Sweden to Algeria and east to India.*

Celery began to be used to flavor broths in the Middle Ages but was used almost exclusively for medicine through the early eighteenth century. Italians grew it by the end of the sixteenth century and it had entered French gardens by 1623.

Transplant celery in spring, moving plants to the garden when they are about 4 to 6 inches tall. Celery grown from transplants have even smaller root systems than those that are direct seeded so you will have to take extra care growing them.

The soil celery is planted in needs to be very high in organic matter. Because the plants are heavy feeders, broadcast fertilizer preplant and sidedress a few times during the season. "Push" their growth to promote development of the tenderest stalks.

Keep the plants cultivated or mulched with straw always, and don't let the weeds gain a foothold.

Because of its origins and small root system, celery needs relatively large quantities of water. Any water stress will yield poor growth and stringiness.

Several nutrient disorders can affect celery. Black heart is due to a calcium deficiency and is made worse by high temperatures, rapid growth, and water stress. The inner leaves and growing point die.

Cracked stem causes a marginal brown mottling of leaves. The petioles become brittle and tissues turn brown due to a boron deficiency.

Pithiness is the result of too-rapid growth. The petiole cells break down, causing corky tissue and cavities.

There are two types of celery: golden and green. Golden

celery is self-blanching and was formerly quite popular. These varieties mature earlier and are less vigorous, stringier, and have thinner petioles than those of the more common green type. Because of celery's long season to harvest, always select shorter-season varieties.

Recommended Celery Varieties

Variety	Days to Maturity	Comments
Conquistador	80	Widely adapted; very vigorous
Utah 52-90 R Improved	90	12-inch stalks; compact

Harvesting: There is no absolute harvest period. Cut the stalks at the soil line when they are large enough for your use. The outer petioles become stringy and tough if you wait too long to harvest.

Blanching produces golden, mild-flavored stalks. You can plant a self-blanching variety or blanch a green variety by covering the stalks with boards or tarpaper several weeks before harvest. Crowding plants in the row will also partially blanch the stalks.

—WHAT HAPPENED HERE?—

MY PLANTS ARE STUNTED AND HAVE YELLOW LEAVES – Because of the plant's small root system this could have many causes: hot weather, dry soil, low soil nutrients, too-deep cultivation.

Chinese Cabbage

Brassica rapa (Pekinensis group) — Heading Napa (Pe-tsai) type
Brassica rapa (Chinensis group) — Leafy (Pak-choi) type
Family: Cruciferae (or Brassicaceae) — Mustard

cool-season vegetable

Direct Seed or Transplant: Transplant
Optimum Range of Soil Temperature for Planting: 60–65°F
Minimum Soil Temperature for Planting: 45°F
Depth of Root System: Shallow
Transplant Spacing Within Row: 10–18 inches
Distance Between Rows: 18–36 inches
Ease of Transplant: Moderately difficult
Consumption of Nitrogen: High
Days to Maturity: 70–80
Average Yield per 10-foot Row: 6 heads
Grow your own transplants:
Optimum Range of Soil Temperature for Germination: 65°–70°F
Approximate Length of Germination Period: 3–4 days
Approximate Time to Grow to Transplant Size: 1 month

The Pak-choi type forms a leafy plant resembling mustard. Pe-tsai types form a headlike lettuce. Both types are sensitive to temperatures below 40°F, grow best between 60 to 70°F, and bolt in long summer days.

Planting and Care: Chinese cabbage has soil fertility requirements similar to those of other crucifers (see cabbage, page 177) and is attacked by the same pests. Transplant plants less than four weeks old to the garden for a spring crop or set them into the garden for a fall crop. If your springs are short, as they are in southwestern Montana, you may have better luck with a fall crop because the plants will mature during cooler weather.

Harvesting: Baby Chinese cabbage may be harvested at any time, or you can cut heads from the stems at the soil line when they are fully developed, about 2 to 3 months after planting. You can harvest the entire plant this way too about 1 to 2 months after planting, or you can simply harvest the outer leaves periodically until frost.

Recommended Chinese Cabbage Varieties

Variety	Days to Maturity	Comments
Blues	57	Pe-tsai type; vigorous; disease resistant
Joi Choi	45	Pak-choi type; very attractive
Toy Choi	30	Pak-choi type; very early; small plants
Greenwich	50	Pe-tsai type; very tall; tasty
Michili	73	Pe-tsai type; sweet, spicy flavor
Jade Pagoda	68	Pe-tsai type; disease and bolt resistant

FUN FACTS

Native to China, Chinese cabbage developed from the wild turnips in the Middle East about 3,000 years ago. It appeared in Europe about 1837.

Collards

Brassica oleracea (Acephala group)

Family: Cruciferae (or Brassicaceae) — Mustard

cool-season vegetable

Direct Seed or Transplant: Either

Optimum Range of Soil Temperature for Germination: 45–95°F

Minimum Soil Temperature for Germination: 40°F

Optimum Range of Soil Temperature for Planting: 60–65°F

Minimum Soil Temperature for Planting: 40°F

Seed Planting Depth: ¼–½ inch

Seed Spacing Within Row: 3 every 8 inches

Depth of Root System: Shallow

Thinned Spacing Within Row: 8 inches

Distance Between Rows: 18–30 inches

Ease of Transplant: Easy

Consumption of Nitrogen: Moderate to high

Days to Maturity: 60–70

Average Yield per 10-foot Row: 7½ lbs.

Grow your own transplants:

Optimum Range of Soil Temperature for Germination: 65–70°F

Approximate Length of Germination Period: 3–4 days

Approximate Time to Grow to Transplant Size: 4–6 weeks

Like many other vegetables, collards are biennials grown as annuals. They are a cool-season crop and are most popular in Southern gardens.

This plant tolerates both heat and cold better than cabbage (down to 15°F if it's acclimated) but it is best grown as a spring or fall crop.

Planting and Care: You can direct seed for a fall crop or set out transplants for a spring crop. Prepare the soil, the same as for cabbage (page 177) and grow collards as you would kale (page 227).

FUN FACTS

Collards, a form of non-heading cabbage, were enjoyed by Greeks and Romans before a banquet with the thought that it prevented one's mind from being clouded by wine.

There are few varieties of collards; 'Champion' and 'Vates' are the most popular.

Harvesting: The greens are ready to harvest about 60 days after seeding. Harvest older, larger leaves and the bud will continue producing leaves as the stem elongates. After several weeks of harvest, the plant will resemble a tuft of new leaves stuck on a long stalk and may need to be staked. If you don't care about multiple harvests, then harvest the entire plant when it is about 6 to 12 inches tall.

Cucumber

Cucumis sativus

Family: Cucurbitaceae – Gourd

Direct Seed or Transplant: Direct Seed
Optimum Range of Soil Temperature for Germination: 60–95°F
Minimum Soil Temperature for Germination: 60°F
Seed Planting Depth: ½ inch
Seed Spacing Within Row: 3–4 inches
Depth of Root System: Moderate
Thinned Spacing Within Row: 8–12 inches
Distance Between Rows: 36–72 inches
Consumption of Nitrogen: Moderate
Days to Maturity: 48–72 (slicing); 48–58 (pickling)
Average Yield per 10-foot Row: 12 lbs.

warm-season vegetable

Cucumber grows best in air temperatures between 65 to 85°F, with 82°F considered ideal. Growth declines substantially in temperatures above 90°F and below 60°F. The plant chills and dies at

temperatures below 50°F.

A moderately deep-rooted annual vine, the cucumber has one of three growth habits. "Indeterminate" varieties form new shoots that extend the entire season, making a sprawling plant. A flower cluster forms at the vine tips on "determinate" varieties and stops their extension. "Compact" varieties are bushy and well suited to small gardens.

Standard cucumbers have male and female flowers on the same plant (monoecious). Male flowers bloom first. Early in the season during times of hot, long days or if they are under stress at any time, more male flowers than female flowers will develop. As the season advances, and the days become shorter and cooler, male and female flowers appear in about equal numbers.

Many new cucumber varieties produce more female flowers than male (denoted as "PF" for predominately female). "Gynoecious" lines produce only female flowers. These varieties ripen all their fruit nearly at once. Since there are no male flowers in gynoecious varieties, seed producers include in the packet a few

FUN FACTS

The cucumber may have originated in Southeast Asia at least twelve thousand years ago. It has been grown for its fruit at least three thousand years and passed from India into Greece and Rome, and more recently into China. Romans raised cucumbers in greenhouses in winter. Roman emperors imported cucumber pickles from Spain and traders spread the plant throughout Europe. It was grown in France in the ninth century and in England in the fourteenth; it was introduced into North America by the middle of the sixteenth century. DeSoto reported the native peoples in Florida were growing cucumbers "better than those found in Spain."

seeds of a monoecious variety that bear male flowers for pollination.

Planting and Care: Soil temperatures of at least 65°F are needed for good plant growth, though 85°F is optimum. Plant seeds about 1 to 1½ feet apart in rows spaced 4 feet apart. Or, plant in hills about 3 to 4 feet apart, dropping several seeds into each and thinning the seedlings to 2 plants per hill. You can also transplant 4-week-old cucumber plants to the garden.

Plant cucumbers on the edges of your garden and let them sprawl into the lawn, or train them to a trellis. Broadcast preplant fertilizer and sidedress once, just as the plants begin to run. They respond well to composted manure so place a handful or two into each hill at planting if you have it.

Cucumbers need large amounts of water in hot weather, especially during bloom and fruiting.

Black plastic mulch increases yields substantially. Organic mulches are fine but don't apply them until the soil has warmed.

Cultivate shallowly and often until the plants begin to run.

Cucumbers come in slicing and pickling types. Slicers are generally long, slender, straight, thick-skinned, and dark green. Their relatively large seed cavities make them soft if they're pickled. Picklers have smaller seed cavities that stay firm during the pickling process. They are light green, short, blocky, thin-skinned, and warty; most newer pickling varieties are gynoecious.

Harvesting: Depending on the variety, harvest begins about sixty days after planting. Pick the fruit while it's still green and several inches long (slicers) or 2 to 4 inches long (picklers). Never let cucumbers ripen and yellow on the vine. These will be seedy and will signal the plant to stop flowering and producing new fruit. If you can't use them all when they're ready, donate them to a food bank.

WHAT HAPPENED HERE?

MY CUCUMBER FRUIT ARE MISSHAPEN AND DROP FROM THE PLANT BEFORE HARVEST – This could be due to poor pollination.

MY NEIGHBOR TOLD ME THAT MY NEARBY CARROTS WILL MAKE MY CUCUMBERS BITTER – Bitterness in cucumbers is caused by compounds known as cucurbitacins, which accumulate in temperatures above 90°F and in abnormally cool, wet weather. Bitterness has nothing to do with carrots.

WE RETURNED FROM VACATION AND OUR PLANTS HAD ONLY A FEW BIG YELLOW CUCUMBERS ON THEM AND STOPPED PRODUCING – Vacation at a different time next year. Cucumber fruit that ripen on the vine shut down the production of new fruit. Keep picking cucumbers as they enlarge and the plant will keep producing.

Recommended Cucumber Varieties

Variety	Days to Maturity	Comments
Straight Eight	58	AAS Selection; heirloom; monoecious slicer; 6–8 inch fruit
Poinsett 76	60	Monoecious slicer; 7½ inch fruit; dark green
Sweet Slice	64	Monoecious slicer; 10–12 inch fruit; burpless
Early Pride	55	Gynoecious slicer; 8½ inch fruit
Olympian	52	Gynoecious slicer; 6–9 inch fruit
Pickalot	54	Gynoecious pickler; bush
Boston Pickling	50	Heirloom; vigorous; open pollinated

EGGPLANT

Solanum melongena var. *esculentum*

Solanaceae — Potato or Nightshade

warm-season vegetable

Direct Seed or Transplant: Transplant
Optimum Range of Soil Temperature for Planting: 70–85°F
Minimum Soil Temperature for Planting: 66°F
Transplant Spacing Within Row:18–30 inches
Distance Between Rows: 24–48 inches
Depth of Root System: Moderate
Ease of Transplant: Moderate
Consumption of Nitrogen: Heavy
Days to Maturity: 50–80
Average Yield per 10-foot Row: 7½ lb.
Grow your own transplants:
Optimum Range of Soil Temperature for Germination: 80–90°F
Approximate Length of Germination Period: 7–14 days
Approximate Time to Grow to Transplant Size: 8 weeks

This very tender plant requires a long growing season of 100 to 140 days from seed. It is killed by light frosts and injured by long periods of chilly weather. Fruit set is poor below 65°F and growth ceases below 63°F. Temperatures below 61°F deform the pollen, producing misshapen fruit. Any slight check in growth decreases fruit quality. Eggplant grows best and has highest fruit quality when daytime temperatures remain between 80 to 85°F and nighttime temperatures hover 70°F.

Typical eggplants are 2 to 8 inches in diameter; oriental types are smaller. Fruit colors may be purple, yellow, white, red, or black, with purple and black being the most common.

FUN FACTS

The common eggplant probably originated in India and Burma (now called Myanmar) while smaller-fruited varieties, such as the snake eggplant (S. melongena var. serpentium), the dwarf eggplant (S. melongena var. depressum), and the Chinese eggplant (S. integrifolium), probably originated in China. It was probably named for the white, egg-shaped fruit of some varieties. The plant was in China as early as the fifth century B.C. Moors introduced the plant into Spain in the seventh century A.D. Arabs and Persians brought it to Africa before the Middle Ages and from there it entered Italy in the fourteenth century. Spanish explorers brought purple- and white-fruited varieties with them to the New World. They were grown in Brazil by 1658. Early New Englanders considered the fruit poisonous and prior to the twentieth century American gardeners grew the plants mostly as ornamentals.

Planting and Care: Set non-hardened, blocky, 7-inch-tall plants in the garden about two weeks after the danger of frost has passed and when daytime temperatures average about 68°F. A cool snap after planting can stunt the plants and, once stunted, they will seldom resume satisfactory growth.

Adding preplant fertilizer will get the plants off to a quick start but eggplant is a heavy feeder. It responds well to soils high in organic matter, so mix some composted manure into the hole at planting and sidedress the plants lightly when growth resumes after transplanting. A small handful of 10-10-10 fertilizer or nitrogen equivalent spread in a broad band about a foot from the base of each plant will do it. Sidedress every six weeks throughout the growing season.

Water stress during flowering can reduce yields substantially and lack of water during fruit maturation will mean a lot of blossom-end rot.

Eggplants don't need staking unless they have a heavy fruit load or you have windy weather.

Eggplant flowering begins after the sixth leaf has opened on early varieties and the fourteenth leaf on late varieties. Spiny, star-shaped, purple flowers give rise to large fruit at temperatures above 65°F.

The most popular varieties bear large, purple, oval-shaped fruit that mature 70 to 80 days after transplanting.

Recommended Eggplant Varieties

Variety	Days to Maturity	Comments
Black Beauty	80	Heirloom; large fruit
Purple Rain	66	Heavy yields; large fruit
Crescent Moon	62	White fruit; delicate flavor
Ichiban	58	Oriental type; long, slender fruit
Fairy Tale	65	AAS Selection; miniature fruit; heavy yields
Millionaire	55	Heavy yields

Eggplants can be divided into four different uncommon types:

Snake Eggplant: Fruit of this distinct botanical variety average about 1 inch in diameter but grow to lengths of about 15 inches.

Dwarf Eggplant: This type produces small, weak plants and small, pear-shaped purple fruit that mature quickly.

Chinese Eggplant: Also called the scarlet-fruited or tomato eggplant, this species is grown for its ornamental fruit.

"Oriental" Eggplant: This type produces small, elongated, slender fruit.

In addition to getting its share of diseases and insects, eggplant is also susceptible to blossom-end rot caused by uneven moisture or by moisture stress. For more information, see the discussion of blossom-end rot under Tomato (page 290).

Most varieties need two to three months to mature their fruit, but fruit can be eaten from the time it is about one-third grown. Don't eat really immature eggplants because they contain the poisonous alkaloid solanine, the same compound found in the skin of "green" potatoes.

——WHAT HAPPENED HERE?——

THE LEAVES OF MY EGGPLANTS HAVE TINY HOLES IN THEM – This is from flea beetle damage. See Chapter 9 for advice.

MY EGGPLANTS WILTED AND DIED – Assuming you watered well and didn't hoe too deeply, you might have *Verticillium* wilt. Destroy affected plants and use a 4- or 5-year rotation.

I TRANSPLANTED MY EGGPLANTS TO THE GARDEN EARLY AND THEY JUST SAT THERE – Eggplants need a warm growing season. If they experienced temperatures below about 60°F their growth may have stopped.

Harvesting: Fruit ready for harvest are firm and glossy. Overly mature fruit become spongy, seedy, and dull. Their seeds darken and fruit color turns a bronzy-green. To determine if your fruit are ready for harvest, look at their sheen and color, and press your thumb into their sides. If the indentation springs back, the fruit is immature; the depression remains in the flesh of mature fruit. Because the fruit bruises easily, don't use the thumb test on all of them, but reserve it for those you believe are probably ripe anyway. Continue to harvest the fruit as soon as they are ready and the plant will continue to bear until frost. Cut eggplants from the mother plant with pruning shears, leaving about an inch of stem and the calyx, or "cap," attached to the fruit.

The fruit of eggplant deteriorates rapidly at warm temperatures and suffers chilling injury below 50°F. Once warmed, chilled eggplants appear pitted, their surface is bronze colored, their seeds are brown, and they rot rapidly.

ENDIVE & ESCAROLE

Chicorium endivia

Family: Compositae (or Asteraceae) — Sunflower

Direct Seed or Transplant: Direct Seed
Optimum Range of Soil Temperature for Germination: 45–95°F
Minimum Soil Temperature for Germination: about 40°F
Optimum Range of Soil Temperature for Best Growth: 55–75°F
Minimum Soil Temperature for Best Growth: 45°F
Seed Planting Depth: ¼ inch
Seed Spacing Within Row: 3 inches
Depth of Root System: Moderate
Thinned Spacing Within Row: 8 inches
Distance Between Rows: 18–24 inches
Consumption of Nitrogen: Low
Days to Maturity: 90
Average Yield per 10-foot Row: about 5 lbs.

cool-season vegetable

Endive is a loose-headed plant with frilly leaves while escarole is simply a marketing term for broadleaved endive. Both belong to the same species *Chicorium endivia.* New red varieties are being developed and both are used in salads or as potherbs. French endive (Witloof) belongs to a different species and is rarely grown in American home gardens.

Endive and escarole are cool-season plants grown as annuals. They withstand cool weather better than lettuce but do not stand heat quite as well.

Endive must grow rapidly for the best quality, growing best at temperatures between 60 to 75°F; it will bolt under long days and high temperatures.

Planting and Care: Sow endive seeds directly in the garden in rows about 18

FUN FACTS

This lettuce-like plant originated in eastern India and was used as a food by the ancient Egyptians before it was introduced into northern Europe at the time of the Crusades. There it was used medicinally and eventually as food in the fourteenth century.

inches apart and thin the plants to about 10 inches apart in the row, or transplant them to the garden in spring. Both are sown to mature in fall because of their long maturity season and their ability to tolerate low temperatures.

The leaves become yellow-white and develop milder flavor if they are blanched, a formerly common practice that has fallen by the wayside in recent years. You can blanch them by crowding them in the row, by tying the outer leaves over the head as you would blanch cauliflower, or by placing tarpaper or boards over the plants for a week or two before harvest.

Recommended Endive & Escarole Varieties

Variety	Days to Maturity	Comments
Clodia	33+	Endive; very early
Salad King	95	Endive; heirloom; slow to bolt; very fancy; curly leaves
Eros	46	Escarole; dense heads
Full Heart	90	Escarole; AAS Selection; heirloom; tolerant of bolting and tipburn

Harvesting: If you want full-sized heads, harvest when they are well developed. Cut the entire plant at the soil line and remove the outer leaves, which are often tough and bitter.

WHAT HAPPENED HERE?

MY ENDIVE PLANTS FORMED FLOWER STALKS – The temperature was too hot.

THE BOTTOM LEAVES OF MY ENDIVE ARE CHEWED – Undoubtedly, this is due to slugs. If you see silvery, slimy trails, set out boards to lure them under the cool cover (whereupon you can pick and squish). Or, set out saucers of beer (to drown the slugs; not to drink!).

GARDEN PEA
(AND OTHER EDIBLE-PODDED PEAS)

Pisum sativum — Garden pea
Pisum sativum vars. — Edible-podded pea
Family: Leguminosae — Pea or Bean

Direct Seed or Transplant: Direct Seed
Optimum Range of Soil Temperature for Germination: 40–75°F
Minimum Soil Temperature for Germination: 40°F
Seed Planting Depth: 1 inch
Seed Spacing Within Row: 1–2 inches
Depth of Root System: Moderate
Thinned Spacing Within Row: 1–2 inches
Distance Between Rows: 24–36 inches
Consumption of Nitrogen: Low
Days to Maturity: 56–75
Average Yield per 10-foot Row: 2 lbs.

cool-season vegetable

Garden peas are legumes but are not the same as cowpeas, which are actually beans. Snap beans and cowpeas are warm-season plants, while peas will not tolerate warm summers unless they have been specially bred for heat tolerance. Pea plants, unlike bean plants, can withstand some frost but the flowers and pods cannot.

There are several types of peas that differ in growth habit and

height. Like tomatoes, pea vines can be determinate or indeterminate. The determinate types, also known as the dwarf or bush peas, are very popular with gardeners. They generally reach heights of 18 to 30 inches and seldom require staking, although staking will make harvest easier. The indeterminate-type peas (also called climbing, telephone, or pole pea) reach heights of up to 6 feet and need support.

Within each type breeders have developed peas with edible pods. Scientists created them by crossing a podded pea with a mutant strain. Snow peas are grown for their flat pods and immature peas. Sugar snap peas have a tender pod that becomes full and succulent and may be snapped and eaten along with the immature peas inside, just like snap beans. When the peas in sugar snaps mature they can be shelled like garden peas.

Planting and Care: While pea plants form taproots that may extend to depths of 3 to 4 feet, many of their feeder roots are near the soil's surface.

Edible-podded peas are more susceptible to mildews and need more careful watering than garden peas. Peas in general need well-drained soil high in organic matter. They are one of the first crops to go into the garden, but don't rush it—pea seeds won't germinate in soil temperatures less than about 40°F and the plants won't grow below 45°F.

Some gardeners plant peas in double rows about 3 to 4 inches apart, with 2 to 3 feet between the double rows. This method provides more space for harvesting. Double rows of peas may also theoretically support each other, but we still use trellising in our garden.

Legumes like peas and beans harbor bacteria (*Rhizobium* spp.) in their root nodules that "fix" atmospheric nitrogen into a form useful to the plant. So, before planting, some gardeners treat their seeds with the proper *Rhizobium* inoculant. (Inoculants are specific to the plants they "infect" so be sure to get "Vetch Group IV" for your peas.) The theory is that if the ground has not been planted with peas within the last five years, the bacteria will not be present, so it must be added. Some scientists don't agree that it's that important and maintain the bacteria are present in soils anyway. The inoculant is inexpensive so if you'd like to try it, do.

Set stakes for supports at planting. Lodging (falling over) increases the amount of bird and slug damage and reduces yields. Stakes or poles set firmly into the ground several feet apart along the row serve as a good trellis framework. String heavy twine between the stakes about every 1 to 2 feet apart vertically, then zigzag the twine between them. The peas grow up the twine. You can also use chicken wire, snow fence, or another material supported by the posts. Keep in mind, however, that if you are going to reuse your trellis material next year, you will need to pick the dead plants off the support this year. An old method is to stick branches into the ground along the row. When the crop is harvested, simply chip and compost, burn, or throw away the branches along with the vines.

Supplemenetal nitrogen is usually not necessary for good pea plant growth due to their ability to fix atmospheric nitrogen. In fact, excess nitrogen may delay pod set in determinate varieties.

FUN FACTS

Peas are thought to have originated in the eastern Mediterranean. Archaeologists dated dried peas buried in Switzerland to at least 7000 B.C. The Chinese were using peas by 2000 B.C. and they spread to Greece, Rome, and Egypt shortly thereafter. Interestingly, only dried peas were used; green peas were considered unfit to eat. Colonists brought the garden pea, by then called the English pea, to America in the early 1600s.

Harvesting: Harvest peas by grasping the pods in your hand and snapping them from the stem. Cool them rapidly to prevent the sugars from converting to starch; we like to harvest early in the morning. If you harvest later in the day, use a large plastic storage bin full of cold water to cool them. The sugar in peas turns to starch more rapidly in warm weather, so you will need to harvest more quickly the hotter the weather becomes. Cool weather stretches the harvest over several days but peas will only hold a day or two when they're ready for picking, so keep an eye on your garden. Garden pea pods that feel hard and look crinkly are too mature. Read the seed descriptions carefully when ordering seeds, as some varieties produce pods containing 5 to 6 seeds, while others may have up to 14 seeds in each pod. Seeds of snow peas should be no larger than BB shot and the pods should be stringless and succulent. If they get ahead of you, you may still use them in your stirfries by slicing them diagonally.

Recommended Pea Varieties

Variety	Days to Maturity	Comments
Knight	62	Garden pea
Little Marvel	58	Garden pea; AAS Selection; heirloom; good for cool springs; easy to shell
Early Frosty	64	Garden pea; good for cool springs
Wando	67	Garden pea; heirloom; tolerates some heat
Sugar Ann	58	Snap pea; AAS Selection; disease resistant
Sugar Sprint	62	Snap pea; very early; very sweet
Oregon Sugar Pod #2	65	Snow pea; early, flat pod

WHAT HAPPENED HERE?

I HAVE STRONG, LUSH PLANTS BUT NO PEAS – They probably just need more time. You can pinch the tips if you want. Or, maybe too much nitrogen fertilizer was applied.

THE PEA PODS ARE SHRIVELED AND SWOLLEN – They're too mature. Next year, harvest at the correct time.

THE LEAF TIPS ARE DYING AND THE PLANTS LOOK LIMP– You may not have been watering enough, or the weather was just too hot for this variety. This could also be a disease. When in doubt, take a sample to your county extension office and ask them to diagnose it.

THERE IS A WHITE, POWDERY LAYER ON THE LEAVES – Powdery mildew is the suspect. Irrigate the soil, not the leaves (meaning water so that you avoid wetting the leaves).

GARLIC

Allium spp.
Family: Alliaceae — Allium

Direct Seed or Transplant: Plant cloves
Optimum Range of Soil Temperature for Growth: 55–75°F
Minimum Soil Temperature for Growth: 45°F
Seed Planting Depth: 1½–2 inches
Seed Spacing Within Row: 4–6 inches
Depth of Root System: Shallow
Thinned Spacing Within Row: 4–6 inches
Distance Between Rows: 12–24 inches
Consumption of Nitrogen: High
Months to Maturity: Variable, 6–10
Average Yield per 10-foot Row: 40–60 bulbs

cool-season vegetable

The garlic bulb is a compound of small bulblets, or cloves, each having two mature leaves and a vegetative bud.

Planting and Care: Plant garlic in very early spring where the spring seasons are long enough; where springs are short, garlic will perform better as a fall-planted crop to be harvested the following summer. It survives cold winters if covered by snow but will not take the summer heat, forming no bulbs at temperatures above 77°F. Be sure the soil is loose and rich; heavy soils cause irregularly shaped bulbs.

Store bulbs at 40 to 50°F for several months before spring planting to break their dormancy. This step is not necessary for fall planting because garlic's dormancy requirements are fulfilled over the winter. Plant as early in spring as the ground can be worked or in fall from September 15 to October 15. Any later planting can increase the number of deformed bulbs. Separate the cloves just before planting, set them into the soil root-end down, and care for them as you would onions. Plant the larger cloves and use the smaller ones for cooking since small cloves form plants that produce small bulbs. Water well because growing garlic in dry soil reduces bulb size.

Harvesting: There are three types of garlic: stiffneck, softneck, and elephant, each with its own harvesting requirements.

FUN FACTS

A native of southern Europe, garlic has been grown for at least five thousand years. It had become an important Egyptian crop by 3200 B.C. and the laborers building the Cheops pyramid about 2900 B.C. ate garlic. They even went on strike when garlic rations were reduced. Homer mentions garlic in The Iliad. *Although Roman and Greek nobles did not prefer it, they offered garlic to their laborers and soldiers to give them strength and courage; Roman gladiators ate garlic before battle. From China and India it had spread by 500 B.C. throughout Asia. Cortez introduced garlic into North America in the early 1500s.*

Stiffneck garlic (*Allium sativum* var. *ophioscorodon*), sometimes called Rocambole, produces a woody scape (seed stalk) that resembles a pig-tail or corkscrew. Remove most of these to increase bulb size, but leave them on a couple of plants as harvest indicators. When the scape straightens, the plants are ready for harvest. This type generally produces smaller bulbs with nicely arranged small cloves compared to the softneck type. The cloves have milder flavor than softneck and the plants are more cold hardy.

Softneck garlic (*Allium sativum*) produces no woody scape and its tops are easily braided for decorative purposes. It is ready for harvest when most of the bottom leaves have browned. This type produces larger bulbs than the stiffneck type with stronger-flavored cloves.

Elephant garlic (*Allium ampeloprasum*) produces very large bulbs up to ½ pound each when given very fertile conditions. Cloves have milder flavor than those of the other garlic types. The plants are somewhat less winter hardy and the bulbs do not store as well as the stiffneck or softneck types.

Recommended Garlic Varieties

Variety	Comments
New York White (Polish White)	Softneck
Elephant	Elephant
German Extra-Hardy	Stiffneck
Chesnok	Softneck; heirloom
Inchelium	Stiffneck; heirloom

WHAT HAPPENED HERE?

MY GARLIC PLANTS GROW POORLY AND DON'T PRODUCE GOOD BULBS – You may not have fertilized enough, or you may have planted too late, or you may not have watered enough.

MY GARLIC BULBS ARE LOPSIDED – Your soil may be too heavy or you did not space cloves far enough apart.

MY GARLIC DID NOT COME UP – You may have planted the cloves root–end up. Garlic will not "right" itself if it's planted upside down.

Garlic is harvested when the pig-tail scape on the stiffneck type straightens, or when at least the lower leaves have yellowed on the softneck and elephant types. Lift carefully with a spading fork and cure them by letting the entire plants dry in a cool, airy spot out of direct sunlight. When the plants have dried and the leaves have turned papery, cut off the bulb, leaving about ½ inch of the stem attached.

GLOBE ARTICHOKE

Cynara scolymus
Family: Compositae (or Asteraceae) — Sunflower

perennial vegetable

Direct Seed or Transplant: Transplant
Optimum Range of Soil Temperature for Planting: 60–65°F
Minimum Soil Temperature for Planting: 45°F
Depth of Root System: Deep
Transplant Spacing Within Row: 48–72 inches
Distance Between Rows: 84–96 inches
Ease of Transplant: Easy
Consumption of Nitrogen: Heavy
Days to Maturity: 85–95
Average Yield per 10-foot Row: 5–10 buds per plant

Globe artichokes are grown as annuals in some northern areas, and as perennials in USDA hardiness zone 7 and above. It is marginally adapted to our region. Use caution when selecting seed to be sure your variety is bred for annual production. Artichokes are space hogs, so be sure you have enough room in your garden. With their beautiful flowers, artichokes are attractive and many gardeners think they're worth the space, but don't give up garden space at the expense of needed food crops.

Globe artichoke buds are killed at temperatures below freezing, and high temperatures toughen and partially separate the budscales.

Planting and Care: A rich, fertile loam produces the best artichokes and water is especially critical during bud formation.

Aphids can be a problem, congregating in hidden masses beneath the outer budscales. Remove a few of the oldest, outer budscales to check for their presence.

Harvesting: Harvest the buds by cutting the stem about two inches below the base of the bud. Terminal buds will be largest, up to 3 to 5 inches in diameter.

FUN FACTS

This herbaceous perennial originated in North Africa along the Mediterranean Sea. The Romans prized its wild form, called cardoon. *First cultivated in Naples for its large flower bud, it had by the sixteenth century become generally popular throughout Europe. It reached England from Italy in 1548. It was brought to the United States before 1800 by French settlers in Louisiana and by Spanish and Italian farmers in California.*

Recommended Globe Artichoke Varieties

Variety	Days to Maturity	Comments
Green Globe	Entire season	For areas with the longest growing seasons; tender thick scales, solid core
Imperial Star	85–100	Specially bred for annual production; produces about 6 buds per plant
Violetto di Romagna	85–100	Italian heirloom; buds about 3 inches wide; deep purple to green in color

——WHAT HAPPENED HERE?——

THE LEAVES OF MY ARTICHOKE ARE CURLED AND DEFORMED – Check the undersides of those leaves for aphids, and if you find them give the plants a good squirt with the garden hose, taking special care to hose the undersides of the leaves.

MY PLANTS SUDDENLY WILTED EVEN THOUGH I GAVE THEM PLENTY OF WATER – *Verticillium* could be the cause. This pathogen clogs the water-conducting channels in the plant and can live for many years in the soil. Follow a long rotation, planting no crops susceptible to verticillium (especially vine crops and the nightshades) in that garden spot for at least five years.

GOURD

Cucurbita, *Lagenaria*, and *Luffa* spp.
Family: Cucurbitaceae — Gourd

Direct Seed or Transplant: Either
Optimum Range of Soil Temperature for Germination: 70–95°F
Minimum Soil Temperature for Germination: 60°F
Optimum Range of Soil Temperature for Planting: 65–75°F
Minimum Soil Temperature for Planting: 50°F
Seed Planting Depth: ½–1 inch
Seed Spacing Within Row: 12 inches (plants); 48 inches (hills)
Depth of Root System: Deep
Thinned Spacing Within Row: 24–36 inches
Distance Between Rows: 84–120 inches
Consumption of Nitrogen: Heavy
Days to Maturity: 85–110
Average Yield per 10-foot Row: Variable
Grow your own transplants:
Optimum Soil Temperature for Germination: 90°F
Approximate Length of Germination Period: 6–10 days
Approximate Time to Grow to Transplant Size: 4–5 weeks

warm-season vegetable

Gourds have cultural requirements similar to those of pumpkins. They are very frost tender, and will not grow at all below 60°F.

Planting and Care: Gourds can be direct seeded or transplanted about 3 feet apart in rows 7 feet apart. Training them to a trellis allows the fruit to hang freely and to maintain their shape. Support the larger fruit in onion bags or old brassieres (at last, a use for them!).

Gourds in the *Cucurbita* genus have thick shells and are difficult to cure. Their color fades after 3 to 4 months. The varieties 'Apple', 'Crown of Thorns',

FUN FACTS

Gourds belong to several genera grown for ornamental, novelty, or utility purposes. Most originated in tropical and subtropical America and were widely distributed before the arrival of Columbus. The Luffa *genus originated in tropical Asia. While many gourds have edible flesh, their original use was for ladles, spoons, and water jugs.*

and 'Spoon' are popular. Varieties in the *Lagenaria* genus, such as 'Calabash', 'Drum', and 'Swan Gourd', make the best dippers, birdhouses, and rattles.

Harvesting: Gourds of the *Luffa* genus, also called "Vegetable Sponge" and "Dishrag Gourd," are grown for their network of fruit fibers that serve as a sponge. Place the fruit in a tub of running water and peel them like an orange. Squeeze the inner core to remove the seeds and flesh and dry the remaining wad of fibers.

You can harvest immature *Lagenaria* fruit about a week after bloom and eat them like summer squash. Or, after a light frost, harvest them when the fruit rind hardens, the fruit feel light, and the tendril next to the fruit stem browns. Cure them for 6 months in a warm, dry room.

Harvest fruit of *Cucurbita* species when a light frost has killed the vine and the fruit are bright and hard. Cure them for several days in warm, dry shade.

WHAT HAPPENED HERE?

Problems with gourds are the same as for squash (page 276).

Recommended Gourd Varieties

Variety	Days to Maturity	Comments
Wooly Bear	85	Bright green, spiny, small fruit
Goblin Egg Mix	95	Small egg-shaped fruit; solid color or multicolored
Crown of Thorns	95	Multifingered, multicolored small fruit
Turk's Turban	95	Scarlet colored, buttercup-type fruit; sometimes classed as a squash
Bottle	125	Large-fruited type suitable for ladles, bottles, and birdhouses

HORSERADISH

Armoracia rusticana

Family: Cruciferae (or Brassicaceae) – Mustard

Direct Seed or Transplant: Transplant
Optimum Range of Soil Temperature for Planting: 60–65°F
Minimum Soil Temperature for Planting: 40°F
Depth of Root System: Deep
Transplant Spacing Within Row: 12–18 inches
Distance Between Rows: 30–36 inches
Ease of Transplant: Easy
Consumption of Nitrogen: Heavy
Days to Maturity: Harvest anytime after killing frost
Average Yield per 10-foot Row: 3 lbs.

perennial vegetable

Horseradish is a perennial that does best where summers are warm and falls cool.

Planting and Care: Plant root cuttings in early spring in fertile, loamy soil well supplied with organic matter. Do not apply a lot of nitrogen fertilizer, since that will cause excessive growth and irregularly shaped roots.

Select fairly straight roots about 10 inches long and nickel-thick and plant them at a 45° angle 4 to 5 inches deep, 18 inches

apart, in rows about 30 inches apart. Position the tops of the roots upward.

Dig the roots when the tops have been killed by frost. Remove the tops and cut the largest sideroots for planting next year, cutting their tops square but making a slanting cut on their bottoms to orient them for planting next spring. Leave them in the ground over winter and dig and set them out in spring before growth begins.

Always grind horseradish outside or in a very well ventilated area.

Recommended Horseradish Varieties

Variety	Comments
Maliner Kren	Crinkled leaf; vigorous
Big Top Western	Smooth leaf; disease resistant
Common	Broad, crinkled leaf; very susceptible to turnip mosaic virus

———WHAT HAPPENED HERE?———

THE LEAVES ON MY HORSERADISH ARE SMALL AND DIS-COLORED AND THE PLANTS LOOK STUNTED – It could be that your plants are infected with white rust or turnip mosaic virus. Remove them from the garden.

MY HORSERADISH ROOTS HAVE BROWN STREAKS INSIDE AND ARE VERY BRITTLE – This sounds like brittle root, for which there is no easy cure. Remove the plants and do not replant new horseradish in the same spot.

IRISH POTATO

Solanum tuberosum

Family: Solanaceae — Nightshade or Potato

Direct Seed or Transplant: Plant tuber pieces
Optimum Range of Soil Temperature for Growth: 60–65°F
Minimum Soil Temperature for Planting: 45°F
Tuber Piece Planting Depth: 4 inches
  Tuber Piece Spacing Within Row: 10–12 inches
Depth of Root System: Shallow
Thinned Spacing Within Row: 10–12 inches
Distance Between Rows: 24–36 inches
Consumption of Nitrogen: High
Days to Maturity: 90–120
Average Yield per 10-foot Row: about 20 lbs.

cool-season vegetable

The potato is a close relative of the tomato, pepper, and nightshade, but is not related to the sweet potato. We grow potatoes for their fleshy underground tubers and treat them as an annual (although they are actually a perennial in their native habitat). Gardeners often find volunteer potato plants in the garden the following year, as the plant propagates vegetatively. Volunteer potato plants should be pulled up and

FUN FACTS

These delicious tubers probably originated in the Peruvian Andes and Bolivia. The Incas cultivated them at least two thousand years before Spanish explorers introduced them to Europe in the early 1500s. Hawkins brought them to North America (Florida) in 1565 and Sir Walter Raleigh introduced them to the Irish in 1585. They were planted in Virginia in 1584, but there is no mention of their use elsewhere until they were brought to Londonderry, New Hampshire, by Presbyterian Irish settlers in 1719, hence their name "Irish" potato. Even then, they were not generally cultivated until the nineteenth century, though they were grown as a field crop in Salem, Massachusetts, in 1762. The impoverished Irish became so dependent upon one type of the potato that an estimated three quarters of a million of them starved to death when their crops were destroyed by infestations of late blight in 1845 and 1846. That blight also sparked a huge wave of Irish emigration to the United States.

destroyed to avoid perpetuating potato diseases, particularly if you live in or near an area where potatoes are grown commercially.

Planting and Care: Potatoes are planted using pieces of seed tubers with at least one bud, also called an "eye." Seed potatoes come in different sizes; each should be about the size of a silver dollar and weigh at least two ounces. Remember that for its first month, the plant will live exclusively on the nutrition it gets from the seed piece. If you buy small seed tubers, you can plant the entire tuber. You *might* get a more vigorous plant by planting larger pieces, but there isn't much difference. Just be sure your tubers haven't sprouted before planting and that they appear to be healthy. Be sure to purchase your seed potatoes from a reputable company and that they are certified disease free. Do not plant potatoes that have been harvested for eating.

Holding the cut seed pieces at 60°F for about a week before planting allows them to cure, making them less apt to rot when they're planted.

Plant the pieces when soil temperature has warmed to about 45°F and after the danger of a hard frost has passed. Set them four inches deep in a trench and fill it slowly as the potato plant grows, lightly covering the apex of the plant until the trench is filled in. Potato tubers grow along the underground stems that grow from eyes on seed pieces.

Some folks modify the trench planting system by covering the plant apex with straw or pine needles instead of soil. This allows them to easily harvest clean spuds by simply pulling away the mulch.

Don't plant when the soil is wet, as potatoes are very sensitive to poor drainage and poor soil aeration. Their roots will not grow into compacted soil.

Potato plants need lots of fertilizer and have small root systems, so turn under composted manure and your cover crop and apply all the fertilizer prior to planting. Never apply fresh manure to potatoes since it may increase the incidence of a disease called scab. If you have very sandy soil, sidedress about a month after planting. Otherwise, sidedressing does little good with potatoes.

At first, one stem grows from each bud, but more can grow as the season progresses. The aboveground stems grow upright during the long days of summer, forming a bushy plant. Flower blossoms range in color and may be a solid color or combination. Potato tubers form just about the time these flowers bloom. The flowers may drop off before they open, especially in tough weather. Not all potatoes flower every year but you should get a crop, regardless. As the season progresses, the plants start to sprawl.

The potato is a cool-season crop that is moderately tolerant of frost. Growing temperature is critical and is one of the most important factors in good yields. The plant stops growing when temperatures fall below 45°F or rise above 75°F, and produces the best yields at 60 to 65°F. Use an organic mulch to cool the soil and help produce a better crop.

Consistent moisture is important for good growth. Yields will be substantially reduced if there is a dry spell for a couple of weeks; conversely, excessive water after the tubers have formed can cause them to rot. Inconsistent or inadequate moisture can cause many physiological disorders in potatoes.

Keep on top of your weeding in the potato patch, but don't cultivate more than two inches deep. In midseason, if you haven't already done so, mound soil over the bases of your potato plants (a process called hilling). Hilling covers the spuds and protects them from the sun's bright rays, which will cause any exposed tuber parts to turn green, bitter, and poisonous (a process called "greening"). The potato tuber is a modified stem, not a root, and plant stems can manufacture the green pigment chlorophyll when they're exposed to light. Now, chlorophyll won't hurt you, but that is not the problem. Green skin and flesh indicates that another compound, solanine, has built up along with the chlorophyll. Solanine tastes bitter and can give you a pretty bad stomachache (or worse) if it's eaten in large quantities. Since most of the chlorophyll and solanine are located near the surfaces of the tubers, peeling will remove much of them. But if you'll take the time to hill the potatoes you can avoid the problem completely.

The potato fruit, a small green berry that grows aboveground, resembles a small tomato and can contain up to about 300 seeds. But don't bother to save them unless you plan to breed your own potato variety. Potato seeds are genetically unstable and will produce many off-type plants. So, if you plant seeds saved from your 'Yukon Gold', you might have many plants, but none will be 'Yukon Gold'. Potato fruits are poisonous, too. Remove and destroy them if you have small children around who might mistake them for tomatoes.

Potato tubers are susceptible to a pathogen that causes scab. The fungus doesn't grow well in acidic soil, so if your soil has a pH of about 4.8 to 5.4, scab will not be prevalent. If your soil pH is high, as are most soils in our region, consider foregoing a spud crop, or find a scab-resistant variety to plant.

Internal black spot is the result of a bruised seed piece in combination with excessive water and nitrogen. The tissue just beneath the skin of the tuber turns black and the potato loses a lot of eye appeal. Be careful not to bruise your seed potatoes at planting time!

Hollow heart is the formation of a cavity near the center of a tuber caused by uneven growth resulting from uneven moisture.

Flea beetles are tiny, shiny, black beetles that overwinter in the soil and feed on your potatoes' leaves. They chew tiny holes that make the leaf look like it received a blast from a tiny shotgun! Their larvae feed on roots and tubers. Rotate your potato crop around your garden.

Many potato varieties are available in different skin and flesh colors. While the most popular to consumers in the United States are white-fleshed, there are yellow, pink, red, and blue-fleshed tubers common in other countries, and they're catching on here.

Recommended Potato Varieties

Variety	Comments
Dark Red Norland	Heirloom; red skin, white flesh; standard early potato
Superior	Early; white skin, white flesh; scab resistant
Adirondack Blue	Purple skin, purple flesh
Yukon Gold	White skin, yellow flesh; midseason; good storage
Kennebec	Heirloom; white skin, white flesh; late season
Red Pontiac	Heirloom; red skin, white flesh; midseason to late

Harvesting: Dig your potatoes about two weeks after the vines have been killed by the first frosts of the season. If you dig too early, when the vines are still living, the spuds' skins will be tender and will skin and bruise easily. Also avoid too much exposure to sunlight before storing your potatoes. To store them, hold them at 50 to 60°F for about a week to allow them to cure. Then lower the temperature to about 40°F, where they will keep for up to six months. While they will not sprout if they're stored below 40°F, their starch will turn into sugar and the potatoes will taste sweet. That is not a problem unless you intend to fry your potatoes, as the sugar that has formed will caramelize and the resulting fried potatoes will be dark brown.

WHAT HAPPENED HERE?

THE LEAVES LOOK BROWN AND HAVE SPOTTED AREAS – This could be blight, especially if it started as a purplish spot. There are many diseases that affect potatoes, so when in doubt, take a sample to your local county extension office for positive identification, particularly if you live in or near an area of commercial potato production. Destroy the plants and follow your county agent's recommendation for control in the future.

MY POTATOES HAVE TURNED GREEN IN THE SUNLIGHT. ARE THEY POISONOUS? – Be sure to hill your potatoes to protect them from sunlight. The green area of potatoes contains a toxic alkaloid, so it's best to cut that green out before preparing your spuds or discard them altogether.

MY STORED POTATOES HAVE BECOME VERY SWEET – Starches in potatoes will turn to sugar if you've stored them in temperatures below 40°F. Move them to an area where the temperatures are above 55°F and the sugars will convert back to starches.

JERUSALEM ARTICHOKE

Helianthus tuberosus

Family: Compositae (or Asteraceae) — Sunflower

Direct Seed or Transplant: Plant tubers
Optimum Range of Soil Temperature for Planting: 50–70°F
Minimum Soil Temperature for Planting: 50°F
Planting Depth for Tubers: 2–3 inches
Depth of Root System: Shallow
Spacing Within Row: 24–30 inches
Distance Between Rows: 36–48 inches
Consumption of Nitrogen: Moderate
Days to Maturity: Harvest anytime after killing frost
Average Yield per 10-foot Row: Highly variable

perennial vegetable

There is some confusion in the literature regarding a type of carbohydrate found in the tubers. Most of the carbohydrates are in the form of "inulin." Don't confuse this with insulin, a protein important in sugar metabolism and often lacking in diabetics.

Planting and Care: The plant's knobby tubers are planted in the early spring 3 inches deep and 3 feet apart in rows 3 to 4 feet apart. Light, loamy soils produce smaller yields than slightly heavier soils but they make harvest easier. Grow the plants as you would potatoes. Plants grow to several feet tall and resemble sunflowers.

Harvesting: The tubers form as days shorten in late summer and early fall and are dug after the tops have been killed by frost. Failure to harvest all of the tubers will lead to a very "weedy" situation as volunteer plants grow in unwanted places. In some neglected patches the only way to clear the ground is to let hogs root out the tubers, which they much enjoy.

FUN FACTS

Scientists believe Jerualem artichoke developed from a wild sunflower species in the Mississippi Valley. Early colonists found the native species growing along the Massachusetts coast and sent specimens to Europe. Europeans gave it the Italian name girasoli articocco *meaning "sunflower artichoke," which was then corrupted and anglicized to "Jerusalem artichoke," the name that first appeared in 1686. By 1806, it had become common in American gardens and varieties bearing white, yellow, and purple skins were grown before the Civil War.*

Recommended Jerusalem Artichoke Varieties

Variety	Days to Maturity	Comments
Stampede	90	One of the earliest maturing; large white tubers up to ½ lb.
Boston Red	Full season	Large, knobby, red-skinned tubers
Kack's Copperclad	Full season	Tubers coppery-purple

WHAT HAPPENED HERE?

MY JERUSALEM ARTICHOKE LEAVES HAVE A WHITE POWDERY COATING ON THEM AND FEEL DRY – This sounds like powdery mildew. Avoid wetting the foliage during irrigation and be sure to rake up and remove from the garden all dead leaves and plant material at the end of the season. Good sanitation is about all you can do here.

THIS YEAR I PLANTED STRAWBERRIES WHERE MY JERUSALEM ARTICHOKES GREW FOR THE PAST FEW YEARS AND I HAVE ARTICHOKES COMING UP EVERYWHERE – This plant can be very pesky, easily becoming a weed if you fail to dig all the tubers in a season. Dig up *all* the tubers every year. Or, dig a trench 18 inches deep at the time of planting and line the sides with double thick polyethylene sheeting to prevent the tubers from spreading. Fill in the trench and repeat the operation every 6 to 8 years.

KALE

Brassica oleracea (Acephala group)

Family: Cruciferae (or Brassicaceae) — Mustard

Direct Seed or Transplant: Either

Optimum Range of Soil Temperature for Germination: 45–95°F

Minimum Soil Temperature for Germination: 40°F

Optimum Range of Soil Temperature for Planting: 60–65°F

Minimum Soil Temperature for Planting: 40°F

Seed Planting Depth: ¼–½ inch

Seed Spacing Within Row: 3 every 8 inches

Depth of Root System: Shallow

Thinned Spacing Within Row: 8”

Distance Between Rows: 18–30 inches

Ease of Transplant: Easy

Consumption of Nitrogen: Moderate to high

Days to Maturity: 60–70

Average Yield per 10-foot Row: 7½ lbs.

Grow your own transplants:

Optimum Range of Soil Temperature for Germination: 65–70°F

Approximate Length of Germination Period: 3–4 days

Approximate Time to Grow to Transplant Size: 4–6 weeks

cool-season vegetable

The two types of kale grown in the United States are "Scotch" kale with its much-curled, crumpled, gray-green foliage, and "Siberian" kale, which has blue-green leaves. Each type has dwarf and tall forms; the dwarf is more popular.

Planting and Care: Transplant kale to the garden in early spring or direct seed it later in summer. Light freezes in late fall improve the quality of the leaves. Do not plant kale to mature in summer's heat.

Kale is a heavy feeder so broadcast preplant fertilizer and sidedress when the

FUN FACTS

This is a winter-hardy, non-heading cabbage that is winterkilled only in very cold weather. Kale was well known to the ancient Greeks, and Romans grew several varieties by 200 B.C. Kale was first noted growing in the New World (in Haiti) in 1565 and was found later in Virginia gardens by the early 1600s.

plants are about a month old. Turn in plenty of manure and compost in the kale bed. Push the plants with water and nitrogen and the leaves will be succulent.

Recommended Kale Varieties

Variety	Days to Maturity	Comments
Vates Blue Curled	55	Heirloom; finely curled leaves; plants 15" tall
Red Russian	50	Heirloom; purple stems; gray-green leaves
Winterbor	60	Very curly blue-green leaves

Harvesting: Harvest the plants before their leaves become tough, or about 40 to 50 days after seeding. You can cut the entire plant or simply remove the older, outer leaves, leaving the inner ones to continue to grow.

WHAT HAPPENED HERE?

MY KALE IS GROWING VERY SLOWLY – It may be too hot, or the soil may lack water or nutrients, particularly nitrogen.

MY KALE IS BITTER AND STRONG–FLAVORED – It's too hot or the kale is too mature; a few light frosts will mellow its flavor.

KOHLRABI

Brassica oleracea (Gongylodes group)
Family: Cruciferae (or Brassicaceae) — Mustard

Direct Seed or Transplant: Either
Optimum Range of Soil Temperature for Germination: 65–70°F
Minimum Soil Temperature for Germination: 35°F
Optimum Range of Soil Temperature for Planting: 60–65°F
Minimum Soil Temperature for Planting: 40°F
Seed Planting Depth: ¼ inch
Seed Spacing Within Row: ½–1 inch
Depth of Root System: Shallow
Thinned Spacing Within Row: 3–6 inches
Distance Between Rows: 12–36 inches
Ease of Transplant: Easy
Consumption of Nitrogen: Moderate to high
Days to Maturity: 50–60
Average Yield per 10-foot Row: 5 lbs.
Grow your own transplants:
Optimum Range of Soil Temperature for Germination: 65–70°F
Approximate Length of Germination Period: 3–4 days
Approximate Time to Grow to Transplant Size: 4–6 weeks

cool-season vegetable

This plant is strange. It looks odd and it's a cool-season plant, developed in northern Europe, that is sensitive to cold. It bolts in temperatures below 45°F and grows best at 60 to 70°F.

Most gardeners direct seed this for fall harvest. For a spring crop, start the plants indoors, as you would cabbage, or in a hotbed and transplant them to the garden when the soil warms.

Prepare the soil as you would for cabbage and give this plant the same care.

FUN FACTS

Kohlrabi is grown for its turniplike swollen stem. It was first definitively described in Italy in 1554; it was introduced from Germany or Greece where it may have evolved from narrow-stem kale. It was cultivated throughout continental Europe by 1570 and was grown in Libya by 1573. It was first grown in Ireland as a field crop both for human food and stock feed by 1734 and was being grown in England by 1837. It was planted in American gardens by 1800.

Recommended Kohlrabi Varieties

Variety	Days to Maturity	Comments
Eder	38	Very early; white skin
Grand Duke	50	AAS Selection; resists becoming woody
Kolibri	42	Purple skin, white flesh

Harvesting: Pull your plants when the swollen stem is about 2 to 3 inches in diameter. Larger stems are woody and strong-flavored and are likely to be cracked. Trim the leaves and the woody taproot and eat the stems.

WHAT HAPPENED HERE?

Check out cabbage (page 180), broccoli (page 173), or any of the other crucifers. Kohlrabi gets the same insects and diseases as they do.

LEEK

Allium ampeloprasum (Porrum group)
Family: Alliaceae — Allium

Direct Seed or Transplant: Either
Optimum Range of Soil Temperature for Germination: 70–75°F
Minimum Soil Temperature for Germination: 35°F
Optimum Range of Soil Temperature for Planting: 55–75°F
Minimum Soil Temperature for Planting: 45°F
Seed Planting Depth: ¼ inch
Seed Spacing Within Row: 2–6 inches
Depth of Root System: Shallow
Thinned Spacing Within Row: 6 inches
Distance Between Rows: 12–36 inches
Ease of Transplant: Easy
Consumption of Nitrogen: Moderate
Days to Maturity: 75–120
Average Yield per 10-foot Row: 20 plants
Grow your own transplants:
Optimum Range of Soil Temperature for Germination: 70–75°F
Approximate Length of Germination Period: 10 days
Approximate Time to Grow to Transplant Size: 9 weeks

Leeks are non-bulbing members of the *Allium* genus grown for their basal leaves. They have a delicate, less onion-y flavor and are prized for cooking.

Planting and Care: Leek plants are started in hotbeds or coldframes, transplanted in early spring, and given the same care as onions (page 246). Hill the soil around their bases to blanch the lower portions as the plants grow through the season, beginning when they are several inches tall.

FUN FACTS

Leeks are an ancient plant; the Israelites complained to Moses that they had no leeks to eat. Nero ate leek soup daily, claiming it strengthened his voice and hence gained him the nickname "leek-mouth." The plants were esteemed by the Welsh, who won a sixth-century A.D. battle over the Saxons by wearing leeks in their caps, by order of St. David, to distinguish them from the enemy. The plants were popular in broths throughout the Middle Ages.

Harvesting: Harvest the plants by pulling them about 75 to 120 days after planting or when they are at least ½ inch in diameter at their base and have 4 to 6 inches of blanched stem.

Recommended Leek Varieties

Variety	Days to Maturity	Comments
King Richard	75	12-in. or greater white stems
Upton	90	Vigorous; 12-in. stems
Lancelot	70 (from transplant)	Bolt resistant; 14-in. stems

WHAT HAPPENED HERE?

MY LEEKS ROTTED AFTER I HILLED THEM – You may have hilled them too soon or you covered the entire plant. Leave the soil loosely mounded over the lower parts of the leeks.

LETTUCE

Lactuca sativa

Family: Compositae (or Asteraceae) — Sunflower

Direct Seed or Transplant: Either
Optimum Range of Soil Temperature for Germination: 40–80°F
Minimum Soil Temperature for Germination: 35°F
Optimum Range of Soil Temperature for Planting: 60–76°F
Minimum Soil Temperature for Planting: 45°F
Seed Planting Depth: ¼ inch
Seed Spacing Within Row: Sow thinly
Depth of Root System: Shallow
Thinned Spacing Within Row: 8–12 inches
Distance Between Rows: 12–24 inches
Ease of Transplant: Easy
Consumption of Nitrogen: Low
Days to Maturity: 45–120
Average Yield per 10-foot Row: 5 lbs.
Grow your own transplants:
Optimum Range of Soil Temperature for Germination: 40–80°F
Approximate Length of Germination Period: 4–10 days
Approximate Time to Grow to Transplant Size: 3–4 weeks

cool-season vegetable

Every gardener knows garden lettuce but few know the less common "stem lettuce." Grown for its stems, it also goes by the names of "asparagus lettuce" and "celtuce." We'll discuss all of them here.

Planting and Care: Lettuce needs warm days ranging from 66 to 73°F and cool nights of about 45 to 52°F to grow well. Temperatures above 75°F soften the heads of head lettuce, and those above 85°F cause all lettuce to become bitter and to bolt. Well-hardened young lettuce can withstand 22°F with little damage,

FUN FACTS

This Mediterranean and Asia Minor native was cultivated for food by the Egyptians at least seven thousand years ago. Before that, oil extracted from the seeds was used medicinally. Lettuce was served to Persian kings by the sixth century B.C. Dozens of varieties of lettuce were grown by the Romans; one particularly popular type was romaine (also known as "cos"). Emperor Augustus had a monument erected to the plant because he thought eating lettuce had helped him recover from illness. It was grown in China by the fifth century A.D. and was brought to the New World by Columbus on his second voyage. Leaf lettuce was the original type; head lettuce was not developed until after discovery of the New World. A "Puerto Rican" type arose from seeds brought to the New World by Columbus and became popular with the first American colonists. Both head and leaf types have been popular in American gardens since the eighteenth century.

but all growth will be very slow at temperatures below 45°F. Lettuce's ability to tolerate cold temperatures decreases with age. (So does ours.)

Lettuce is an annual crop, with the plant growing the most in the twenty days or so preceding maturity. Heads of lettuce, like cabbage, develop from the inside out, so the outermost leaves remain the outermost leaves throughout the plant's life.

A common problem is lettuce bolting before you can pick it all. When exposed to typical summer conditions following cool springs, it sometimes acts as though it is in its second season and produces a seed stalk. It's a plant for spring or fall harvest, not for a summer harvest.

Most gardeners direct seed lettuce in early spring. Because lettuce seeds require light for germination, do not bury seeds. Remember—spacing affects the size of the lettuce head, so don't crowd it. As you thin, transplant the seedlings to other areas of the garden.

Lettuce transplants easily, and plants propagated this way mature a few weeks ahead of seeded plants. This is particularly advantageous with head lettuce since it requires a long season.

Lettuce uses only a small amount of nutrients from the soil but it is a poor forager because of its small root system. So nutrients must be made easily available near the plants. Apply preplant fertilizer and sidedress lightly when the plants are thinned. Because you are after the succulent leaves, be sure to give your lettuce plenty of nitrogen.

Lettuce requires plenty of water, but excessive amounts during hot days late in the season will cause head lettuce to become "puffy."

Four types of lettuce are commonly grown in America: loose-leaf (bunching), crisphead (iceburg), butterhead (Boston, bibb), and romaine (cos). Looseleaf is a short-season lettuce. It's easiest to grow and the most popular in our gardens. Crisphead is the most popular in markets but the most difficult to grow because of its long season and heat sensitivity. Butterhead is a semi-heading lettuce. Romaine forms a long, upright plant more tolerant of weather than other heading types.

Recommended Lettuce Varieties

Variety	Days to Maturity	Comments
Black Seeded Simpson	46	Loose leaf; heirloom; susceptible to bolting
Red Salad Bowl	51	Loose leaf; heirloom; burgundy-colored
Ithaca	72	Crisphead; heirloom; disease tolerant
Summertime	70	Crisphead; good tolerance to hot weather
Buttercrunch	64	Butterhead; AAS Selection; slow bolting
Cimmeron	60	Romaine; plum-red leaves with green veins
Green Towers	74	Romaine; very dark green color

Lettuce does suffer from some environmental disorders. Tipburn causes brown spots along the leaf margins, is common in hot weather, and is associated with a calcium deficiency. Slower plant growth reduces the problem. Crisphead is more tolerant than other types.

Bolting results from exposure to long days, high temperatures, or extreme environmental stresses such as drought.

Harvesting: Looseleaf lettuce is harvested about 40 to 50 days after seeding, butterhead and romaine are harvested 55 to 70 days after seeding, and crisphead is harvested about 70 to 120 days after seeding. Baby lettuce may be harvested anytime. Use scissors to harvest entire plants, leaving at least an inch of stem. The plants will regrow for 2 or 3 more harvests.

Sometimes brown spots develop on the lower midrib of lettuce leaves in the refrigerator. Called "russet spotting," it's caused by the plant's reaction to ethylene.

——WHAT HAPPENED HERE?——

MY LETTUCE IS BITTER – This is probably due to high temperatures.

THE LETTUCE FLOWERED BEFORE WE COULD HARVEST – This is due to high temperatures or drought; plant earlier and water well next year.

MY HEAD LETTUCE DID NOT FORM HEADS – Thin your plants well and give them enough room to form heads.

MY HEAD LETTUCE ROTTED – The weather could be too warm and damp from overirrigation. Time your lettuce planting so it will mature in cool weather.

MUSKMELON

Cucumis melo (Reticulatus group)
Family: Cucurbitaceae — Gourd

warm-season vegetable

Direct Seed or Transplant: Either, but usually direct seeded
Optimum Range of Soil Temperature for Germination: 80–90°F
Minimum Soil Temperature for Germination: 60°F
Optimum Range of Soil Temperature for Planting: 65–75°F
Minimum Soil Temperature for Planting: 60°F
Seed Planting Depth: ½ inch
Seed Spacing Within Row: Several per hill
Depth of Root System: Moderate
Thinned Spacing Within Row: 18 inches
Distance Between Rows: 60–84 inches
Ease of Transplant: Requires special care
Consumption of Nitrogen: Moderate
Days to Maturity: 85–95
Average Yield per 10-foot Row: 10 melons
Grow your own transplants:
Optimum Range of Soil Temperature for Germination: 80–90°F
Approximate Length of Germination Period: 4–8 days
Approximate Time to Grow to Transplant Size: 4 weeks

Muskmelons belong to the same species as honeydew, casaba, true cantaloupe, and Persian melon, and all intercross readily within the species, resulting in many gradations among the fruit. (The watermelon, on the other hand, belongs to a different genus and will not cross with any of these melons, nor will cucumber, which belongs to a different species.)

Muskmelons require a long, hot growing season with optimum temperatures of 65 to 75°F.

FUN FACTS

Muskmelons probably originated in western Africa or the Middle East. Columbus brought them to the New World in 1494 and colonists reintroduced the plants into North America in the 1600s. Very few true cantaloupes are grown in the United States. Rather, you have a muskmelon with your breakfast, not a cantaloupe. Blame the marketers who changed the name to increase consumption of the fruit, since "cantaloupe" sounds so much more exotic than "muskmelon."

Muskmelons are *andromonoecious*; that is, they bear both perfect and male flowers, with male flowers appearing first. Unlike watermelon, which only produces one or two fruits per vine, muskmelon vines bear several fruit.

Planting and Care: To direct seed, plant several seeds in a hill and space the hills about 18 inches apart in the row, with about 6 feet between rows. A handful of composted manure in the bottom of each hole gets plants off to a good start.

If space is at a premium, train the melon vines onto trellises, supporting each fruit with a sling or something similar, or plant them at the edge of the garden and let the vines sprawl onto the lawn.

While muskmelons are not particularly heavy feeders, they should have nutrients sufficient to sustain uninterrupted growth through the season. Good vine growth supplies ample sugar to the fruit. Apply preplant fertilizer and sidedress the plants just before the vines begin to run.

Keep melon foliage dry by using drip irrigation or a soaker hose, for all melons are highly susceptible both to powdery and downy mildews. These diseases destroy the leaves and produce bitter or tasteless melons.

In addition to the mildews, all melons are notorious for becoming infected with wilts. Breeders have released varieties that have built-in resistance to many of the diseases that made growing good melons difficult in the "old days." Select one of these resistant strains or varieties.

Keep the weeds under control while your plants are young; once the vines begin to run they smother the weeds.

Harvesting: Muskmelon fruit matures in about 6 to 8 weeks after pollination. When fully mature and at its highest sugar content (10 to 12 percent) muskmelon fruit separates from the stem. This is called the full slip stage of development. Wait for this; then pick your melons.

Recommended Muskmelon Varieties

Variety	Days to Maturity	Comments
Ambrosia	86	Orange flesh; 4-lb. fruit
Hale's Best	80	Orange flesh; heirloom
Sweet Granite	70	Orange flesh; bred for mountain climates
Rocky Ford	84	Green flesh; heirloom; 2-lb. fruit

——— WHAT HAPPENED HERE? ———

MY MELON LEAVES DRIED UP AND THE FRUIT WAS TASTELESS – This is probably due to powdery mildew; moisture and humidity are the culprits. Look for white powder on the leaves and use an appropriate fungicide. Also, keep irrigation water off the leaves. (If the leaves are dead they cannot produce sugars for the fruit.)

I HAVE BITTER MELONS – Bitterness can be caused by cool weather during ripening; it's hard to control the weather.

MUSTARD

Brassica juncea

Family: Cruciferae (or Brassicaceae) — Mustard

Direct Seed or Transplant: Direct Seed

Optimum Range of Soil Temperature for Germination: around 77–95°F

Minimum Soil Temperature for Germination: around 50°F

Seed Planting Depth: ¼–½ inch

Seed Spacing Within Row: 1 inch

Depth of Root System: Moderate

Thinned Spacing Within Row: 5–10 inches

Distance Between Rows: 12–36 inches

Consumption of Nitrogen: Moderate

Days to Maturity: 35–55

Average Yield per 10-foot Row: 10 lbs.

Mustard is a hardy annual grown for its foliage. Like some other leafy greens, it will bolt in summer heat.

Planting and Care: Sow the seeds directly in the garden in very early spring or sow them in late summer for fall use. Like other crucifers, it prefers fertile, well-drained soil high in organic matter.

Mustard varieties run the gamut from having very curled leaves to nearly smooth leaves.

Harvesting: Begin harvesting about 40 to 50 days after planting, cutting the entire plant at the soil line or by snapping off the older outer leaves.

FUN FACTS

White mustard, leaf mustard, and spinach mustard are all grown for their leaves. The commercially prepared mustard, the condiment, is made from the seeds of the distantly related black mustard. Once quite popular, mustard (also known as mustard greens) has lost some of its popularity to spinach and kale, especially in northern gardens, but it remains popular in India and central Africa as well as in the southern United States.

Recommended Mustard Varieties

Variety	Days to Maturity	Comments
Southern Giant Curled	48	AAS Selection; heirloom; bolt-resistant; popular; curled-leaved
Savannah	25	Mild flavor; rapid growing
Red Giant	40	Purple-red leaves; white midrib

WHAT HAPPENED HERE?

MY MUSTARD GOES TO SEED VERY EARLY – If this is happening to your spring planting, you may be running into hot weather; try fall plantings.

MY MUSTARD IS VERY STRONGLY FLAVORED – The weather is too hot or the soil is too dry.

NEW ZEALAND SPINACH

Tetragonia tetragonioides

Family: Tetragoniaceae — Carpetweed

warm-season vegetable

Direct Seed or Transplant: Direct seed

Optimum Range of Soil Temperature for Germination: 60–75°F

Minimum Soil Temperature for Germination: around 50°F

Seed Planting Depth: 1½–2 inches

Seed Spacing Within Row: 1–2 feet

Depth of Root System: Shallow

Thinned Spacing Within Row: 10–20 inches

Distance Between Rows: 36–60 inches

Consumption of Nitrogen: Moderate

Days to Maturity: 70

Average Yield per 10-foot Row: Variable

This is the only warm-season potherb that's relatively common in American gardens. It is drought and heat resistant but is chilled by cool nights. It provides tasty greens after early summer when spinach has bolted.

This large, spreading plant forms a canopy 1 to 2 feet tall and 3 to 4 feet wide and bears inconspicuous white or yellow flowers.

Planting and Care: Plant seed after all danger of frost has passed and the soil has warmed. The "seed," like that of beet and Swiss chard, is actually a dried fruit containing several seeds. It requires from 2 weeks to 3 months to germinate, so soak them in water for 24 hours before planting to hasten germination.

FUN FACTS

Sir Joseph Banks, on Captain Cook's 1770 expedition to the South Seas, discovered New Zealand spinach growing along the shores of Queen Charlotte Sound, New Zealand. Sailors used the boiled leaves as a substitute for spinach. Specimens were brought to Kew Gardens in 1772 and by 1820 English gardeners were growing it. Seeds were sent to New York in 1827 and the plant found its way into American seed catalogs in 1828. "New Zealand Spinach" was not used for food in New Zealand and is not related to true spinach.

Using a preplant fertilizer should be adequate. If the lower leaves begin to yellow, however, sidedress each plant with a small handful of fertilizer.

Usually, this plant is simply listed in the catalogs as "New Zealand Spinach" with no varieties offered.

Harvesting: Begin harvest about 40 to 50 days after seedlings emerge. Clip about 3 to 4 inches of the tender branch tips with their leaves as you need them, stimulating the plant to produce new branches and foliage.

——WHAT HAPPENED HERE?——

MY NEW ZEALAND SPINACH SEED DID NOT GERMINATE – You probably planted when the soil was too cold.

OKRA

Abelmoschus esculentus

Family: Malvaceae — Mallow or Cotton

warm-season vegetable

Direct Seed or Transplant: Either

Optimum Range of Soil Temperature for Germination: 80–90°F

Minimum Soil Temperature for Germination: 60°F

Optimum Range of Soil Temperature for Planting: 70–85°F

Minimum Soil Temperature for Planting: 65°F

Seed Planting Depth: ½ inch

Seed Spacing Within Row: 2 inches

Depth of Root System: Deep

Thinned Spacing Within Row: 6–12 inches (Dwarf); 24 inches (Tall)

Distance Between Rows: 24–36 inches (Dwarf); 60 inches (Tall)

Ease of Transplant: Requires special care

Consumption of Nitrogen: High

Days to Maturity: 50–60

Average Yield per 10-foot Row: Variable

Grow your own transplants:

Optimum Range of Soil Temperature for Germination: 80–90°F

Approximate Length of Germination Period: 13–27 days

Approximate Time to Grow to Transplant Size: 4–5 weeks

Okra requires a warm season and yields poorly in short northern seasons. It tolerates temperatures as low as 65°F and as high as 95°F but grows best at those above 85°F.

The woody dwarf types reach heights of about three feet while the tall types can grow to ten feet. Some have spines but spineless types are popular. The plants begin to flower about 35 to 60

FUN FACTS

This cousin of cotton is a perennial grown as an annual. It originated near the Upper Nile region of Sudan and was brought to Spain by invading Moors in the eighth century. It was introduced into the New World by African slaves, first to Brazil by 1658 and then into the United States by the early 1700s. Thomas Jefferson mentions okra being grown in Virginian gardens in 1781. Confederate soldiers used the ripe seeds as a substitute for coffee during the Civil War.

days after emergence. The beautiful flowers each bear a single, pod-shaped fruit. Pod shapes vary from short and round to long and pointed and their colors range from white to dark green and purple. Okra normally flowers under short days, (which is why the crop is difficult to grow in northern gardens); fortunately, 'Clemson Spineless' is day neutral and better adapted to colder areas.

Planting and Care: Soaking the seeds in water at room temperature overnight just before planting speeds germination. If you forget to soak them the night before soak them in 110°F water for two hours just before planting.

Plant the seeds after the danger of frost has passed and the soil has warmed to at least 75°F. Alternatively, set transplants in the garden but, as with the cucurbits, take care not to disturb their roots. Okra does not tolerate poorly drained soils or those that are highly acidic, which is not a problem for most of us.

The fertilizer you broadcast before planting will get the seedlings off to a good start, but sidedress them when the first pods begin to form. Don't use a high-nitrogen fertilizer since it will encourage excessive vegetative growth at the expense of fruit production; a 5-10-10 formula will do nicely.

Harvesting: Cut the pods when they are 4 to 6 days old and about 2 to 4 inches long and their color is bright. Quality deteriorates rapidly after the seventh day. For continuing harvest, be sure to pick regularly, and if you've planted the spiny type, wear gloves and a long-sleeved shirt.

Recommended Okra Varieties

Variety	Days to Maturity	Comments
Clemson Spineless	55	AAS Selection; heirloom; the major variety grown
North & South	50	Tolerates cool weather; highly productive
Cajun Delight	49	AAS Selection; excellent for northern gardens; widely adapted
Red Burgundy	55	Red stems and pods

——WHAT HAPPENED HERE?——

I PLANTED SEEDS IN SPRING AND NOTHING HAPPENED – If you planted too early and soaked the seeds beforehand they probably rotted.

MY PLANTS PRODUCED A FEW FRUIT, THEN STOPPED – Old fruit that matures on the plant causes flowering to cease.

MY PLANTS ARE VIGOROUS BUT THEY PRODUCE FEW FRUIT – You may have used too much high-nitrogen fertilizer.

ONION

Allium cepa (Cepa group)

Family: Alliaceae — Allium

cool-season vegetable

Direct Seed or Transplant: Sets or plants

Optimum Range of Soil Temperature for Germination of Seed: 50–95°F

Minimum Soil Temperature for Germination of Seed: 35°F

Optimum Range of Soil Temperature for Planting: 55–75°F

Minimum Soil Temperature for Planting: 55–75°F

Set Planting Depth: 2–3 inches

Set Spacing Within Row: 1–2 inches

Depth of Root System: Shallow

Thinned Spacing Within Row: 3–4 inches

Distance Between Rows: 15–24 inches

Ease of Transplant: Moderate to Easy

Consumption of Nitrogen: Moderate

Days to Maturity: 90–150 (also see text)

Average Yield per 10-foot Row: 10 lbs.

FUN FACTS

The Pharaoh supplied laborers building the Great Pyramid with onions, garlic, and radishes. The Roman author Juvenal claimed the Egyptians worshipped sweet, mild onions. The Israelites complained to Moses that they could find no onions to eat in the wilderness. In 430 B.C. Greece, Hippocrates reported that onions were popular and several varieties were grown. Onions were used in Europe during the Middle Ages but they were not as popular as leeks or garlic. Columbus brought onions to Isabela Island in 1494 and from there they spread through the Americas, becoming especially popular with Native Americans. Massachusetts's colonists grew them in 1629, and Virginia harvested its first crop in 1648. Polish king Stanislas I popularized French onion soup during the reign of Louis XV.

Grow your own transplants:

Optimum Range of Soil Temperature for Germination: 50–95°F

Approximate Length of Germination Period: 10 days

Approximate Time to Grow to Transplant Size: 9 weeks

The common garden onion is a biennial grown as an annual. Its bulb is an accumulation of leaf bases; the bulb forms when plants are exposed to the proper daylength.

Onions grow best at temperatures from 55 to 75°F and do poorly when the temperature rises to 85°F or more, or drops below 45°F. Ideally, the weather should be cool during the early phases of onion development and warm during bulbing.

Onion bulbing is a response to daylength and onions are divided into three groups based on this. Short-day types grow best in southern gardens below 28°N latitude as fall and winter crops. Long-day types do best when exposed to 14- to 16-hour days (hours of sunlight). These are grown in northern gardens above 35°N latitude and are planted to mature in late summer. Intermediate types do best when given 13- to 14-hour days in latitudes between 28° and 35°N. We typically plant long-day types in northern gardens where bulbing begins in late June. Leaf growth stops when bulbing begins and the process depends upon existing leaves for bulb nourishment. It's important to plant onions early to get as much top growth as possible before the onset of bulbing.

Planting and Care: Onions grow best in rich soil high in organic matter and nutrients so work in composted manure and

compost and broadcast some preplant fertilizer. The plant's small, shallow root system is a poor competitor for water and nutrients.

Planting methods depend upon the onion use. If you want them for dry bulbs you can plant either seeds or sets in very early spring after the danger of hard freezes has passed. Onion sets produce a crop 3 to 4 weeks earlier and yield more than seeded onions. Plant the sets right-side up about 3 inches apart in the row and cover them lightly with soil. The best sets are dormant and dime-sized. Smaller sets yield poorly and plants from larger sets will likely bolt.

If you choose to seed, plant thinly in the row and don't thin. Bear in mind that onion seedlings are more prone to onion smut infection than onion sets.

Pencil-thick onion plants about 6 inches tall and 8 to 10 weeks old are planted 3 to 4 inches apart.

Sidedress the young plants about a month after planting, but nutrients, especially nitrogen, added after this time delay maturity.

Onion plants must be well watered throughout the season, but excess water, like excess fertilizer, delays maturity and results in soft bulbs that store poorly. Stop watering when the onion tops begin to fall over to encourage the plants to "harden up."

A premature seed stalk is the result of improper storage temperatures. Large sets stored at 40 to 50°F are most likely to produce plants that bolt.

There are different types of dry bulb onions: round, flat, and globe-shaped bulbs in red, white, and yellow colors. They can be pungent (American type) or mild (foreign type) and short-day, intermediate-day, or long-day sensitive.

Pungent onions are small, dense, and strong-flavored. Though all three colors exist within this type, the most popular are yellow bulbs. The pungent type stores far better than the mild type.

Mild onions are best typified by the Bermuda, a short-day type grown widely in the South.

Recommended Onion Varieties

Variety	Days to Maturity	Comments
Candy	85	Intermediate; mild, sweet flavor
Red Burgermaster	112	Red color; excellent quality
White Sweet Spanish	120	White skin; mild flavor; poor keeper
Stuttgarter	102	Long storage life
Ebenezer	105	Heirloom; mild, sweet flavor; long keeping

Harvesting: Any densely planted onions can be pulled for green onions starting when they are about pencil thick.

Pull onions for dry bulbs when the tops on most of the plants have fallen over but before the foliage has dried completely. If you delay harvest the bulbs may sprout new roots and will not store well. Do not break the tops over but let them fall naturally, as breaking them over reduces yield. After harvest you must cure the plants.

Here's how to cure onions: Pull the plants and put them into long, narrow piles in the garden with the tops of one row covering the bulbs of another to reduce bulb sunburn. Leave them alone until the tops are completely dry, between 5 to 14 days depending upon the weather. If the weather is wet, cure them under cover, such as in a shed, on a piece of 1-inch mesh poultry fencing supported by 2 x 4s laid between two sawhorses so that air can circulate around the bulbs.

When the tops have dried completely, cut them off, leaving about an inch above the bulb, and place the sound, firm bulbs into a mesh bag with large holes. Be sure they have good ventilation all around. Store them in a cold, dry place that does not freeze. Damaged bulbs and those with thick necks will not store well.

WHAT HAPPENED HERE?

I HAVE VERY SMALL ONION BULBS – They did not receive enough water or fertilizer or there were too many weeds during bulb formation. The plants may also have been crowded in the row.

SHOULD I BREAK THE TOPS OF MY ONIONS TO SPEED HARVEST? – No.

PARSNIP

Pastinaca sativa

Family: Umbelliferae (or Apiaceae) — Parsley

Direct Seed or Transplant: Direct Seed
Optimum Range of Soil Temperature for Germination: 50–70°F
Minimum Soil Temperature for Germination: 35°F
Seed Planting Depth: ½ inch
Seed Spacing Within Row: 3 inch
Depth of Root System: Deep
Thinned Spacing Within Row: 2–4 inches
Distance Between Rows: 18–36 inches
Consumption of Nitrogen: High
Days to Maturity: 120
Average Yield per 10-foot Row: 7½ lbs.

cool-season vegetable

Parsnips require a 100- to 130-day season. They are not as heat tolerant as carrots and grow best at cool temperatures from 60 to 65°F.

Planting and Care: Parsnips require a deep soil free from hardpans and stones. Their roots become crooked in shallow soils. Heavy (clay) soils, especially if the surface crusts before the seeds germinate, produce a poor stand with roughened roots.

Prepare a fine seedbed and plant in early spring. If the plants are crowded the roots will be small, but tender; if they're too far apart, they'll grow too large and rapidly become woody and fibrous.

Parsnip seeds take up to three weeks to germinate and you'll usually have to weed before the parsnip seedlings

FUN FACTS

This root native to Europe and Asia was relished by the Greeks and Romans. Pliny extolled the medicinal value of parsnip. The emperor Tiberius liked it so much he had it imported fresh from Germany. Parsnips grown during ancient times did not have the large, white, fleshy root we know today. This characteristic developed during the Middle Ages when the English ate the roots during Lent. Parsnips were brought to North America by the early colonists and were cultivated in Virginia in 1609 and in Massachusetts by 1629. General Sullivan, in his 1779 punitive expedition against the Six Nations in New York, found the Native Americans growing parsnips.

appear. Use radish as a nurse crop and continue to cultivate to control weeds. You can also cover the seeds with peat moss, vermiculite, sand, or a board to keep the soil from crusting over them until the seedlings emerge.

Fertilize parsnips as you would carrots (page 181). Begin cultivation as soon as weeds emerge and continue until the plants' foliage shades the area between the rows.

Recommended Parsnip Varieties

Variety	Days to Maturity	Comments
Hollow Crown	105	Heirloom; medium-long roots
Harris Model	120	Heirloom; fine grained; sweet flesh
Javelin	110	Vigorous; canker resistant

Harvesting: Starch in a parsnip root is converted to sugar when temperatures fall below about 37°F. The roots are very long so you can't pull them like carrots; dig them after several hard frosts and store them in your root cellar. Alternatively, leave them in the garden, mulched with leaves, and dig them throughout the winter into early spring before the tops resume growth; growing tops indicate shriveled, tasteless roots.

──WHAT HAPPENED HERE?──

MY PARSNIP ROOTS ARE FULL OF TUNNELS AND WORMS – They have root maggots or wireworms. Try planting a trap crop of radishes near the parsnips next year or, better still, avoid planting root vegetables in that part of the garden for at least three years.

I BOUGHT NEW PARSNIP SEEDS THIS YEAR BUT HAD VERY POOR RESULTS – Parsnips are notorious for having poor germination and seedlings. The seeds lose their viability very rapidly and the seedlings are weak. Prevent soil crusting by keeping soil organic matter levels high and/or by planting a nurse crop like radish along with the parsnip seeds.

PEPPERS

Capsicum annuum var. *annuum*

Family: Solanaceae — Potato or Nightshade

Direct Seed or Transplant: Transplant
Optimum Range of Soil Temperature for Planting: 70–75°F sweet; 70–85°F hot
Minimum Soil Temperature for Planting: 65°F
Depth of Root System: Moderate
Transplant Spacing Within Row: 12–24 inches
Distance Between Rows: 18–36 inches
Ease of Transplant: Moderate
Consumption of Nitrogen: Moderate
Days to Maturity: 65–80
Average Yield per 10-foot Row 5–7 lbs.
Grow your own transplants:
Optimum Range of Soil Temperature for Germination: 65–95°F
Approximate Length of Germination Period: 5–7 days
Approximate Time to Grow to Transplant Size: 8 weeks

warm-season vegetable

Peppers are perennial tropical plants grown as annuals. They are more chill-sensitive than tomatoes and don't tolerate prolonged periods below 50°F, nor will they set fruit below 60°F. Sweet peppers make their best vegetative growth between 65 and 85°F. Temperatures above 85°F cause misshapen fruit and those above 90°F cause flowers to abort.

Hot peppers grow best above 75°F with consistently warm nighttime temperatures above 70°F. Temperatures above 90°F actually increase fruit set. But like sweet peppers, hot peppers will not set fruit when temperatures fall below 60°F.

All peppers quickly abort their flowers if they are growing in waterlogged soils.

Common peppers are determinate, erect, bushy plants 1 to 3 feet tall. They have moderately sized root systems and cannot forage widely for nutrients. Their stems and leaves are brittle and break when soil moisture is high and/or the plant has a heavy fruit load. Stake the plants as you would tomato plants when there's a chance of windy conditions.

FUN FACTS

There are sweet peppers and pungent peppers, but all peppers grown in the United States—except one, tabasco (C. frutescens)—belong to the same species. None are closely related to the spice black pepper (Piper nigrum). Peppers were gathered from the wild at least seven thousand years ago and cultivated at least two thousand years ago in their native Central America, where most wild types are very hot. Columbus brought chili peppers to Europe in 1493 and their use spread rapidly. The fruit were dried, ground, and used as a substitute for expensive black pepper. Peppers became so valued that jalapeños were bartered and used to pay taxes during the Spanish conquest of Mexico. Chili peppers were being cultivated extensively in India by the late 1500s.

The plant is day-neutral but flower buds form faster under long days and warm temperatures. Fruit forms following pollination.

Planting and Care: Because of their need for lots of heat, peppers are transplanted to the garden well after the danger of frost has passed. Large transplants produce a large, early yield but may not give as much of a total yield as slightly smaller transplants. Overhardening stunts plants and reduces total yields.

Use a liquid transplant fertilizer and sidedress with a dry fertilizer when the plants have set several fruit. Using manure or compost in the planting hole never hurts but peppers do not respond to them as well as do some other vegetables.

Excess water causes the flowers and small fruit to abort while too little water increases the incidence of blossom-end rot. Soaker hoses or watering the soil (not the pepper's leaves) with a watering can is best.

Mulching is the best way to control weeds in the pepper patch. Black plastic mulch increases the yield of high-quality fruit. If you choose to use straw, leaves, or another organic mulch, let the soil warm up before you apply them.

The many varieties of peppers can be confusing.

Bell Types: The plants produce large, sweet, blocky fruit up to about 4 inches wide and 4 inches long. Immature green fruit turn red or another color at maturity, but most are eaten green.

Pimento: These plants produce sweet, round to slightly pointed fruit about 2 inches wide and 3 to 4 inches long. The fruit is used to stuff into green olives and is also eaten in salads.

Celestial: Plants bear small fruit up to 2 inches in diameter. These stand upright on the plant. The fruit may be red, yellow, orange, or purple and fruit color can be mixed on a single plant. The plants are used as ornamentals and hot fruit are often ground for chili powder.

Cayenne: Fruit from these plants are slender, curved, pointed, and 2 to 12 inches long. They are green when they're immature and red when they're mature. Fruit of the sweet types are ground into paprika while those of the hot types are used in chili powder.

Cherry: These plants produce cherry-shaped fruit that are orange or red at maturity and can be sweet or hot. They can be pickled or ground for chili powder.

Tomato: Fruit resemble small, green tomatoes and are pickled when they are immature.

Tabasco: These plants produce slim, very hot fruit up to 3 inches long. They are used as ornamentals, pickled, or ground for use in chili powder.

The fruit of most pepper varieties are green when they are immature and red when they are mature, particularly those of the open-pollinated types. Seeds are inexpensive to produce and the large number of good-quality varieties means that there is little demand for hybrid varieties. Lately, however, consumers have been introduced to bell-type fruit that are yellow, orange, chocolate-brown, or purple; these are hybrid varieties.

The pungency or "hotness" of pepper fruit is expressed in Scoville Heat Units. The non-pungent, sweet bell types are rated 0; the Anaheim, 150–2,500; and the cayenne and jalapeño, 10,000–18,000. Tabasco peppers are rated in the vicinity of 40,000 units. The variety 'Berbere' from Ethiopia rates up to *100,000 units*. This pungency is due to the presence of an alkaloid called capsaicin. This compound is extracted and used to produce the "warmth" in some topical balms used to treat sore muscles. It is the irritant in "mace" and, as "pepper spray," can be an effective animal repellent.

Scientists believe hot peppers are so popular because they increase our general metabolism, salivation, and the release of endorphins in the body, creating a sense of wellbeing.

Peppers develop only a few disorders that should not be problems for most gardeners. Blossom-end rot can occur under very dry soil conditions and is related to poor calcium distribution in the fruit. See the discussion of this disorder under the Tomato profile (page 288).

Sunscald shows up as off-white blotches and papery dead skin on fruit exposed to direct sun. This can be a problem when the plants are partially defoliated.

Recommended Pepper Varieties

Variety	Days to Maturity	Comments
California Wonder	75	Sweet bell type; heirloom
Big Bertha	70	Sweet bell type; very large fruit
Gypsy	65	Sweet bell type; great for stir-frying
Sweet Banana	66	AAS Selection; heirloom; pimento type; ripens red; sweet
Thai Dragon	75	Dries easily; very hot
Red Rocket	65 green / 85 red	Cayenne type; very hot
Sahuaro	70 green / 90 red	Cayenne type; mild
Hungarian Wax	70	Cayenne type; medium hot
Jalapeño	65 green / 80 red	Cayenne type; very hot; red at maturity
Cherry Bomb	62 green / 87 red	Cherry type; very hot
Ancho	68 green / 88 red	Medium hot
Habanero	75 green / 100 ripe	Very hot

Harvesting: Pepper fruit are harvested from 60 to well over 100 days after planting, provided you have the season for it. If you want red bell peppers, wait for the fruit to mature before picking. Otherwise, pick the fruit at any time it has reached an acceptable

——WHAT HAPPENED HERE?——

ALL THE FLOWERS DROPPED FROM MY PEPPER PLANTS – The weather has been too cold or very hot or you waterlogged your soil by overwatering.

LATE IN THE SEASON, MY BELL PEPPER FRUIT ACQUIRE A PURPLE CAST – If it's got a purple cast it won't turn red. This off color is common on green bell peppers near the end of the season and is caused by cool weather and shorter days, but the fruit remains edible.

HOW DO I KNOW WHEN TO PICK MY PEPPERS? – When a pepper has developed the color and size you want, pick it.

size, usually 3 to 4 inches in length. Harvest all peppers by snapping the stem from the plant. (Be sure to support the rest of the plant when you snap off the fruit.) Pick the largest fruit every 7 to 10 days. Green fruit will ripen off the plant if it's stored above 50°F but bacterial soft rot can become a problem. Wear gloves when you harvest or cook with hot peppers.

RADISH

Raphanus sativus

Family: Cruciferae (or Brassicaceae) — Mustard

cool-season vegetable

Direct Seed or Transplant: Direct Seed
Optimum Range of Soil Temperature for Germination: 45–90°F
Minimum Soil Temperature for Germination: 40°F
Seed Planting Depth: ½ inch
Seed Spacing Within Row: Thinly
Depth of Root System: Shallow
Thinned Spacing Within Row: ½–1 inch
Distance Between Rows: 8–18 inches
Consumption of Nitrogen: High
Days to Maturity: 22–30
Average Yield per 10-foot Row: 10 bunches

Easy-to-raise radishes are grown as annuals for their fleshy, often pungent roots. They may be grown for a spring or fall harvest in our region, but they will not tolerate summer's heat. Any halt to their growth will cause the roots to become woody and too pungent. Warm weather may also cause the plants to bolt.

Generally, there are two types of radishes; the more familiar of the two is called a "spring" or "salad" radish, which matures in 3 to 6 weeks. The winter radish is less common and slower growing, requiring 45 to 70 days to mature.

One of the fastest seeds to germinate, radishes are good for novice gardeners and children to plant. But beware! A child who pulls a beautiful red radish, washes it, and takes a bite just might not want to repeat the experience. Because radish seeds germinate quickly, you can use them as a nurse crop with slower-to-germinate seeds, such as carrot, beet, and parsnip.

Planting and Care: Radishes perform best in light, loamy soils. You will end up with oddly shaped roots if your soils are stony. And, if you forget to thin, you may find no radish "root" at all.

Spread fertilizer before you plant radishes; there'll be no time to sidedress during their short growing season.

Spring radishes are most popular. The little globe-shaped red

FUN FACTS

We know the Pharaohs enjoyed radishes four thousand years ago, but this vegetable actually originated in Asia and Europe. They were well loved by Greeks, who cast small golden replicas of the roots. New forms were developed in China after their introduction to that country in 500 B.C. Radishes were introduced into England in 1548 and were cultivated in the United States by the early seventeenth century.

roots are attractive in salads and as garnishes. Radishes come in many shapes and colors, as well as pungencies, so be sure to read the descriptions in your catalog. Late summer radishes are not widely grown in the United States but you can try some in your garden. They take slightly longer to mature than the spring varieties. Winter radishes generally take about twice as long to mature as do spring varieties and are grown for a fall crop. They also come in different pungencies and colors.

Harvesting: Harvest spring radishes when roots reach 1 to 1½ inches in diameter. If you leave them in the ground too long they'll get strong flavored and crack.

You can store spring radishes in the refrigerator for a few weeks, but remove the tops prior to storage or you'll end up with a vegetable drawer full of mush. The leaves don't store well.

Recommended Radish Varieties

Variety	Days to Maturity	Comments
Cherry Bell	24	AAS Selection; heirloom; very attractive; high quality
Early Scarlet Globe	22	Heirloom; very crisp white flesh
French Breakfast	25	Heirloom; olive-shaped; bright scarlet color
White Chinese Celestial	60	Mild winter radish
China Rose	50	Heirloom; pure white 5–6 in. roots; for winter storage
Black Spanish	55	Heirloom; black skin; long-keeper; 4 in. diameter roots

RHUBARB

Rheum rhabarbarum

Family: Polygonaceae — Buckwheat

Direct Seed or Transplant: Plant crowns with at least one "eye"
Optimum Range of Soil Temperature for Planting: 50–70°F
Minimum Soil Temperature for Planting: 50°F
Planting depth for crowns: place eyes 2 inches below soil surface
Depth of Root System: Extensive
Spacing Within Row: 24–48 inches
Distance Between Rows: 36–48 inches
Consumption of Nitrogen: Very high
Average Yield per 10-foot Row: 20 leaf stalks

perennial vegetable

Rhubarb is highly resistant to drought and severe cold and grows best in spring and fall where summer temperatures average 75°F and winter temperatures, 40°F. It begins growing when temperatures reach 45°F. In the cool spring the leaf stalks develop their characteristic red color. Vegetative growth slows considerably in summer, the leaf stalks turn green, and the plant produces a long flower stalk. Vegetative growth resumes in fall and the

stalks become red again, finally dying back when temperatures drop to about 26°F.

Planting and Care: Rhubarb is a very heavy feeder and does best in a well-drained, high-organic soil.

Cut crown divisions into as many pieces as there are strong buds on the outer portion of the old crown and plant these in spring or in late fall. Set the divisions 2 to 4 feet apart and 2 inches deep, firming the soil around their sides but leaving the soil directly over their bud loose. Water well after planting.

Once established, sidedress the plants in spring with a complete fertilizer. Some gardeners cover the plants for winter with composted manure, but using manure or heavy organic winter mulch is not advised where foot rot is a problem because this pathogen thrives in soils that remain damp for long periods of time.

Harvesting: Initially, harvest for a week or two from vigorous plants in their second season but by their third season a harvest of up to 8 to 10 weeks may be possible if plants remain vigorous. Don't harvest for longer than that and harvest in either spring or fall (preferably the former) but not in both.

FUN FACTS

Rhubarb is grown for its tart petioles (leaf stalks). It first was brought to Italy from Siberia about 1608. It appeared in America in 1778 and was commonly grown by 1806. When the Nazi army overran the rich fruit growing districts of Russia during World War II, Joseph Stalin authorized the importation of tons of rhubarb seeds from the United States. These were planted in secure northern regions of the country and supplied Soviet citizens with plenty of "fruit."

Pull the leaf stalks from the plant and remove the leaf blades before storage; the leaf blades contain toxic amounts of oxalic acid. Discard them and eat only the leaf stalks.

The plants will become crowded after 8 to 10 years and their leaf stalks will become spindly. Divide the plants, transplant the divisions to new areas, and give the old plants a good dressing of manure and fertilizer.

Recommended Rhubarb Varieties

Variety	Comments
Ruby	Bright red leaf stalks
Valentine	Bright red leaf stalks; better adapted to slightly warmer sites; bolt resistant
Canada Red	Bright red leaf stalks; better adapted to slightly warmer sites
McDonald	Old Canadian variety; produces pink leaf stalks
Victoria	Very old Canadian variety; large plant produces green leaf stalks

—WHAT HAPPENED HERE?—

MY PLANTS PRODUCED SEED STALKS – The weather got too hot and the days too long. Remove and discard the seed stalks.

CAN I START RHUBARB FROM SEEDS? – Seed viability is terrible; go with crown divisions.

CAN I USE RHUBARB LEAVES LIKE SWISS CHARD? – *Absolutely not*; the leaf blades are poisonous.

RUTABAGA

Brassica napus (Napobrassica group)
Family: Cruciferae (or Brassicaceae) — Mustard

cool-season vegetable

Direct Seed or Transplant: Direct Seed
Optimum Range of Soil Temperature for Germination: 45–95°F
Minimum Soil Temperature for Germination: 40°F
Seed Planting Depth: 1 inch
Seed Spacing Within Row: 1–2 inches
Depth of Root System: Moderate
Thinned Spacing Within Row: 5–8 inches
Distance Between Rows: 18–36 inches
Consumption of Nitrogen: Moderate
Days to Maturity: 90–95
Average Yield per 10-foot Row: 15 lbs.

People confuse the rutabaga and the turnip, but savvy vegetable gardeners know the difference. They do have similar cultural requirements, and both are grown for their enlarged fleshy root. Rutabagas found in a local grocery store typically have yellow flesh, while turnips are typically white-fleshed, but both boast varieties with flesh of other colors. The turnip is a smaller plant with smaller roots that may be round, elongated, and sometimes slightly flattened. They have no neck, and are usually white to tan in color, with purple near their tops. Leaves of a turnip plant are typically hairy, rough, thin, and green. A rutabaga has a larger, round root with a thick neck and smooth, blue-green leaves, and the root is usually tan.

FUN FACTS

Rutabagas are closely related to turnips, and are native to northern Asia, the Near East, and Afghanistan. They are more nutritious than turnips and many turnip lovers are turning to rutabagas for a tasty treat. It's thought that the rutabaga evolved in Europe from a cross between kale and turnip. It was introduced into England about 1790 and America around 1800. The rutabaga is also known as Swede, Swede turnip, and winter turnip.

Planting and Care: Rutabagas tolerate low temperatures and do poorly when temperatures get too warm. Like turnips, they are biennial, so young plants exposed to temperatures of 50 to 55°F will bolt. Time the planting so that the roots will mature during cool weather. Rutabagas require from 85 to 95 days to mature and are better grown as a fall harvest in the Rocky Mountain region.

Like turnips, rutabagas are sensitive to boron. Watch for brown heart or water core, which is characterized by breakdown of flesh at the center of the root. It typically shows up during periods of rapid growth. Have your soil tested professionally and follow the recommendations of the soil lab before applying too much of any boron-containing compound.

Harvesting: Rutabagas taste best when the roots are 3 to 5 inches in diameter and when they mature in cool weather.

Recommended Rutabaga Varieties

Variety	Days to Maturity	Comments
American Purple Top	90	Heirloom; excellent fresh or stored for winter use
Laurentian	95	Mild flavor
Helenor	90	Very high yielding; sweet orange flesh

──WHAT HAPPENED HERE?──

Rutabagas and turnips have similar problems (page 294).

SHALLOT

Allium cepa (Aggregatum group)
Family: Alliaceae — Allium

cool-season vegetable

Direct Seed or Transplant: Sets
Optimum Range of Soil Temperature for Planting: 55°-75°F
Minimum Soil Temperature for Planting: 45°F
Set Planting Depth: ¾ their length deep
Set Spacing Within Row: 4-8"
Depth of Root System: Shallow
Distance Between Rows: 36-48"
Ease of Transplant: Easy
Consumption of Nitrogen: High
Days to Maturity: 80-100
Average Yield per 10-foot Row: Variable

Shallots are perennial plants native to western Asia that are grown as annuals for their cluster of bulblets or cloves. They may also be used as green onions.

Planting and Care: Shallots are planted in early spring and grown as a summer crop in our region, where their green tops may be harvested anytime they're ready.

Dry bulbs are harvested about 60 to 100 days after planting. Grow shallots as you would onions.

Harvesting: To harvest as "green onions," blanch the stems if you would like a mild flavor. Mound the soil about 2 inches deep around the plants about 2 months prior to harvest. Wait 2 weeks, then mound soil another 2 inches deep. Pull the plants when the tops are 6 to 8 inches tall.

FUN FACTS

Shallots were probably introduced into Europe by returning Crusaders in the twelfth and thirteenth centuries. The French introduced shallots into New Orleans by 1800.

For dry bulbs, harvest when the tops have fallen over and cure as you would onions.

Recommended Shallot Varieties

Variety	Days to Maturity	Comments
Pikant	80	High yields
Ambition	100	Red skin; long storage
Picador	105	Red-brown skin; white flesh

WHAT HAPPENED HERE?

Not surprisingly, problems affecting shallots are the same as those for onions (page 246).

SNAP BEAN

Phaseolus vulgaris

Family: Leguminosae – Pea or Bean

Direct Seed or Transplant: Direct Seed
Optimum Range of Soil Temperature for Germination: 60–85°F
Minimum Soil Temperature for Germination: 60°F
Seed Planting Depth: 1–1½ inches
Seed Spacing Within Row: 1–2 inches (bush); variable (pole)
Depth of Root System: Moderate
Thinned Spacing Within Row: 2–4 inches (bush); variable (pole)
Distance Between Rows: 18–36 inches (bush); variable (pole)
Consumption of Nitrogen: Low
Days to Maturity: 48–62
Average Yield per 10-foot Row: 8 lbs. (bush); 15 lbs. (pole)

warm-season vegetable

Beans grow best at soil temperatures of 60 to 85°F. Seeds will not germinate well below 50°F or above 95°F and seedlings will not emerge from the soil if days have fewer than about 16 hours of sunlight.

Bean plants will be damaged if temperatures fall below 50°F, high humidity increases diseases, and high temperatures during flowering cause the flowers to abort. Hot, dry winds also injure the flowers, reducing pod set.

Planting and Care: Beans have one of three growth habits. Indeterminate varieties produce climbing vines several feet tall. These pole, or runner, beans must be trellised. Bush beans are determinate and reach a height of 8 to 24 inches. They are less likely than pole beans to suffer damage in windy locations. The stem tips end with a flower cluster, thus limiting vegetative growth. The half-runner is semi-determinate and reaches heights of several feet. Bush beans are the favorites of many of our gardeners.

The bean root system has nodules that contain the *Rhizobium* bacteria. These bacteria convert atmospheric nitrogen into a form

FUN FACTS

Beans were grown in Central America at least seven thousand years ago. Columbus introduced them into Europe, from whence they were carried throughout the world by the Portuguese and Spanish explorers. Colonial settlers in New England adopted Native American ways of growing and preparing beans. Succotash and Boston baked beans are Native American dishes. The snap bean is also called the string bean, though most varieties today have no strings. (Strings were the fibrous material in the pod that had to be removed to make the bean palatable.) This characteristic was selected out of varieties over a century ago but the name persists.

useful to the plant. You can buy packages of these bacteria to treat your bean seeds before planting, but you really don't have to. The bacteria are usually present in the soil and there is no conclusive evidence that adding this inoculant increases yields.

Snap bean pods are cylindrical or flat, 3 to 8 inches long, and green to yellow to purple in color. Yellow-podded beans are called wax beans. Seed colors can be yellow, white, purple, red, green, black, or brown.

Trellis pole beans when you plant the seeds, or center a tripod over each hill made of eight-foot poles, 1 to 2 inches in diameter. You'll damage the root systems if you try to erect a trellis after the plants are up.

Beans are low to moderate feeders and respond little to fertilizer. Preplant fertilizer will satisfy their needs for the season. They are very sensitive to salts so keep all fertilizers at least eight inches away from the plant stems. Excessive nitrogen causes excessive vine growth, reduces pod set, and delays maturity.

Beans are very sensitive to moisture stress, as well. Lack of water, especially during flowering, decreases yield.

Besides classifying beans as pole or bush, we group snap beans by pod shape (cylindrical or flat), or by whether they will be shelled. Beans grown for their immature green seeds are called "horticultural" beans, while those grown for their mature seeds are called "dry" beans.

Harvesting: Bush beans have shorter seasons and ripen all at once, while pole beans ripen over an extended period, making them more useful for smaller families.

Harvest snap beans about 50 to 80 days after planting, depending upon the variety and growing conditions, picking the pods when they are about 3 to 5 inches long and while their seeds are still small and tender. Large bumps along the pods indicate seeds that are too mature.

──WHAT HAPPENED HERE?──

MY BEAN PLANTS DROPPED THEIR FLOWERS AND SMALL PODS – Hot weather and moisture stress during flowering causes this.

MY BUSH BEANS LOOK LIKE SMALL POLE BEANS – You may have applied too much nitrogen.

MY BEAN LEAVES HAVE COTTONY PATCHES ON THEIR UNDERSIDES – This sounds like mildew. Pull up and discard infected plants (do not compost).

Dry shell beans should remain on the plants until the pods mature and dry.

Recommended Snap Bean Varieties

Variety	Days to Maturity	Comments
Tendercrop	54	Heirloom; green, bush; 5–6-in. pods
Jade	53	Green, bush; 6–7-in. pods; stress tolerant
Provider	50	Green, bush; 5-in. pods; widely adapted
Goldrush	53	Yellow, bush
Rocdor	52	Yellow, bush; 6-in. pods
Royal Burgundy	55	Purple, bush; 5-in. pods
Kentucky Wonder	64	Heirloom; green, pole; 9–10-in. pods
Romano	65	Green, pole; freezes well

SPINACH

Spinacea oleracea

Family: Chenopodiaceae — Goosefoot

Direct Seed or Transplant: Direct Seed
Optimum Range of Soil Temperature for Germination: 45–75°F
Minimum Soil Temperature for Germination: 35°F
Seed Planting Depth: ¼ inch
Seed Spacing Within Row: 1 inch
Depth of Root System: Shallow
Thinned Spacing Within Row: 2–6 inches
Distance Between Rows: 12–36 inches
Consumption of Nitrogen: Moderate
Days to Maturity: 37–45
Average Yield per 10-foot Row: 4 lbs.

There are two types of spinach leaves. Savoy-type spinach has very crinkly and thick leaves with good tooth appeal. Unfortunately, the crinkly nature of Savoy-type leaves holds more soil, making careful washing necessary. For this reason, some gardeners prefer to plant the smooth-leaf spinach.

Spinach is an annual plant that forms a rosette of leaves when it's grown under cool conditions, but in the long days and high temperatures of summer it will quickly bolt. It is shallow rooted, with most of its roots within two inches of the soil surface.

This hardy crop withstands light freezes to 20°F, though it makes its best growth at temperatures of 60 to 65°F and doesn't tolerate temperatures above 77°F well. It is grown as a spring and fall crop in the Rocky Mountains.

FUN FACTS

This native to central Asia was first cultivated by the Arabs. The plant spread into China, where it was being cultivated by the seventh century. The Moors carried it into Spain around 1000 A.D. and from there it had spread into the rest of Europe by the fourteenth century. It was not widely grown in northern Europe until the eighteenth century. Its use on church fast days was first recorded in 1351, and it graced the table of King Richard II in 1390. Its precise date of introduction into the United States is not known, but it was commonly grown here by 1800.

Planting and Care: For baby spinach, sow seeds as close as ¾ inch apart and snip the plants, leaving an inch or so of stem, as they get to your perfect size. Plants will regrow and give you several harvests of delicious greens. Sow seeds for fall crops about six weeks before the first frost. Plants are usually ready to begin thinning and harvesting within 21 to 35 days after planting.

Spinach does well in most soils, but plants grown in soil with a pH above 6.5 may become yellow and, if the soil pH is lower than 5.5, plants will be severely stunted.

This crop does best with high fertility, so spread manure in fall prior to spring planting and turn under a green manure crop as well. Broadcast some fertilizer before planting and sidedress when the plants are a few inches high.

Keep the soil uniformly moist with a soaker hose to avoid wetting the foliage. Spinach is very susceptible to air pollution. Both ozone and sulfur dioxide will cause the leaf edges to die, as well as leaf speckling to occur.

Harvesting: If you want large, uniform plants, thin them about 4 to 6 inches apart in the row. If you care only for the greens and do not care about the shape or size of the plants, don't bother. Instead, thin by harvesting the largest plants for dinner and let the smaller ones grow. You may harvest single leaves or entire plants. Begin to harvest your crop when it has developed 5 to 6 leaves and continue until just before it bolts, cutting the plants at the soil line.

Recommended Spinach Varieties

Variety	Days to Maturity	Comments
Melody	42	AAS Selection; most popular Savoy type; low bolting susceptibility
Whale	37	Moderately tolerant to bolting; smooth leaf
Bloomsdale Longstanding	48	Heirloom; holds quality; smooth leaf; low bolting susceptibility
Tyee	40	Bolt resistant; Savoy type

WHAT HAPPENED HERE?

THE PLANTS GREW TALL AND FLOWERED BEFORE THE HARVEST WAS OVER – Spinach bolts in warm weather. You can try planting earlier in spring or later in the season for a fall crop.

MY SPINACH LEAVES HAVE TUNNELS IN THEM – Leaf miner adults are small flies that lay their eggs inside the leaves. The maggots hatch and burrow between the upper and lower surfaces of the leaves. Try using row covers at planting to prevent the adults from laying eggs. Pick and remove heavily infested leaves from your garden. Tear off the small tunneled areas and eat the rest of the leaf.

SUMMER SQUASH

Cucurbita spp.

Family: Cucurbitaceae — Gourd

warm-season vegetable

Direct Seed or Transplant: Either, but usually direct seeded

Optimum Range of Soil Temperature for Germination: 70–95°F

Minimum Soil Temperature for Germination: 60°F

Optimum Range of Soil Temperature for Planting: 65–75°F

Minimum Soil Temperature for Planting: 60°F

Seed Planting Depth: ½–1 inch

Seed Spacing Within Row: 12 inches (plants); 48 inches (hills)

Depth of Root System: Moderate

Thinned Spacing Within Row: 24–36 inches (also see text)

Distance Between Rows: 36–48 inches (also see text)

Ease of Transplant: Requires special care

Consumption of Nitrogen: Moderate

Days to Maturity: 40–50

Average Yield per 10-foot Row: 20 lbs.

Grow your own transplants:

Optimum Range of Soil Temperature for Germination: 70–95°F

Approximate Length of Germination Period: 6–10 days

Approximate Time to Grow to Transplant Size: 4–5 weeks

Squash do better in cooler climates than cucumbers and melons. Summer squash need only about 40 to 60 days to produce a crop and are eaten at an immature stage before their rinds harden.

Dry, sunny weather is important for good pollination, though drought conditions reduce fruit set. Most summer squash form bushy plants that are easy to control.

All squash plants are *monoecious*; that is, they bear separate

FUN FACTS

Squash belong to four species—Cucurbita pepo, C. maxima, C. moschata, and C. mixta—all originating in the area from the southwestern United States to the Andes Mountains. All squash have fine-grained flesh and summer squash are eaten as vegetables with meals. Summer squash mature in a relatively short season but store poorly.

male and female flowers in the ratio of about three female to one male. The male flowers appear first in the season. Plants within a species intercross, and certain species will cross with other species. For example, plants in *C. moschata* will cross with those in *C. pepo* and *C. mixta*. Don't worry about strange fruit unless you save the seeds for planting the following season. See the profile on winter squash (page 302) for a complete table on squash intercrosses.

Planting and Care: Be sure the soil has warmed to at least 60°F (warmer is better) before planting. Drop several seeds into a hill and thin to 2 to 3 plants when they have formed their first leaves. Squash are best thinned by pinching out unwanted plants rather than pulling them out if sown close together. You can also transplant squash to the garden. Space hills 48 inches apart.

Squash are heavy feeders. Summer squash do well in soil supplied with high amounts of organic matter; add a spadeful of composted manure or compost to each hill at planting. Broadcast preplant fertilizer and sidedress when the first flowers bloom.

You must supply plenty of moisture to summer squash with watering cans or soaker hoses; wetting the foliage with sprinklers encourages diseases.

Summer squash come in many colors and shapes. Most common are fruit that are green, yellow, or white and that are round and flat (patty pan), straight (straight-necked), club-shaped (zucchini), or curved (crook-necked). Yellow crook-necked squash are passing out of favor because so much of the fruit is lost in trimming the crooked neck.

Recommended Summer Squash Varieties

Variety	Days to Maturity	Comments
Ambassador	47	Zucchini type
Raven	48	Zucchini type; very dark green fruit
Multipik	50	Yellow straightneck
Early Prolific Straightneck	50	AAS Selection; heirloom; yellow; heavy yields
Meteor	49	Golden zucchini
Patty Pan	50	Heirloom; patty pan type; "meaty"
Scallopini	48	AAS Selection; Zucchini/ patty pan hybrid
Early White Bush Scallop	53	Heirloom; patty pan type

Harvesting: Pick summer squash 2 to 8 days after bloom (40 to 60 days after planting) when the fruit is 4 to 8 inches long, 2 inches in diameter (3 to 4 inches in diameter for patty pan squash), and the rind is still soft. Never let the fruit mature on the vine as doing so signals the plant to stop flowering. Besides, mature summer squash are seedy and lousy to eat. If you can't use all the squash then give some to your neighbors until you wear out your welcome.

WHAT HAPPENED HERE?

I HAVE WONDERFUL LOOKING SQUASH VINES, BUT LITTLE FRUIT – This is probably due to poor pollination. **MY SQUASH VINES GROW WELL, THEN THEY SUDDENLY WILT** – Look for a little hole with sawdust–like material in the stem at the soil line. If you find one, slit the stem lengthwise with a razor blade, passing through the hole and cutting the worm, a squash vine borer. Mound soil over the slit and the plant will root at that spot.

SWEET CORN

Zea mays var. *saccharata*

Family: Gramineae — Grass

Direct Seed or Transplant: Direct Seed
Optimum Range of Soil Temperature for Germination: 60–95°F
Minimum Soil Temperature for Germination: 50°F
Seed Planting Depth: ½–1 inch
Seed Spacing Within Row: 4–6 inches
Depth of Root System: Shallow
Thinned Spacing Within Row: 8–12 inches
Distance Between Rows: 30–42 inches
Consumption of Nitrogen: Heavy
Days to Maturity: 64–95
Average Yield per 10-foot Row: 2 dozen ears

warm-season vegetable

Corn is a tropical and subtropical plant that does not grow in soil temperature below 50°F and grows very slowly at 60°F and at 95°F. The best soil temperatures for corn are between 70 to 85°F. Corn does not grow well in hot nights, contrary to popular myth. Nearly the entire stalk of a corn plant is telescoped back into the seedling; much of the plant's growth is simply an elongation of the internodes. Tasseling begins at the seven-leaf stage. Each tassel produces up to 50,000 pollen grains for each silk produced by the ear.

Each strand of silk (female flower) is attached to one kernel. Each corn stalk produces 1 to 3 ears and 1 tassel. The first ear forms in the middle of the stalk and will be the largest. After pollination, ears rapidly enlarge, collecting sugars from the leaves. The more leaves, the more sugar (and the sweeter the fruit).

FUN FACTS

Corn is one of the few native American vegetables. The plant grew in Mexico at least eighty thousand years ago and was cultivated in southern Mexico at least seven centuries ago. Ancestors of our modern corn type had a tassel at the tip of each ear. Columbus brought corn to Europe in 1493, where it was called "turkey corn," and eventually introduced it back into the United States.

The corn of historical record is the dent corn (also called "cow corn" or "field corn"), grown for feed and meal. Lt. Richard Bagnal, a member of General Sullivan's 1779 expedition against the Six Nations, found the Iroquois raising sweet corn and brought some back to New England. It immediately was accepted and by 1820 had become a major crop. Sweet corn is a mutant "cow" corn wherein the conversion of sugar to starch is retarded. Until the twentieth century people preferred white corn, feeling that yellow corn was fit only for animal feed.

Flowering in corn is a function of daylength. Long, hot days favor stalk growth, while short, cool days favor flowering and ear formation. Tropical varieties won't flower in temperate areas until daylength shortens to about twelve hours. Northern varieties flower under long days and cooler temperatures; select northern varieties for your garden.

Planting and Care: Corn seeds will not germinate in soil temperatures below 50°F. At 55°F, it takes about three weeks for the seeds to germinate; at 75°F, only about four days.

Plant corn seeds in short "blocks" to aid pollination. Short rows should be spaced three feet apart. Thin the corn plants when they are about 5 inches tall to stand 10 inches apart. Overcrowded plants produce small ears with poor tipfill.

Plant early-, midseason-, and late-ripening varieties at the same time, or make successive plantings of the same variety about ten days apart to extend the harvest season.

Corn has a shallow, fibrous root system and is moderately tolerant of soils with higher pH as long as the soils are fertile. Broadcast preplant fertilizer, and improve the soil with large amounts of organic material. Sidedress your corn at least once during the season, especially if the lower leaves begin to yellow.

Corn doesn't tolerate flooding or drought. Drought will stunt the stalks, rot the silk, and ears will be poorly filled and stubby. A tip: if you see that the corn leaves are tightly rolled, you'd better water right away.

There are huge numbers of corn varieties available: white, yellow, and bicolor. Most of these are hybrids selected for their increased pest resistance and sugar content. Many of their classes have confusing names. Classes are constantly changing, and catalogs use different systems. Here is a small sampling.

Sugary class ("normal," "traditional," "sugar," "standard," and "su" class): This is the standard sweet corn we know from the old days. It contains 10 to 15 percent sugar and has a creamy texture. The sugar turns into starch rapidly during maturation and the corn goes downhill fast.

Sugary-enhanced class ("su se," "se+," or "se" class): This corn has twice as much sugar as those in the sugary class and the kernels have the same creamy texture. Although the sugar converts to starch at the same rate as in the sugary class, this type of corn has more to begin with, so it remains sweeter longer.

Shrunken-2 class ("sh2," "supersweets," and "extrasweets"): These develop 2 to 3 times more sugar than the su type, which is converted to starch more slowly. Because of its lower starch content, the kernels have a crunchy rather than creamy texture. Further, seeds germinate poorly in cool soil and under water stress. Plant them later than those of the se or su types. These varieties usually don't yield as much as the su and se varieties and some folks find this corn far too sweet.

Augmented class: Here breeders have combined different sweetness genes. These are sweeter than the su types and have the same creamy texture.

ADX class: These contain a combination of three sweetness genes and the sugar levels are as high as those of the supersweets, but there are few good varieties available.

Now, which class is right for you? If you have a sweet tooth, choose one of the sweeter types. If you like the old-fashioned creamy taste, stick with the sugary class. But remember, sweet corns cross-pollinate and that could spell trouble. A supersweet pollinated by a sugary variety will become "normal." So, isolate the supersweet (sh2) varieties from other types. Follow these rules:

1. You may plant different varieties of the same class near each other, for most classes, without influencing the sugar content.

2. Isolate varieties of Shrunken-2 and ADX types since cross-pollination will make their kernels starchy. Pollen from these makes kernels of the sugary and sugary-enhanced starchy too.

3. Different colored corns can cross-pollinate. Pollen from a yellow variety landing on the silks of a white variety will cause the kernels to which those silks are attached to become yellow. If it lands on silks of a bicolor, it will increase the number of yellow kernels. Pollen from a white variety will not change the color of kernels. To be sure, isolate varieties by at least 250 feet or plant them to ripen at least 14 days apart.

In addition to a number of diseases, sweet corn is troubled by a couple of physiological disorders.

Poor tipfill results from poor pollination. Hot winds, temperatures above 96°F, and drought stress interfere with pollination.

Shriveled kernels near the tip indicate a lack of nitrogen.

As corn matures from the edible "milk" stage (about 20 days after pollination) to the dry "dent" stage, sugar converts to starch and quality decreases. Examine the corn about 20 days after silking. Silks will have begun to dry and the kernels will feel plump. Crush a kernel with your finger. If clear liquid comes out and the kernels are small, the corn is in the immature "pre-milk" stage. If "milk" (starchy semi-liquid) squirts out, the ear has reached prime eating quality. Corn passes from the "milk" stage into the starchy "early dough" stage in less than a week. You can still eat it in this stage but it is noticeably less sweet and much more "pasty." When it has reached the "dough" stage it's ready for the birds.

Harvesting: Harvest the ears by snapping them from the stalk and cool them to 32°F immediately by plunging them into ice water. The best way to eat corn is to have the pot boiling when you pick it.

Recommended Sweet Corn Varieties

Variety	Days to Maturity	Comments
Spring Treat	66	se+; yellow; very early; good in cold soil
Sugar Buns	70	se+; yellow; 7-in. ears; long harvest
Silver Queen	91	su; white; standard late season
Xtra Tender 270A	71	sh2; bicolor
Earlivee	67	Heirloom; su; yellow; adapted to cold soil; 8-in. ears
Early Sunglow	66	Heirloom; su; yellow; 7-in. ears
Northern Xtra Sweet	63	sh2; yellow; 8-in. ears
Butter and Sugar	73	su; bicolor; 7-in. ears
Bodacious	75	se+; yellow; 8-in. ears

WHAT HAPPENED HERE?

I GET VERY FEW GOOD EARS OF CORN – The corn may have had poor pollination. Plant corn in small blocks and remember, you'll only get a couple of ears on each stalk anyway unless you plant 'Six Shooter'.

THE KERNELS AT THE TIPS OF THE EARS DO NOT DEVELOP – This is due to poor tipfill. It's usually caused by poor pollination and/or bad weather during silking.

MY CORN SEEDLINGS ARE ALL LYING ON TOP OF THE SOIL AND THE SEEDS ARE MISSING – Birds probably pulled out the seedlings to get to the seed. Get a cat, but remember the problem disappears as the seedlings grow.

MY CORN PRODUCES LITTLE EARS IN THE TASSEL AND LITTLE TASSELS IN THE EAR – Climatic stress, such as long, cool springs following early periods of warm weather, produce these abnormalities.

HOW DO I CONTROL EARWIGS IN MY CORN SILK? – They really aren't damaging your corn. Pull the husks off the ears outside and flick them to the side.

SWISS CHARD

Beta vulgaris

Family: Chenopodiaceae — Goosefoot

cool-season vegetable

Direct Seed or Transplant: Either
Optimum Range of Soil Temperature for Germination: 50–85°F
Minimum Soil Temperature for Germination: 40°F
Optimum Range of Soil Temperature for Planting: 60–65°F
Minimum Soil Temperature for Planting: 40°F
Seed Planting Depth: ½ inch
Seed Spacing Within Row: 2 inches
Depth of Root System: Moderate to deep
Thinned Spacing Within Row: 4–12 inches
Distance Between Rows: 24–36 inches
Ease of Transplant: Easy
Consumption of Nitrogen: Moderate
Days to Maturity: 50–60
Average Yield per 10-foot Row: 5 plants

This cool-season vegetable crop tolerates high temperatures better than other greens (except New Zealand spinach) and is grown through the summer in our region. Grow it as you would beets.

Planting and Care: You can easily transplant Swiss chard as soon as the danger of hard frost has passed but there is really no need to do so. Most gardeners direct seed it. Thin the young plants to stand about 4 inches apart at first, then 10 inches apart as they begin to crowd. Transplant the thinnings or use them as tender greens. If you use the small Swiss chard leaves leave the plants at closer spacings. If you want larger

FUN FACTS

Swiss chard is a beet grown for its tops only; it does not develop a swollen root. Aristotle and Theophrastus described several varieties in the fourth century B.C. and Pliny described one grown for its thick stems.

plants and leaves then thin plants to stand farther apart.

Spring planted Swiss chard lasts through summer and well into fall. It is adaptable to soil types so long as they are fertile and well drained, but it does respond well to large amounts of organic matter. Broadcast preplant fertilizer and sidedress at least once if you plan on carrying the plants into fall.

Regular Swiss chard varieties have thick, dark-green crumpled leaves and green-white leaf stalks, though some interesting varieties have brilliantly colored or multicolored stalks.

Recommended Swiss Chard Varieties

Variety	Days to Maturity	Comments
Fordhook Giant	60	Heirloom; green leaves, thick stalks
Virgo	60	Green leaves, thick bright white stalks; crinkled leaves
Bright Lights	60	AAS Selection; multicolored stalks
Rhubarb	60	Heirloom; bright red leaf stalks

Harvesting: Harvest about 60 days after planting by cutting the entire plant at the soil line or by removing the outer stalks over time about 1 to 2 inches above the soil line. Take care not to damage the small bud at the center of the plant and the plant will continue to produce new leaves until fall. Swiss chard freezes very well and maintains its wonderful flavor.

---WHAT HAPPENED HERE?---

MY SWISS CHARD HAS LIGHT BROWN TUNNELS IN THE LEAVES – These are leaf miner tunnels. Remove and destroy heavily infested leaves. Snip out damaged portions of lightly infested leaves and eat the good portions. Keep the garden area clear of lambsquarters, a weed that harbors leaf miners.

I CUT MY SWISS CHARD BUT IT DID NOT RESPROUT – You can harvest a few leaves of the Swiss chard plant or you can harvest the whole plant. If you cut the plant a few inches off the ground it will form new stems and leaves for later harvest; cutting it to the ground prevents satisfactory regrowth.

TOMATO

Lycopersicon lycopersicum
Family: Solanaceae — Potato or Nightshade

Direct Seed or Transplant: Either, but usually transplants
Optimum Range of Soil Temperature for Germination: 60–85°F
Minimum Soil Temperature for Germination: 50°F
Optimum Range of Soil Temperature for Planting: 70–75°F
Minimum Soil Temperature for Planting: 65°F
Seed Planting Depth: ¼–½ inch
Seed Spacing Within Row: 12–24 inches
Depth of Root System: Deep
Thinned Spacing Within Row: 18–24 inches staked
Distance Between Rows: 36–60 inches
Ease of Transplant: Easy
Consumption of Nitrogen: Moderate
Days to Maturity: 60–90
Average Yield per 10-foot Row: 15 lbs.
Grow your own transplants:
Optimum Range of Soil Temperature for Germination: 70–75°F
Approximate Length of Germination Period: 4–9 days
Approximate Time to Grow to Transplant Size: 5–6 weeks

warm-season vegetable

The tomato requires a growing season of 60 to 120 days from transplant. Daytime temperatures of about 70°F are best. The plant stops growing at temperatures above 95°F and below 53°F and is killed by long exposure to temperatures below 50°F. Plants require ample water throughout the season, but water droplets falling on the surface of ripening fruit can crack them.

Tomato plants have one of three growth habits in varying degrees: indeterminate, determinate, and semi-determinate. A determinate vine produces several flower clusters each separated by a leaf or two, then terminates with a flower cluster. This results in many side branches. The growth of each side branch is similar to that of the main stem. This gives a compact plant with a concentrated period of fruit ripening. For ease of harvest, you can use a tomato cage for determinate types.

Plants with the indeterminate habit have a central shoot that continues to grow throughout the season. Side shoots are short with few branches. Flower clusters, usually separated by 3 to 4 leaves, are produced along the vine. Fruit produced on older, lower clusters ripen first, followed by fruit on progressively younger clusters. The vine sprawls but it can be trellised, and the fruit ripen over a long period of time.

Semi-determinate types have characteristics between the other two. They may have several lateral flower clusters with the main stem ending in a flower cluster as well. Flower clusters develop directly from the stems and not in the leaf axils. The flowers are borne in groups called inflorescences, each having 4 to 12 or more flowers. Fruit develop after pollination but development on the plant is uneven since not all flowers are pollinated at the same time.

Optimum pollination temperatures are between 60 and 70°F. Daytime temperatures above 85°F and nighttime temperatures above 70°F or below 55°F during bloom reduce fruit set. Low humidity, wind, excess nitrogen, insufficient light, and drought cause flowers to abort.

Planting and Care: Many gardeners in our region transplant to start their tomatoes. Good tomato sets should be 6 to 8 inches tall and have stocky, pencil-thick stems with 4 to 6 dark-green leaves. Properly hardened plants have a slight purpling on the stem and the leaf veins.

Tomato sets that have become too tall dry out rapidly and may blow over if planted at the usual depth. Instead, plant them deeply or dig a small trench within the row and lay their stems along the bottom with the top several inches of the plant aboveground. Fill in the trench and roots will sprout along the buried stem. When planting deeply, pinch off any leaves that would be buried to reduce the chances of rot. Don't plant tomato transplants that are in bloom or that have small fruit, for their growth will be slow and the plants will produce poorly.

Tomatoes respond well to moderately high fertility, but excess

FUN FACTS

Tomatoes probably originated in the Andes Mountains of Bolivia and Peru and the Aztecs and Incas developed these early types into today's large-fruited forms. Early European explorers carried tomato seeds to Italy where the plants had gained notice by 1544 and whence it spread into France, Germany, and other continental countries by 1600. The French and the southern Italians relished it, but the British thought it poisonous, probably because of its relationship to belladonna. This prejudice carried over into the American colonies. While the tomato was grown in the Carolinas and Georgia in the early 1700s and even had its virtues extolled by Thomas Jefferson in 1781, the plant was not generally cultivated in the United States until 1835. It was not until the latter part of the nineteenth century that it came under extensive commercial cultivation. The 'Mikado' tomato was the first commercially available hybrid vegetable (in 1882).

nitrogen delays maturity and results in "vineyness" and too many small green fruit. Broadcast fertilizer just before planting and sidedress when plants have become established and again after they have set several fruit. Don't fertilize again.

Plants under water stress during their early development may

 never recover, and plants that receive insufficient water during bloom time may develop blossom-end rot.

Sprinklers are satisfactory for watering during the first half of the plant's development and they won't knock off the flowers as some people believe. During the second half of development, however, use soaker hoses since wetting the fruit during ripening can crack them.

Red plastic mulch is ideal for tomato plants and promotes earlier maturity. Straw mulch or grass clippings are also fine but may slow growth in cooler soils.

Tomato plants will trail along the ground unless they're supported. Sprawling vines do bear the most fruit, but they ripen later and are more damage-prone. If you decide to let them sprawl, apply a thick layer of straw mulch around the plants to keep the fruit off the ground.

Supports increase the yield of good fruit, make picking easier, save space, and reduce the chances of stepping on vines. The most common method is to drive a 6-foot stake 2 feet into the ground 3 to 4 inches from the plant at transplanting. When plants have reached 12 to 15 inches in height, prune them to 2 to 3 stems by pinching off the lateral stems as they appear. Continue to pinch out these "suckers" to avoid overgrowth of flowering stems producing fruit that won't ripen. Fruit on pruned plants can ripen up to 14 days earlier than those on nonpruned plants, though pruned plants won't bear as many fruit and their fruit may have a higher evidence of blossom-end rot. You may prune to only one main stem, but that leaves no security for the crop should that stem be injured. Tie the stems loosely to the stake with soft twine. Knot the twine tightly to the stake about 2 inches above a leaf stem, then wrap it loosely around the stem just below the leaf base. As the plant grows, make new ties about every 12 inches along the stem.

You can buy tomato cages or make them yourself from 4-foot-wide lengths of 4 x 6-inch mesh stock-fencing or concrete reinforcing wire. A piece of fencing 5 feet long will make a cage that's about 18 inches in diameter. Vinyl-covered wire and plastic cages resist rust. Set the cage over a young tomato plant and tie it to four 4-foot stakes driven into the ground. Fruit on caged plants ripen later but are more perfectly shaped than those on staked plants.

Tomato varieties vary according to vine habit, fruit color, size, shape, season of ripening, the area of the country to which they are adapted, and pest resistance, but they can be subdivided into types according to their uses and characteristics.

Beefsteak: There is a 'Beefsteak' variety, but the term is generally applied to any large tomato that has thick, solid flesh with few seed cavities. Most of these require long seasons (about 100 days) to ripen their fruit and are not well adapted to our region.

Container: Although any tomato plant can be grown in a container, varieties that produce small fruit less than 2 inches in diameter on plants less than 24 inches tall are best suited to this method.

Main Crop: This type produces medium to large fruit with varying days to maturity. Most common varieties are of this type.

Paste: Fruit of these contain less water and more meat and are used for paste, canning, and catsup. They are also wonderful to eat fresh.

Salad: These are "cherry" tomatoes with fruit up to 1½ inches in diameter.

White: These are actually a light yellow color.

Recommended Tomato Varieties

Variety	Days to Maturity	Comments
Beefsteak	85	Heirloom; large fruit; indeterminate
Brandywine	78	Heirloom; pink fruit; indeterminate
Abraham Lincoln	75	Heirloom; indeterminate
Better Boy	75	Indeterminate
Early Girl	59	Main crop; indeterminate
Celebrity	70	AAS Selection; main crop; heavy yield; determinate
Roma	76	Heirloom; paste type; classic; indeterminate
Golden Mama	68	Paste type; yellow; indeterminate
Sun Cherry	58	Cherry type; very sweet; indeterminate
Sweet Baby Girl	65	Cherry type; indeterminate
Gold Nugget	56	Cherry type; yellow; very sweet; determinate
Sun Gold	57	Cherry type; orange; extra sweet; indeterminate

Tomatoes can get several physiological disorders. Blossom-end rot is the result of tissue breakdown near the blossom end of the fruit characterized by a sunken, dark brown leathery spot that enlarges as the fruit matures. It is caused by a calcium deficiency in the fruit that is aggravated by fluctuations in soil moisture, excessive nitrogen fertilization, and root damage. It's more of a problem on staked or pruned plants and those that have not been mulched.

Catfacing is most likely to occur on early ripening fruit when the faded blossom sticks to the fruit tissue during cool, cloudy weather, causing the blossom end to become malformed.

Sunscald occurs when green fruit are exposed to direct sun.

This causes a greenish-white patch to develop on the exposed shoulder and is most apt to occur on fruit of pruned or partially defoliated plants.

Growth cracks occur when the fruit skin cannot stretch fast enough to accommodate growth. This results from extreme changes in fruit growth rate due to large and sudden moisture fluctuations and temperatures above 90°F. Radial cracking begins at the stem end and radiates out over the fruit surface. Concentric cracking occurs in concentric circles around the stem end of the fruit. Never water tomatoes heavily following an extended drought and never sprinkle water onto the surfaces of maturing fruit. Also, plant crack-resistant varieties.

Harvesting: Tomato fruit ripen 6 to 8 weeks after bloom. The lowest temperature at which they will ripen properly is 55°F though the optimum temperature is 68°F. Even a brief exposure of green fruit to 40°F destroys the enzyme responsible for proper ripening. Temperatures above 80°F inhibit the development of red color and otherwise "red" fruit turn yellow-orange. Leave fruit on the vine until they are fully ripe and just begin to soften. If temperatures are expected to remain above 80°F or if frost is expected, harvest the fruit when they begin to develop mature color and ripen them indoors at about 70°F.

——WHAT HAPPENED HERE?——

MY TOMATO PLANTS LOOK VERY HEALTHY AND GROW TALL AND BUSHY, BUT THEY PRODUCE FEW FRUIT THAT NEVER RIPEN – You might be fertilizing with too much nitrogen, watering too much, or the nights might be too hot. Pinch the terminal shoot and decrease the watering and fertilizing.

MY TOMATO PLANTS TOOK FOREVER TO BEGIN GROWING – Tomato plants will not grow when night temperatures fall into the 50s; planting them early will not necessarily give you an earlier crop, so don't jump the gun.

MY TOMATO PLANTS' BLOSSOMS DROP OFF BEFORE PRODUCING ANY FRUIT – This is common on cool nights when the temperatures fall into the 50s or when night temperatures remain in the mid–80s.

TURNIP

Brassica rapa (Rapifera group)
Family: Cruciferae (or Brassicaceae) — Mustard

cool-season vegetable

Direct Seed or Transplant: Direct Seed
Optimum Range of Soil Temperature for Germination: 60–105°F
Minimum Soil Temperature for Germination: 40°F
Seed Planting Depth: ¼–½ inch
Seed Spacing Within Row: ½–1 inch
Depth of Root System: Moderate
Thinned Spacing Within Row: 2–6 inches
Distance Between Rows: 12–36 inches
Consumption of Nitrogen: High
Days to Maturity: 40–75
Average Yield per 10-foot Row: 5 lbs.

Like rutabaga, the turnip is grown for its large, tasty root and both have varieties with yellow and white flesh. The two vegetables have similar cultural requirements. Turnip roots may be round, elongated, or conic in shape, and are slightly flattened. The greens sprout directly from the roots, which are usually white to tan with purple near their top. Turnips may also have green or bronze skin. The leaves are hairy, thin, and green.

Planting and Care: Turnips tolerate low temperatures and you must time planting so the roots mature during cool weather; roots get bitter and woody in hot weather, but prolonged exposure of young plants to 50 to 55°F will cause them to bolt.

You can plant turnips as a spring or fall crop but a fall crop usually has better flavor. Spring crops usually need fairly high amounts of fertilizer to mature before warm weather hits. Broadcast fertilizer before planting and sidedress your plants when you thin them. High fertility is not so important for fall as the weather cools and plant growth slows. Turnips are sensitive to boron deficiency but before adding boron, have your soil levels tested for boron and watch for brown heart, an indicator of low boron.

FUN FACTS

The turnip has been used for food since prehistoric times and grows wild in Siberia. The Romans grew it for its leaves and enlarged root and later introduced the plant into other parts of Europe, where it was widely grown in France in the Middle Ages. It was introduced into England in the middle of the sixteenth century. Turnips were brought to Canada in 1540 by Cartier and were being cultivated in Virginia by 1609. The turnip is slowly being replaced on American tables by the tastier potato and by its close relative the rutabaga, which has higher nutritional value.

Brown heart is a browning and breakdown of flesh at the center of the root that typically shows up in warm weather when the plants are growing rapidly. It can be corrected for your next crop by adding borax to the soil but there is a fine line between not having enough boron and having too much! Excessive levels of boron will sterilize your soil. Always follow the recommendations of a professional soil-testing lab before applying any boron-containing compound to your soil.

Harvesting: Turnip roots are tastiest when they are 2 to 3 inches in diameter and mature in cool weather. Harvest the entire crop before the weather gets too hot. If you're growing turnips for their greens, harvest them about 4 to 6 weeks after planting.

——WHAT HAPPENED HERE?——

THERE IS BROWNING OF THE ROOT CORE – This is typically caused by a boron deficiency. Have your soil professionally tested and follow the lab's instructions regarding any amendments.

THERE ARE "SHOT HOLES" IN THE LEAVES – Shot holes in the leaves of plants are usually caused by flea beetles. Flea beetles are small (1/16"), usually dark-colored beetles that travel on the wind. Row covers applied at planting are effective in protecting your garden.

MY TURNIPS HAVE TUNNELS IN THEIR ROOTS – Root maggots cause damage to many root crops. They overwinter in the soil, so rotate your vegetables next year and don't plant susceptible vegetables in that spot. The adult of the root maggot is a flying insect, and may be excluded from an uninfested location with the use of row covers at planting. Row covers will not help if they are placed over an area where the root maggot has overwintered.

Recommended Turnip Varieties

Variety	Days to Maturity	Comments
Purple Top White Globe	60	Heirloom; nicely shaped; excellent for fresh or winter storage; white-fleshed roots
Shogoin'	70	Heirloom; grown for leaves and roots
Seven Top	50	Heirloom; grown for leaves; roots are inedible

WATERMELON

Citrullus lanatus
Family: Cucurbitaceae — Gourd

Direct Seed or Transplant: Transplant
Optimum Range of Soil Temperature for Planting: 70–85°F
Minimum Soil Temperature for Planting: 65°F
Depth of Root System: Deep
Transplant Spacing Within Row: 24–36 inches
Distance Between Rows: 6–8 feet
Ease of Transplant: Requires special care
Consumption of Nitrogen: Heavy
Days to Maturity: 75–95
Average Yield per 10-Foot Row: 7 melons
Grow your own transplants:
Optimum Range of Soil Temperature for Germination: 80–90°F
Approximate Length of Germination Period: 3–12 days
Approximate Time to Grow to Transplant Size: 4 weeks

warm-season vegetable

Watermelon seedlings are damaged very easily. Young plants will be set back by any frost or cultivation damage during their first week of growth. Vine growth is upright at first, but after the first six leaves have formed, the plants begin to run.

As in cucumbers, watermelons are *monoecious,* meaning they have both male and female flowers; the male flowers are the first to bloom, followed by the female flowers several days later. Watermelon plants usually bear only 1 or 2 good-sized fruit.

Planting and Care: Set each transplant at the indicated spacings and if you use peat pots be sure to plant the entire pot containing the plant. Do not remove the plants from the pots, since any damage to their root system may doom your crop.

Watermelons should receive enough fertilizer to sustain uninterrupted growth throughout the season. Good vine growth is important to supply sugar to the fruit. Apply a preplant fertilizer and sidedress the plants just before they begin to run.

Watermelons are more drought tolerant than muskmelons, but all melons should receive plenty of water throughout their season. Water is especially critical during fruit set and growth. Avoid wetting the foliage by using drip irrigation whenever possible. All melons are highly susceptible to both powdery and downy mildews, which destroy the leaves and leave your melons bitter or tasteless.

Melons do a fine job of weed control once they begin to run, but until that time, it's up to you to keep weeds away. Allow the soil to warm prior to any mulching. Use plastic tunnels to increase both your early and total yields.

Northern and high elevation gardeners should try the "icebox"

FUN FACTS

Watermelons are heat-loving, long-season members of the same family as muskmelons. They are thought to have originated in Africa, where, in the nineteenth century, the famous explorer Dr. David Livingstone discovered fields of wild melons. They were also reported by European settlers in the United States as being grown in the Illinois River Valley by Native Americans in the early 1600s. Since it is fairly unlikely the watermelon originated in the Americas, perhaps the "Indian melon" was actually a native citron and not a watermelon.

types of watermelons. These are small (about 10 pounds) and round and require only 70 to 80 days to ripen their fruit.

Most seedless watermelons require a longer growing season and gardeners in our region will have to start their plants early. You'll also have to plant a "normal" variety alongside the seedless plants for pollination. Seedless watermelons are not always completely seedless and some seeds may form under stressful conditions.

Harvesting: Watermelon fruit mature about ten weeks after pollination. When fully mature, muskmelon fruit separate from their stems, but watermelons do not. There are a number of indicators to use to tell when watermelons are ripe. First, check the groundspot; this will turn from white to yellow as the fruit matures. The tendril opposite the melon will turn brown or black when the fruit is ripe. And then, there's the not-so-accurate thumping test. When thumped, ripe melons give a dull thud instead of a higher pitched, almost metallic sound of unripe melons. The thumping sound is highly subjective, though, so consider thumping one of your last options (although it is fun). Ripe melons will be brightly colored, juicy, and have a sugar content of about 14 percent (yummy!).

Recommended Watermelon Varieties

Variety	Days to Maturity	Comments
Sugar Baby	70–80	Icebox type
Yellow Baby	70–80	AAS Selection; icebox type
Crimson Sweet	130	Standard size
Charleston Grey	130	Heirloom; standard size

──WHAT HAPPENED HERE?──

THE BLOSSOMS ON MY WATERMELONS DROP AND NO FRUIT SETS – Like cucumbers, the first flowers that appear are male and therefore do not set fruit. Wait.

WINTER SQUASH & PUMPKIN

Cucurbita spp.

Family: Cucurbitaceae — Gourd

Direct Seed or Transplant: Either

Optimum Range of Soil Temperature for Germination: 70–95°F

Minimum Soil Temperature for Germination: 60°F

Optimum Range of Soil Temperature for Planting: 65–75°F

Minimum Soil Temperature for Planting: 60°F

Seed Planting Depth: ½–1 inch

Seed Spacing Within Row: 12 inches (plants); 48 inches (hills)

Depth of Root System: Deep

Thinned Spacing Within Row: 24–36 inches

Distance Between Rows: 7–10 feet

Consumption of Nitrogen: Heavy

Days to Maturity: 85–110

Average Yield per 10-foot Row: 20 lbs.

Grow your own transplants:

Optimum Range of Soil Temperature for Germination: 90°F

Approximate Length of Germination Period: 6–10 days

Approximate Time to Grow to Transplant Size: 4–5 weeks

Also see the Summer Squash profile (page 274) for more information on the growing culture of squash.

Winter squash and pumpkins require a long, warm season from 80 to 140 days. Dry, sunny weather is important for good pollination, though drought conditions can reduce fruit set.

Most winter squash and pumpkin plants are vines, though some bush types are entering the marketplace.

All squash bear separate male and female flowers in the ratio of about three female to one male. The male flowers appear first. Plants within a species can intercross, and certain species will cross with other species. Melons and cucumbers will not cross with squash and pumpkins. Don't worry about it unless you save seeds.

Planting and Care: Be sure the soil has warmed to at least 60°F before planting. Plant seeds of the bush or small vine- forming varieties about 2 feet apart in rows about 5 feet apart, but give the large vine varieties at least 3 feet within rows spaced 7 to 9 feet apart. Drop several seeds into the hill and thin to 2 to 3 plants when they have formed their first leaves. You can also transplant squash to the garden to get a jump on the season.

Winter squash (and pumpkins) grow well when supplied with high amounts of organic matter and moisture, so add a spadeful of composted manure or compost to the bottom of each hill. Broadcast preplant fertilizer and sidedress when the plants begin to run

FUN FACTS

Winter squash, pumpkin, and summer squash originated in the area from the southwestern United States to the Andes Mountains. Columbus brought specimens to Europe, and noted that native peoples allowed vines to climb corn stalks and trees. Pumpkins and squash are botanically inseparable and vary only by cultural methods, use, and flavor. Winter squash have mild, fine-grained flesh and are eaten in pies or as vegetables with meals. Although they are edible, pumpkins are used for stock feed and for decorations primarily. They have stronger-flavored coarse flesh, and orange rinds. Commercially prepared "pumpkin pie" filling is actually made from squash.

(vine types), or when the first flowers open (bush types).

You must supply plenty of moisture to squash with watering cans or soaker hoses; wetting the foliage with sprinklers will only encourage diseases.

Breeders have worked hard to adapt squash to today's gardens and families. Both are generally smaller than those of our grand-parents as there is often no room for large vines and no need for large fruit. For example, the large fruit of 'Hubbard' have been shrunk to manageable size.

Pumpkins are typically round and orange and winter squash are often green, golden, or buff-colored and more or less globed-shaped or cylindrical. Like summer squash, there are several main types of winter squash. Hubbard types have the typical 'Hubbard' shape and may be blue-green or golden and standard sized (up to 50 pounds) or dwarf (several pounds). Delicious types resemble 'Butternut' squash with long, curved necks. Acorn squash form bushy plants with acorn-shaped fruit that may be deep green, white, or golden. Buttercup squash actually look more like acorns than the acorn squash and come complete with the "cap." Every-one knows what the buff-colored butternut squash looks like. The flesh of these holds its firmness in stews. Pumpkins are tradition-ally large and orange but also are available today as large white-fruited types and as miniature orange- and white-fruited types.

Harvesting: Harvest pumpkins and winter squash when they are fully mature (80 to 140 days after planting), and a deep color. You should see no green "veins" on butternut fruit. The fruit rinds should be so hard that your fingernail cannot puncture them. Har-vest them before a frost since even a slight freeze will damage the fruit. Butternut types are especially sensitive to chilling at tem-peratures of 35 to 45°F. Cut them and other squash from the vine, leaving a two-inch piece of stem (a handle) attached to the fruit. Cure the fruit before storage by placing it under cover at 80°F for

10 days. This aids in sealing wounds in the rind. Then, remove them to a dry room at 50°F and about 60 percent relative humidity where they will keep for several months, depending upon type.

Recommended Winter Squash & Pumpkin Varieties

Variety	Days to Maturity	Comments
Blue Hubbard	100	Heirloom; standard large Hubbard type; 12–15 lb. fruit
Dwarf Blue Hubbard	95	Small Hubbard type; 4–6 lb. fruit
Golden Delicious	100	Heirloom; Delicious type
Table Ace	85	Bush acorn type
Table Queen	80	Heirloom; Bush acorn type
Buttercup	95	Heirloom; Buttercup type; 3–5 lb. fruit
Sweet Mama	95	AAS Selection; Buttercup type
Waltham	105	AAS Selection; large-fruited Butternut type; 3–4 lb. fruit
Connecticut Field	120	Heirloom; large orange pumpkin; 20 lb. fruit
Lumina	110	Medium-sized white pumpkin
Baby Boo	95	Miniature white pumpkin
Godiva	110	Pumpkin with hulless seeds for the toasted pumpkin seed trade
Big Max	120	Giant pumpkin; 100 lb. fruit

──WHAT HAPPENED HERE?──

I HAVE WONDERFUL LOOKING SQUASH VINES, BUT FEW FRUIT – This is probably due to poor pollination from lack of bees or from poor weather during bloom.

MY SQUASH VINES GROW WELL, THEN THEY SUDDENLY WILT – Look for a hole filled with sawdust-like material in the stem where the plant leaves the ground. Slit the stem lengthwise, passing through the hole and the small worm that made it.

Some commonly grown cucurbit varieties and their species

Varieties within the same species will cross freely, as will varieties within species with the same superscript.

Cucurbita pepo [a]	*Cucurbita moschata* [a,b]	*Cucurbita maxima* [b]	*Cucurbita mixta* [a]
Pumpkin: Baby Boo, Baby Pam, Cal. Sugar, Big Tom, Caserta, Cheyenne Bush, Cinderella, Conn. Field, Cow, Happy Jack, Halloween, Howden, Jack-Be-Little, Jack o'Lantern, Lady Godiva, N.E. Pie, Pankow	**Pumpkin:** Cheese, Dickinson, Kentucky Field, Long Island, Longfellow, Quaker Pie, Tenn. Sweet Potato	**Pumpkin:** Amish Pie, Atlantic Giant, Big Max, Big Moon, Burgess Giant, German Sweet Potato, Harvest Moon, King of Mammoths	**Pumpkin:** Green Striped Cushaw, Jonathan, Pennsylvania Crookneck, White Cushaw, White Crookneck
Squash: Acorn, Cocozelle, Crookneck, Delicata, Patty Pan, Spaghetti, Straightneck, Sweet Dumpling, Vegetable Marrow, Zucchini	**Squash:** Butternut, Golden Cushaw, Orange Cushaw, Penn. Dutch Crookneck, Small Flat Cheese	**Squash:** Banana, Boston Marrow, Buttercup, Golden Delicious, Hubbard, Hokkaido, Kabocha, Lakota, Turk's Turban	**Squash:** Cushaw

(Source: Gough and Moore-Gough. 1999; Ashworth, 2002.)

Glossary

AAS: All-America Selections. A plant variety that has been tested by a network of independent judges who determine if its garden performance is superior under many conditions. (Visit http://www.all-americaselections.org).

ANNUAL: Plants that complete their entire life cycle in one year.

APEX: The growing tip of a plant part. This could be a root or shoot.

BIENNIAL: Plants that require two growing seasons to complete their life cycle.

BLACKHEART: Disorder of celery caused by a calcium deficiency wherein the inner leaves and growing point turn black.

BLOSSOM END ROT: A disorder caused by a calcium deficiency and often related to water movement. BER affects fruiting plants, especially tomatoes, peppers, and cucurbits, and causes the flower end of a fruit to become brown and leathery.

BOLT: A plant that goes to seed as a result of daylength or temperatures.

BUTTONING: The premature formation of a small curd on cauliflower. No further curd expansion occurs.

CAP: The group of sepals (calyx) of an eggplant fruit.

COLE CROPS: Members of the Mustard family, also known as Cruciferae or Brassicaceae. These crops are also sometimes referred to as "crucifers."

COTYLEDON: A seed leaf. The first "leaf."

CROSS-POLLINATION: The spread of pollen from anthers of one plant to the stigma of another, resulting in the production of a seed with the genetic characteristics of both parents.

CULTIVAR: A cultivated variety of a plant. Cultivars are nearly always the result of selective breeding by man.

CURD: The "head" of a cauliflower.

DAMPING OFF: A fungal disease causing seedling stems to collapse at the soil surface and the plant to fall over and die.

DAYS TO HARVEST: The number found on seed packaging that may be used to compare the earliness or lateness of harvest of the variety to other varieties. The actual number of days to harvest of an individual plant is based on climate, watering, fertility, and many other factors.

DETERMINATE: Growth habit where plants stop apical growth, flower, and fruit all at once. See "Indeterminate."

ETHYLENE: A gas that promotes ripening of fruit.

FAMILY: A wide grouping of related plants, usually including several genera.

FERTILIZER ANALYSIS: The percentages of nitrogen, phosphorus pentoxide, and potassium oxide, or "potash", in a fertilizer blend. For example, a fertilizer analysis may be 10-10-10.

FERTILIZER EQUIVALENCY: Used to determine relative quantities of two fertilizers of differing nitrogen analyses.

FERTILIZER RATIO: The proportion of numbers in a fertilizer analysis. For example: 5-10-10 fertilizer has a 1-2-2 ratio.

FUNGICIDE: A substance, usually a chemical, that is used to kill fungi.

GENUS: A grouping of plants or animals encompassing one or more species.

GERMINATION: The beginning of growth of a seed, spore, or other structure such as pollen.

GROUND HEAT: Heat stored in the earth that may be trapped by row covers late in the growing season.

GROUNDSPOT: The place where melon or squash fruit skin contacts the earth. The groundspot is used to determine the ripeness of the fruit.

GROWING SEASON: The period of time between the last killing frost of spring and the first killing frost of fall for a particular area.

HARDENING OFF: The process of preparing transplants for the transition from a greenhouse to outdoors. Hardening off usually consists of withholding of moisture and exposure to cooler temperatures, air movement, and sunlight.

HARDPAN: An impermeable layer of soil often found under the topsoil.

HEAT OF RESPIRATION: The heat that is given off by ripening produce. It must be controlled during storage to delay spoilage.

HEAT SINK: A substance (or location, such as a city) that absorbs heat, then dissipates or releases it.

HEIRLOOM: Any cultivar more than fifty years old that has a documented history, often a colorful name, and has retained its traits through open-pollination.

HILL: Several seeds planted in a single hole, as in the case of squash. These hills are not elevated.

HILLING: Mounding soil over the bases of some plants such as leeks (for blanching), potatoes (to prevent sunburn), or corn (for support).

HYBRID: A cross of two parental types which produces a unique offspring in the next, or first filial (F_1) generation. Seeds saved from a hybrid will not come true and will produce plants that may resemble one of the ancestral types.

INCIPIENT WILT: A temporary, drought-induced wilt from which a plant will recover during the cool of the night or from judicious watering. Large-leaved plants such as squash and beans may wilt during midday but recover at night. Incipient wilt will become permanent wilt if the plants are not watered.

LONG-DAY PLANT: A plant that flowers only after a certain number of hours of daylight. Spinach is a long-day plant.

MILK STAGE: The stage in the development of sweet corn wherein the kernels, when punctured, excrete a milky, very slightly viscous sap. This stage usually coincides with that of the greatest sugar accumulation in the sap.

NODE: The point of attachment of a leaf to a stem.

OPEN-POLLINATED: A nonhybrid variety that will produce off-spring true-to-type from its own seeds. Heirloom vegetables are open-pollinated.

PERENNIAL: A plant that continues to grow, flower, and set seeds every year. Rhubarb and asparagus are perennials.

PERFECT FLOWER: Flowers that contain both male and female parts.

PERMANENT WILT: Drought-induced wilt from which a plant does not recover.

PHYTOTOXICITY: Literally "plant toxicity." A compound applied to a plant that damages the foliage or other plant parts is said to be phytotoxic to that plant.

RAGDOLL TEST: A way to test the viability of seeds. Seeds are wrapped in moistened toweling and placed in a jar in a warm spot. After a week or so the toweling is unwrapped, the number of germinated seeds counted, and the germination percentage calculated.

RESISTANCE CODES: Short letter codes for pest resistance that follow the name of variety. For example, an "F" following a tomato variety name indicates that variety is resistant to Fusarium wilt.

RHIZOME: An underground stem by which some plants, such as asparagus, asexually propagate and spread.

RICINESS: In cauliflower, the condition in which the curds have begun to flower and discolor to a gray or pink from being too mature.

ROOT CROPS: Vegetables such as carrots and parsnips grown for their fleshy roots.

SEED TAPE: A convenient device for planting very small seeds. The seeds are positioned along a "tape" at proper intervals and the entire tape is laid along the row.

SETS: Transplants

SIDEDRESS: To apply fertilizer along a row of plants or in a circle around individual plants.

SILK: In sweet corn, the elongated portions of the female flower that emerge from the ear. Each silk is attached to a kernel and each must be pollinated before the kernel can develop.

SURFACTANT: A compound mixed with a spray to lessen surface tension to allow more even coverage of a plant's tissue.

TASSELING: In sweet corn, the emergence of the male flower stalk, or tassel, from the top of the corn stalk.

TIPBURN: Characterized by a dry brown or black area at the tip of a leaf.

TIPFILL: In sweet corn, the complete development of kernels at the distal end (tip) of the ear.

TUBER: A swollen, underground stem and storage organ. The Irish potato is a tuber.

U.S.D.A. HARDINESS ZONES: The United States Department of Agriculture has divided North America into 11 zones based on average minimum winter temperatures. A range of 10°F separates each zone. This term is most applicable when discussing perennial plants but can influence growing seasons indirectly, thus impacting vegetables.

VARIETY: The "given" name for a plant. In the cultivar names 'Straight 8' cucumber and 'Butter and Sugar' corn, both 'Straight 8' and 'Butter and Sugar' are the varieties, which are set off by single quotation marks. The term was replaced by the more proper term "cultivar" nearly fifty years ago but remains commonly used.

VINE CROPS: Includes melons, squashes, cucumbers, gourds, and all members of the Cucurbitaceae family. Also sometimes referred to as "cucurbits."

Colorado Climate Profile

City	Elevation (feet)	Average growing season (days)	Range in season length (days)	Average Date Last Frost	Average Date First Frost
Boulder	5,344	153	90–197	May 3	October 7
Castle Rock	6,210	125	55–172	May 22	September 23
Colorado Springs	6,008	152	110–191	May 7	October 6
Durango	6,523	110	70–178	June 2	September 19
Estes Park	7,522	94	17–128	June 3	September 9
Ft. Collins	5,003	142	89–182	May 8	September 29
Glenwood Springs	5,762	130	85–165	May 19	September 26
Grand Junction	4,597	170	132–221	April 30	October 16
Greeley	4,664	138	94–164	May 11	October 1
Gunnison	7,703	62	7–98	June 26	August 30
Loveland	4,982	145	125–165	May 7	September 29
Steamboat Springs	6,728	47	7–99	July 2	August 23

(Source: www.wrcc.dri.edu.)

Idaho Climate Profile

City	Elevation (feet)	Average growing season (days)	Range in season length (days)	Average Date Last Frost	Average Date First Frost
Bonner's Ferry	1,850	122	80–169	May 14	September 19
Council	3,150	132	104–171	May 25	September 24
Coeur d'Alene	2,160	141	86–209	May 12	September 30
Kilgore	6,160	36	7–81	July 10	August 21
Lewiston	738	196	152–235	April 15	October 21
May	5,070	77	53–137	June 17	September 7
Moscow	2,630	134	61–201	May 18	September 24
Powell	3,630	86	47–129	June 11	September 8
Salmon	3,950	93	15–143	June 5	September 12
Twin Falls	3,730	147	107–191	May 6	October 2
Wallace	2,770	110	57–161	May 28	September 19
Warren	5,910	11	1–59	July 25	August 2

(Source: www.wrcc.dri.edu.)

Montana Climate Profile

City	Elevation (feet)	Average growing season (days)	Range in season length (days)	Average Date Last Frost	Average Date First Frost
Billings	3,567	151	111–180	May 15	September 22
Bozeman	4,900	112	61–155	May 29	September 14
Glendive	2,080	137	95–192	May 28	September 25
Great Falls	3,363	141	107–169	May 11	September 24
Hamilton	3,575	119	69–173	May 23	September 21
Havre	2,584	131	83–179	May 13	September 20
Helena	3,828	128	83–165	May 15	September 20
Kalispell	2,965	123	80–150	May 23	September 18
Lewistown	4,940	117	100–146	May 27	September 15
Miles City	2,629	147	102–195	May 7	September 27
Missoula	3,197	115	69–161	May 26	September 20
Plentywood	2,040	119	108–138	May 19	September 16

(Source: www.wrcc.dri.edu.)

Utah Climate Profile

City	Elevation (feet)	Average growing season (days)	Range in season length (days)	Average Date Last Frost	Average Date First Frost
Alton	6,875	110	64–151	June 7	September 24
Beaver	5,898	105	48–154	June 6	September 17
Brigham City	4,320	160	111–206	May 1	October 13
Cedar City	5,834	130	75–173	May 26	September 25
Gunnison	5,120	109	49–154	June 6	September 17
Logan	4,535	160	80–203	May 6	October 16
Moab	4,025	182	143–239	April 17	October 18
Ogden	4,350	164	116–271	May 3	October 14
Orem	4,510	181	140–234	April 21	October 17
Provo	4,490	150	118–188	April 22	October 14
Salt Lake City	4,260	204	175–233	April 13	October 31
Vernal	5,260	117	69–155	May 25	September 21

(Source: www.wrcc.dri.edu.)

Wyoming Climate Profile

City	Elevation (feet)	Average growing season (days)	Range in season length (days)	Average Date Last Frost	Average Date First Frost
Casper	5,112	122	77–165	May 19	September 16
Cody	5,020	126	53–178	May 16	September 20
Cheyenne	6,250	119	93–149	May 15	September 26
Evanston	6,860	62	17–116	June 26	August 31
Green River	6,080	100	46–150	June 1	September 12
Lander	5,560	127	91–171	May 17	September 22
Newcastle	4,380	133	89–181	May 14	September 24
Powell	4,390	132	91–179	May 14	September 23
Rawlins	6,850	129	56–145	June 7	September 20
Rock Springs	6,270	111	75–155	May 26	September 14
Thermopolis	4,350	129	66–179	May 13	September 25
Worland	4,060	133	91–179	May 11	September 21

(Source: www.wrcc.dri.edu.)

References

Ashworth, S. *Seed to Seed*. Iowa: Seed Savers Exchange, 2002.

Babb, M.F. and J.E Kraus. *Home Vegetable Gardening in the Central and High Plains and Mountain Valleys*. USDA Farmers' Bulletin 2000, 1949.

Boswell, V. and H.A. Jones. "Climate and Vegetable Crops." in Climate and Man. *Yearbook of Agriculture 1941*. Washington, D.C.: United States Government Printing Office, 1941.

Coleman, E. *Four-Season Harvest*. Vermont: Chelsea Greens Publishing Co., 1999.

Fletcher, R.F. *Growing Vegetable Transplants*. Pennsylvania State University Cooperative Extension Service Circular 562, 1975.

Gough, R.E. *A Glossary of Vital Terms for the Home Gardener*. Binghamton, New York: The Haworth Press, 1993.

Gough, R.E. and C. Moore-Gough. *Harvesting and Saving Garden Seeds*. Montana State University Extension MontGuide MT199905AG, 1999 (Rev. 2008).

Gough, R.E. and C. Moore-Gough. *Montana Master Gardener Handbook*. Montana State University Extension Publication EB0185, Fourth Edition, 2008.

Krug, H. "Environmental Influences on Development, Growth, and Yield" in Wein, H. *Physiology of Vegetable Crops*. New York: CAB International, 1997, pp. 101–180.

Lutz, J.M. and R.E Hardenburg. *The Commercial Storage of Fruits, Vegetables, and Florist and Nursery Stocks*. USDA Agricultural Handbook No. 66, 1968.

MacGillivray, J.H. *Home Vegetable Gardening*. University of California Agricultural Extension Circular 26, 1948.

Maynard, D.N. and G. J. Hochmuth. *Knott's Handbook for Vegetable Growers: Fourth Edition*. New York: J. Wiley and Sons, 1997.

Nissley, C. *The Pocket Book of Vegetable Gardening*. New York: Pocket Books Inc., 1942.

Orzolek, M.D., P.A. Ferreti, W. J. Lamont, K. Demchak, A. A. MacNab, J.M. Halbrent, S. J. Fleischer, L. LaBorche, K. Hoffman, and G. J. SanJulian. *Commercial Vegetable Production Recommendation*. University Park, Pennsylvania: Pennsylvania State University, Penn State Cooperative Extension, Pennsylvania Agricultural Experiment Station, 2003.

Rubatsky, V. and M.Yamaguchi. *World Vegetables: Second Edition*. New York: Chapman and Hall, 1997.

Scopel, A.L., C.L. Gallare, and S.R. Radosevich. 1994. "Photostimulation of seed germination during soil tillage." New Phytologist 126(1), 1994, pp. 145–152.

Splittstoesser, W. E. *Vegetable Growing Handbook*. Connecticut: AVI Publishing Co., 1979.

Swaider, J.M. and G.W. Ware. *Producing Vegetable Crops: Fifth Edition*. Illinois: Interstate Publishers Inc., 2002.

Tate, H.F. *Arizona Home Gardening*. Arizona Cooperative Extension Circular 130, 1964.

Thompson, H. C. and W.C. Kelly. *Vegetable Crops: Fifth Edition*. New York: McGraw-Hill, 1957.

Tworkoski, T. "Herbicide effects of essential oils." *Weed Science* 50(4), 2002, pp. 425–431.

Wein, H. *Physiology of Vegetable Crops*. New York: CAB International, 1997.

Index

Meet Bob & Cheryl

Dr. Bob Gough holds a doctorate in botany and is associate dean for academic programs and professor of horticulture at Montana State University. A prolific writer, Bob is the author of 13 gardening books, 500 extension service publications, and numerous

articles for magazines such as *Fine Gardening*, *Country Journal*, *National Gardening*, *Zone 4 Magazine*, *Montana Magazine*, and *Harrowsmith*. He served as state extension horticulturist in Montana, hosted the popular *Dr. Bob's Northern Gardening Tips* radio program for ten years, and has been a panel member on the PBS show *Montana Ag Live* for fifteen years.

Cheryl Moore-Gough holds a master's degree in horticulture, is adjunct assistant professor of horticulture at Montana State University, and has served as Montana state extension horticulturist, Montana Master Gardener Instructor and Coordinator, and Montana State University plant disease diagnostician. Cheryl hosts *Northern Gardening Tips* radio program and is a regular panelist on *Montana Ag Live* on PBS. Cheryl's gardening articles are regularly published in scores of regional newspapers and in such popular magazines as *Fine Gardening*, *Montana Magazine*, *Big Sky - Small Acres Magazine*, and *American Nurseryman*.

Cheryl and Bob have written three books together on Rocky Mountain gardening and are experts for a website dedicated to monthly gardening tips for the Rocky Mountains and northern Great Plains.

Bob and Cheryl collectively have nearly a century of gardening experience. When not writing about gardening, they can be found—where else—in the garden!